THE EDGE OF THE SOUTH

*Life in
Nineteenth-Century
Virginia*

The Edge of the South

Life in Nineteenth-Century Virginia

EDITED BY

EDWARD L. AYERS

AND

JOHN C. WILLIS

University Press of Virginia

CHARLOTTESVILLE AND LONDON

THE UNIVERSITY PRESS OF VIRGINIA

Copyright © 1991 by the Rector and Visitors
of the University of Virginia

First published 1991

Library of Congress Cataloging-in-Publication Data
The Edge of the South : life in nineteenth-century Virginia / edited
   by Edward L. Ayers and John C. Willis.
      p.   cm.
   Includes index.
   ISBN 0-8139-1298-9 (cloth)
   ISBN 0-8139-1322-5 (paper)
      1. Virginia—History.   2. Virginia—Social life and customs.
   I. Ayers, Edward L., 1953–   .   II. Willis, John C., 1961–   .
   F230.E34   1991
   975.5—dc20

90-12825
CIP

Printed in the United States of America

Contents

Acknowledgments

The editors would like to thank Cindy Aron, Paul Gaston, Stephen Innes, Armstead Robinson, and D. Alan Williams of the University of Virginia's Department of History for their advice and encouragement. James Tice Moore of Virginia Commonwealth University and Peter Wallenstein of Virginia Tech offered insightful criticism, as did Jon Kukla, Sandy Treadway, and John Kneebone of the Virginia State Library. At the University Press of Virginia, John McGuigan has been a steadfast ally from the beginning.

Contributors

MELINDA S. BUZA received her B.A. from Carnegie-Mellon University in 1985 and her M.A. from the University of Virginia in 1987. She is currently employed as a technical writer and lives in Beacon Falls, Connecticut.

JOHN C. WILLIS received his B.A. from Baylor University in 1983 and his M.A. from the University of Virginia in 1987. His doctoral dissertation examines the development of his native region, the Yazoo-Mississippi Delta, from wilderness to plantation empire.

T. LLOYD BENSON received his B.A., M.A., and Ph.D. from the University of Virginia (in 1981, 1983, and 1990, respectively) and is Assistant Professor of History at Furman University. His doctoral dissertation is a comparative study of life in antebellum Mississippi and Indiana.

KEVIN CONLEY RUFFNER received his A.B. at the College of William and Mary in 1982 and his M.A. from the University of Virginia in 1987. The author of *The 44th Virginia Infantry*, Ruffner is pursuing his Ph.D. at George Washington University.

GREGG L. MICHEL received his B.A. from the University of Chicago in 1988 and his M.A. from the University of Virginia in 1989. He currently teaches anthropology and history at St. Stephen's Episcopal School in Austin, Texas.

LAWRENCE L. HARTZELL received his B.A. from Duke University in 1983 and his M.A. from the University of Virginia in 1985. His doctoral dissertation is a study of life in post–Civil War Petersburg, Virginia.

ELIZABETH ATWOOD received her B.S. from West Virginia University in 1981 and her M.A. from the University of Virginia in 1983. A native of Luray, Virginia, she is currently working as a news reporter at the Baltimore *Evening Sun* and pursuing her Ph.D. in communication at the University of Maryland.

ROBERT WEISE received his B.A. from the University of Wisconsin in 1986 and his M.A. from the University of Virginia in 1990. His doctoral dissertation is a social history of the Appalachian coal region.

BETH B. SCHWIEGER received her B.A. from Stephen F. Austin State University in 1983 and her M.A. from the University of Virginia in 1988. Her doctoral dissertation is a history of Southern religion in the nineteenth century.

ANGIE PARROTT received her B.A. from the University of Tennessee in 1988 and her M.A. from the University of Virginia in 1989. She is currently employed at the Tennessee State Library and Archives in Nashville.

EDWARD L. AYERS received his B.A. from the University of Tennessee in 1974 and his Ph.D. from Yale University in 1980. He is the author of *Vengeance and Justice: Crime and Punishment in the 19th-Century American South* and is Associate Professor of History at the University of Virginia.

THE EDGE OF THE SOUTH

Life in
Nineteenth-Century
Virginia

EDWARD L. AYERS

Introduction:
The Edge of the South

THE CHAPTERS IN THIS VOLUME EXPLORE DIVERSE SCENES of nineteenth-century Virginia: the big house and the slave quarters, small farms and battlefields, freed slaves in the country and freed slaves in the city, dark coal mines and brightly illuminated caverns, raucous political rallies and genteel meetings of the United Daughters of the Confederacy. Each essay offers a new perspective on a past which refuses to fit familiar ways of thinking about the nation and the South.

This book has its origins in the University of Virginia's graduate program in history. Beginning as explorations of discrete topics in social and political history, most of the essays started modestly as master's theses. Each author worked with historical materials close at hand, relying on the received wisdom of Southern history to make sense of manuscripts, newspapers, census reports, tax records, military documents, voting returns, and business ledgers in libraries, historical societies, and courthouses across the state. In each case, the evidence and the conventional categories of analysis failed to align in reassuring ways. Each author fashioned an argument which attempted to reconcile matters as effectively as possible, fulfilled the requirement, and went on with life. Some of the authors proceeded to become journalists, editors, and teachers, while others remained in academia.

As their disquieting discoveries accumulated, it began to seem that we might reverse the equation and use Virginia's unknown history to revise some of our basic assumptions about the South. The editors invited the authors, scattered from Connecticut to Texas, to revise their earlier work into chapters addressed to a larger readership. Some essays have been substantially condensed, some have been rethought entirely, and all have been buttressed with additional research. Yet their common theme reflects each author's independent discovery: nineteenth-century Virginia was seldom what we expected.

As the conclusion to this book argues, these studies of a Virginia which repeatedly appeared anomalous under close scrutiny urge us to reconsider some of our ideas about the South in general. Once we abandon the notion of a South whose history can be strung along some central theme or reduced to some lowest common denominator, we can see many "edges" throughout the region. Mississippi and Alabama, as well as Virginia and Missouri, had their own anomalies that the generalities of unified arguments cannot embrace. A central notion of this book is that we can learn as much about people in the past by looking at the parts of their experience that do not fit easy generalizations as we can by settling for reassuring coherence.

The ten chapters move across the entirety of the nineteenth century and across the face of Virginia. The story told here begins in the age of Jefferson and ends in the Progressive Era. During that century, Virginia changed as much as any state in America, beginning as the oldest slave society in the continental United States and evolving into a state altered by the deep economic and cultural ferment of the transatlantic industrial age. People in the mountainous southwest corner of the state or in the Shenandoah Valley witnessed as many changes as the more thoroughly studied Piedmont and Tidewater. Women experienced history no less than men, blacks no less than whites. Change came in the cultural realm as well as the economic and political, the personal as well as the public. Read consecutively, these chapters tell a story of Virginia in the nineteenth century quite different both from the state's official folklore and from historians' generalizations about the South as a whole.

Early in the nineteenth century, everything was tied to slavery. Visitors felt palpable differences between the plantation areas of Virginia and the states in the North, the overwhelming sense of a society built around slavery. The effect was heightened by the many faces of bondage in the Old Dominion. Unlike slaves in the deep South, few in Virginia labored on cotton plantations. Instead, they were scattered among tobacco fields and towns, wheat farms and oyster boats, coal mines and iron foundries. This diffused economic demand for the institution made slavery in nineteenth-century Virginia seem anachronistic, a relic from a different age. Yet slavery was everywhere.

If Virginia could seem old-fashioned, even antediluvian, from the perspective of the North, from the Southern point of view it could seem the face of the future. White Virginians had profited from slavery longer than any other Americans, repeatedly adapting the institution to the opportunities of a diversifying economy. These Virginians struggled with the justice and wisdom of slavery long before it took root in most of the cotton states; they were creating elaborate rationalizations for bondage even as Virginia's excess slaves were being shipped to Alabama and Louisiana. The debates over the future of slavery in the Virginia legislature in 1831 and 1832 seemed to inoculate whites in the state against public anxiety and protest. A visitor to Virginia from the newer slave states might be struck at how malleable slavery was in the Old Dominion and how effectively it worked in a society of diverse agricultural and industrial enterprises. Virginia contained a number of cities where free blacks and hired slaves spent much of their time unsupervised by whites, where slaves labored in factories and commerce. But a white visitor might also wonder whether slaves so often out of the master's view would continue to endure enslavement. The Virginia slave debates had, after all, been triggered by the bloodiest slave revolt in United States history, and no one knew whether the newly legislated constraints on slaves and free blacks could prevent another outbreak.

Even as elite white Virginians struggled to domesticate slavery, they wrestled with more private concerns as well. Faced with complex and subtle changes in gender relations, elite Virginians at the beginning of the nineteenth century found themselves questioning traditional roles and attitudes. Members of this elite, after all, could draw on several different traditions. They might model themselves on the great Tidewater aristocrats from the golden age of the early eighteenth century, when imperious slaveowners built vast plantations and conducted themselves with the air of British gentry. They could also model themselves on the statesmen-planters of the Revolutionary War era, precariously balancing slaveholding and the latest Enlightenment philosophy. Or they could try to create a new cultural style, one specifically tailored to the new century.

The first chapter, by Melinda S. Buza, explores the creation of that new style, one that tried to reconcile the sentimental sensibilities of the early nineteenth century with a slaveholding society, one that tried to bring the male-dominated traditions of Virginia planters into line with evolving Anglo-American conceptions of women as moral paragons and centers of the household. The essay, with its focus on relationships within prominent Virginia families, shows the formation of a standard which soon spread throughout the slave South. Buza finds that the letters and diaries of these members of the Virginia gentry challenge the portrayal of the Old South as a land of sharp patriarchal authority. Instead, women and men worked to find emotional sustenance in a time of heart-wrenching mortality among mothers and children.

The slave quarters of the plantations where Buza's masters and mistresses lived saw different kinds of struggles. Although slaves enjoyed far less latitude than whites, they too had to decide where to stand on matters of family, religion, and assertiveness. Slaves did not react uniformly to bondage. As John C. Willis shows, nineteenth-century slave quarters were divided between men and women, among generations, and between Christians and non-Christians, as each person grappled with the meaning of lifelong enslavement. While some embraced the promise of redemption, others spurned salvation in the hereafter for precedence in the present. The contest between honor and the values of Christianity in the slave quarters suggests that we might rethink the working of honor in the Old South, even as we rethink the way slaves approached Christianity.

The struggles in the manor and the quarters affected most white Virginians only indirectly, for the majority did not live on plantations before the Civil War. The typical white farmer ran a relatively small farm, perhaps with one or two slaves, perhaps hiring slaves from neighbors, perhaps with white tenants, perhaps with only the labor of his own family —a far cry from the fine plantations described in the first two chapters. In fact, the gap between yeoman farmers and the wealthier planters troubled Virginians. White Virginians no less than other Americans prided themselves on their freedom and political equality, and some worried that the concentration of wealth made possible by slavery mocked claims of equality, allowed planters to dominate their counties, engrossing the best land and relegating poorer neighbors to the margins. T. Lloyd Benson investigates these problems in a central Virginia county in the late antebellum era. Through a close examination of local records, he discovers complex spatial juxtaposition and intermingling of white classes, a portrayal which challenges easy conceptions of the social order in the antebellum South.

Virtually all the tensions and concerns Virginians held about their society came to the surface in the Civil War. Tied to the North by economic, kinship, and social connections, Virginia was reluctant to heed calls for Southern separatism. State leaders worked frantically to forestall conflict between the North and the South, even when other states had given up hope. One of the last states to secede, Virginia entered the Confederacy reluctantly. Yet some of the very attributes that set Virginia apart from the rest of the South—industrial cities and proximity to the North—also made it essential to the Confederacy's survival. The state that backed into the Southern cause so reluctantly found itself the capital and the industrial heart of the Confederacy. Richmond, with its large immigrant population, tobacco factories, and iron mills, was an unlikely focus for Southern nationalism, but such it became.

Virginia, as its leaders had feared, became the major battlefield of the war. Union and Confederate armies cut across the state, stripping formerly prosperous farms and towns. Isolated and obscure courthouses, farms, and creeks became famous overnight and forever as the sites of horrible engagements. More than half the war's battles were waged within Virginia's borders. And as the conflict intensified, some white Virginians who had been skeptical of the Confederacy and the war abandoned their earlier reservations and became ardent supporters of the cause; others bitterly watched the state reap the fruit of the secession they had opposed and gave the cause only tenuous support. Ironically, the conflicting loyalties felt so acutely by Robert E. Lee and other Confederate soldiers later made their measured devotion to the Southern cause seem all the more noble. Lee's doubts and anxieties freed him from the stigma of fanaticism and imparted to his actions the serene dedication to duty that Virginians claimed as their special character.

Common men found their devotion to the cause challenged from the very beginning. If any of the soldiers in the Confederacy had reason to doubt their loyalty to secession and the war for Southern separation, surely it was Virginia's. Fighting so close to their homes, their families in constant danger of battle, scavengers, and hunger, many Virginia soldiers were tempted to desert. The unusual diversity of the state fed their temptation: Did an Irish immigrant working in the factories of Richmond have reason to die for the Confederacy? A nonslaveholding mountaineer? An illiterate tenant farmer working on some other man's land? The proximity of the Union forces and their own families encouraged potential deserters to try their luck. Kevin C. Ruffner's essay shows how one Virginia regiment was organized, how it changed over the course of the war, how its men were tempted to leave their posts, and why some did. Desertion measured in concrete terms the conflicts that tore at white Virginians in the era of the Civil War. But the divisions uncovered by Ruffner's innovative research do not correspond to the fault lines of the antebellum and Confederate South sketched by previous historians. From the perspective of the 44th Infantry Regiment, Virginia was both unified and divided in ways more subtle than our usual categories can describe.

Black Virginians experienced their own conflicts in the war years, conflicts that often bore little resemblance to those among whites. When a Federal unit arrived on a plantation, some slaves claimed the soldiers as their liberators, grasping freedom in whatever tenuous form it came. Others bided their time, keeping on good terms with the white people they lived among, protecting a relationship which might prove critical to an ex-slave's success in freedom. On plantations and farms across Virginia, hundreds of thousands of black people prepared to make these decisions on the spur of the moment and endure the consequences for the rest of their lives.

Slaves carefully watched the plantation and its owners as they struggled to adapt to the events of war, emancipation, and surrender. On tobacco and wheat plantations, former masters approached black Virginians to strike deals. Some planters offered as little change as possible, maintaining gang labor, slave quarters, and sharp constraints on black freedom; some planters allowed valued workers and their families the chance to farm a piece of land with little supervision. These decisions turned not only on the kindness of the master but also on the ambition of the former slaves, on the prices the crops brought, and on the scarcity of labor. Gregg Michel follows a large wheat plantation through the Civil War and the decades beyond to see how such a place evolved in these years of tumult, to see how whites and the black people who worked their land dealt with one another as the state moved from war into the years of the New South. The experience of black and white Virginians at Hickory Hill shows the limitations of models of the Southern economy focused only on the cotton regions.

Black Virginians in the state's major cities faced a set of choices and compulsions quite different from those confronting rural slaves. Virginia's cities offered former slaves unusual opportunities: opportunities to work in a far broader range of occupations than blacks in the cotton South, to take part in a social life in which blacks ran their own organizations, to vote for a party which had considerable strength and possibility for success. Moreover, urban blacks tended to be more skilled and more literate than their rural counterparts. Lawrence L. Hartzell examines the attempts of blacks in Petersburg to build new lives for themselves, their efforts hindered by the decline of Petersburg from one of the largest and most prosperous Southern cities before the Civil War into a stagnant backwater. The Petersburg story reveals a black community which was both active and divided, as common people and leaders alike constantly negotiated their way among conflicting opportunities and aspirations.

A Virginia weakened by poverty, defeat, and the massive departure of former citizens of both races saw some more promising changes and innovations in the decades after the Civil War. Postbellum railroad building brought a variety of new opportunities to Virginia, opening large parts of the southwestern part of the state to mining and lumbering, creating towns virtually overnight, rearranging the economic lives of farm families for miles around, and bringing blacks from cities to the coalfields.

Virginia's new railroads brought travelers in search of diversion and relaxation as well as men on the make in the decades after the Civil War. Its warm springs had attracted visitors long before the war, but now the state offered new and more modern attractions. Virginia welcomed tourists who traveled from Boston, New York, or Washington to visit luxurious resorts. Huge hotels arose in Virginia's mountains and valleys, and soon wealthy men and women were strolling through impressive lobbies and carefully tended gardens. The chapter by Elizabeth Atwood tells of the development of Luray in the Shenandoah Valley, where enterprising outsiders discovered and promoted massive caverns. The history of the Luray Caverns reveals the growth of tourism to be as contested as the growth of more traditional industries, as locals and Northern businessmen maneuvered for commercial advantage and for control of the town and its future.

The mountains of southwest Virginia saw the new order arrive with a startling rapidity. In a matter of a few years, places such as Wise County went from farming economies only loosely connected to commercial agriculture to outposts of heavy industry. Towns by the dozen were founded along the railroads, and mining shafts were driven deep into mountains that had seen only the grazing of cattle and hogs. In this rapid change, local people had to make decisions of far-reaching importance: to what extent would they cast their lot with the new order, the new men, the new money? Robert Weise's chapter examines the decisions people made in Wise County and offers a bold reinterpretation of their motives and of Appalachian history in general.

Throughout the years when Virginia was undergoing all these social and economic changes, the state also experienced deep and unusual political change. While states to the south passed through years of turbulent Reconstruction, white conservative leaders in Virginia managed to harness the forces of change. The state saw only a brief and mild form of political control by Republicans, but then, unlike any other Southern state, Virginia witnessed the closest thing to a political revolt by men of both races and of all classes. The Readjuster movement of the early 1880s was unique in the South, a successful broad-gauged assault against the regime of the conservative whites. Those conservatives sought to tax the state's people to pay wealthy bondholders on debts accrued by the state years before, and they were willing to beggar the public schools to meet the payments. The coalition that sought to lower or "readjust" the debt—a coalition of Republicans and Democrats, blacks and whites, poor and privileged—could hold on only briefly to the power they won. Their defeat made it even more difficult for subsequent dissidents to gain a hearing in the state; while neighboring states were convulsed by the Populist movement in the 1890s, Virginia experienced only the mildest forms of political revolt in that decade.

As in other Southern states, though, Virginia Democrats maneuvered to prevent anything resembling Readjusterism or Populism from ever happening again. Throughout the nineteenth century, white Virginians enjoyed telling themselves and anyone else who would listen that their state was more moderate and less cruelly racist than states farther south. Indeed, Virginia saw relatively few lynchings in the heyday of that barbarity, was late to segregate its railroads, and waited until 1901 to hold a constitutional convention to deprive its black citizens of their votes— more than a decade after the first state in the South had done so. As the chapter by Beth B. Schweiger reveals, the debates and doubts about the reduction of the vote showed Virginia leaders' ambivalence about their actions, an ambivalence missing from virtually every other account of Southern disfranchisement. Hope for a vibrant democracy of educated white men warred with dreams of a firmly controlled biracial society and fears of white dissension. Virginia ended the century the way it had started, anxiously negotiating between national ideals and Southern problems, between a vision of an illustrious past and a present which always seemed full of ambiguity and disappointment.

The final chapter in the book, by Angie Parrott, chronicles the attempts of a visible and determined group of Virginia women to resolve their state's problematic identity. The United Daughters of the Confederacy sought to overcome the forgetfulness toward Confederate veterans displayed by so many white Southerners near the turn of the century. Although Richmond became more like a Northern city every year— with streetcar suburbs, corporation headquarters, and college football games—women in the city worked to provide constant reminders of a more Southern past. Monitoring schoolbooks for evidence of Northern bias, taking care of elderly veterans neglected by the new generation, and building monuments to remind the young of the heroes of an earlier age, the Daughters took an active hand in shaping the way Virginians recalled the past. While the UDC was far more active than stereotypes of Southern women would lead us to believe, they were active in a self-consciously reactionary cause. By and large, the Daughters and their many allies in historical revision succeeded in their crusade. Virginians of the twentieth century forgot how complex a heritage their white and black ancestors had bequeathed to the state, and each generation felt itself the first to confront the full dilemma of being both Virginian and American. We hope this book can help reclaim some of that complexity.

1

MELINDA S. BUZA

"Pledges of Our Love": Friendship, Love, and Marriage among the Virginia Gentry, 1800–1825

"HIGH HO," WROTE YOUNG SALLY KENNON IN NOVEMBER 1809, pondering her approaching marriage, "it makes me feel very strangely whenever I think that perhaps in a month or two I may no longer be Sally Kennon, but have assumed a new name and in some measure a new character." She confided to her longtime friend Ellen Mordecai, "you may depend I have some very serious reflections on the occasion."[1] Sally's ambivalence was not unusual, for in early nineteenth-century Virginia marriage posed many confusing questions. In this era of change men and women attempted to forge new social and cultural patterns of gender relations out of tradition, myth, and convention.[2] As members of the Southern gentry, Sally and her fiancé, Captain Arthur Sinclair, were both immersed in a genteel honor culture which often exaggerated divisions between genders. Theirs was also a time when the inescapable dangers of childbirth threatened the happiness of every young family. In the opening decades of the new century, antebellum Virginians like Sally, Arthur, and their friends created styles of courtship and marriage that set the tone for generations of white Southerners.

Two opposing views emerge in the current scholarship on relationships between antebellum Southern men and women like Sally and Arthur Sinclair. One view contends that restrictive Southern genteel society provided only limited opportunities for interaction between men and women. Hampered by strict gender conventions, pristine Southern ladies and self-consciously chivalrous male patriarchs viewed each other as drastically different beings and lived hostile, estranged lives. With only vague and incorrect understanding of each other, antebellum men and women were often trapped in unsatisfying, confining, and unequal marriages. These unions between strangers could become desperate struggles between insensitive, overbearing men and frustrated, overburdened, idealized Southern women, relations one historian describes as "intense, competitive, and almost antagonistic."[3]

For scholars at the other end of the spectrum, however, antebellum Southern family life was cooperative, caring, sentimental, and emotionally fulfilling. While the sexes pursued different tasks and duties, their shared fears of mortality and fluctuating economic fortunes combined to promote close and egalitarian family ties with loving marriages and caring childrearing. Relations between these Southern men and women, while guided by gender conventions, were far from cold or malevolent.[4]

Despite these contradictory interpretations of Southern marriage, most historians agree that divergent gender roles encouraged close bonds of deep friendship between members of the same gender, particularly among women. Especially for those portraying relations between men and women at their most embattled extreme, these same-gender networks were crucial to women's lives, often the only warmth women experienced. Their intimate, intense, and long-lived female bonds were an essential and accepted pattern of behavior in nineteenth-century society and are viewed as women's antidote to distant and unfulfilling connections with men. These networks created a way of life in which men made but "a shadowy appearance."[5]

A reading of Virginians' personal writings from the opening decades of the nineteenth century reveals a complex and multifaceted picture. The close and intimate network of female friendships thrived, as did an equally vital male network; but at the same time men and women saw considerable interaction between these two worlds of same-sex friendships. Men emerge from the shadows in these writings, revealing a culture of sentimental associations with members of their own gender as well as an emotional involvement in the lives of their female loved ones. Separate male or female networks coexisted within the wider circle of association between men and women. All three of these relationships interacted in the emotional lives of these antebellum Virginians, lives often consumed by the questions and problems of marriage under the conditions of their time.

Same-sex worlds were thus much more than a substitute for unattainable intimacy with men or an antidote to "social restrictions" inhibiting relations between men and women.[6] Since both men and women developed deeply cherished, long-standing relationships with members of their own sex, both possessed an understanding of companionability, love, and intimacy. This, in turn, helped them overcome the socially prescribed divisions between the sexes once they joined in marriage and actually fostered the development of "companionate marriage."[7] Their personal writings suggest that same-sex relationships served as a learning ground for emotional commitments, as a way to alleviate the sadness of unpreventable tragedies, and as a way to explore their feelings about the problems of marriage. With their background in loving friendships, these antebellum Virginians created marriages—despite limited knowledge of each other, despite the attitudes and realities governing their time—with the same sense of companionability, understanding, and commitment that they showed in their same-sex networks. Both worlds thus intertwined in the intricate fabric of daily emotional life.

Virginia's genteel families of the early nineteenth century constituted the "cultural elite" of their time. They were often descendants of the state's founders, whose names dominated the political and military honor rolls from the Revolutionary War through the twentieth century. Bound together in a web of friendship, business association, and intermarriage, they were also the people with the time, inclination, and education to record their feelings and experiences in letters and diaries.[8]

The letters exchanged between the elite women attest to strong, loving relations—friendships that played an important part in their lives for decades. The letters between the young Sally Kennon and Ellen Mordecai, for example, were filled with shared secrets and assurances of trust.[9] Sally wrote in March 1809 of family news and her excitement over the coming summer's Fourth of July Ball. She girlishly talked of dresses and beaux and then admonished, "for God's sake let no eye glance over this but your own if you love me." She later gave the same caution regarding less trivial matters; in July she became engaged and wrote to Ellen with the news, closing: "If you love me dear Ellen let no eye glance over this but your own and no person know the contents but your family." Such closings demonstrate how easily Sally employed the word "love" to describe the bond between her and Ellen. In fact, she even seemed to see their girlish love for each other as superior to what she perceived as the love between men and women. In the March 1809 letter she wrote: "And tho' we are not lovers, my beloved girl, we are what is better, friends; and are as much pleased with reading each others letters as any of the sighing swains, or love sick damsels could with the effusions of their pens."[10]

Sally's mother, Elizabeth Kennon, expressed comparable sentiments in her writing. In September 1808 she wrote to Ellen Mordecai telling of Sally's return from a trip. "News, Ellen, news," she wrote, "good news I have to tell; Sally came yesterday." She continued by expressing her worry over Sally's "ague and fever" and apologized for writing such a "humdrum sort of letter" but noted, "to confess the truth, I am so delighted to see and chat with my Pet that I can hardly spare time to write to you and my doing so at this time ought to convince you how much I love you." A touching footnote, revealing just how long-lived such friendships could be, was added across the back of the letter, written in pencil by an older, unsteady hand: "Dear old letters, reperused at the close of 1862, arranged according to dates on New Year's Day 1863 by her who loved the writer," signed "Ellen Mordecai." [11]

Significant attachments were expressed by other women who found themselves separated by time and distance from those they held dear. In 1802 Mary Walker Carter wrote to Nancy Barraud: "Indeed my dear Nancy may believe me when I say that my love for her and my anxiety when we are separated to keep up a more regular intercourse of letters increases everyday, or rather every hour." These women were deeply attached to each other and felt pain when separated by long distances. "You cannot conceive how I have felt your loss since I have been here," Mary continued, "for every thing reminds me of you so much that sometimes I am almost tempted to go and look for you, but I am obligated to stop in my hunt and recollect that you are far far away from me. Oh my dear Nancy, I cannot describe to you how I feel when I remember that there are so many mountains to cross before we meet again." [12]

Sisters often enjoyed very close relationships. An 1817 letter from Margaret Daniel to her sister, Mary Baldwin, is one example. In 1817 Mary was watching out for Mrs. Daniel's two children, Cornelia and William, while they were away from their mother at school in Lynchburg. Margaret's love for Mary linked both maternal and sororal feeling. "We shall certainly be in Lynchburg by the 25th of December," she wrote. "I am as much delighted at the prospect of seeing you my dear children as you can possibly be, and feel quite impatient for the time to arrive for us to start. I say my dear children for you appear to me my dear sister in no other light—your affectionate and dutiful attentions to me, your dear brother, and my beloved children, has excited in my breast feelings which I can in no way so fully describe as by saying they are parental." Margaret concluded: "I love you my dear Mary most sincerely and affectionately and I trust in God we may always live near each other. I wish you and my sweet amiable Cornelia could always live as you now do, in the continual interchange of sisterly offices." [13]

Margaret expressed her love for the now-pregnant Mary again in an August 1822 letter she sent to her husband William. "Mary is still about," she wrote, "contrary to hers and my expectations. I lament that it has so happened, for I shall not feel satisfied to leave her 'till she is safely over her confinement, . . . [I] should have been pleased to have returned home with you." Margaret, unable to leave Mary so close to the child's birth or to dismiss her "considerable anxieties for the result," found herself caught between the love and responsibilities of her woman's world and the love for her husband and children. In September, Mrs. Daniel wrote to her husband: "I have felt a desire several times since you left me to address a few lines to you although it has been but a few days since you left me, but I have really been so constantly engaged attending on Mary and her Baby, that I could not leave the room long enough. I have had a most fatiguing time of it and I have never undressed to go to bed, or had any rest to do me any good, since I saw you."[14] Clearly, Margaret felt similarly loving ties to both her sister and her husband but was compelled by her sense of women's duty to remain with Mary.

Virginia Randolph Trist and her newly married sister Ellen experienced very deep bonds. In 1825, shortly after Ellen's departure for the North, Virginia wrote: "Dearest Sister, . . . you know what a valuable friend and tender daughter and sister you have made me; you have counseled wisely, comforted in distress, smoothed the difficulties which cropped my path in learning, and excited the desire which daily grows upon me to resemble you in all that I can." She went on, "Your figure is constantly before me in every part of the house and I almost fancy when I go out of it that I shall see you in some of your favorite haunts; what would I not give to see you, to hear the sound of your voice, once more to feel you encircled by my arms."[15]

Mothers and daughters also shared particularly close bonds, like that between Ellen Wayles Randolph and her mother, Martha Jefferson Randolph, daughter of Thomas Jefferson. Ellen wrote often when they were apart, and her letters frequently expressed a deep desire to please her mother. She often stressed fears and insecurities—that she wrote too little or too much, that she was too dull or too impersonal. Yet Ellen's writing was also affectionate and suggested a close relationship. She expressed her feelings beautifully in a March 1814 letter home. "Adieu my dearest mother," she closed, "I am never happier than when I am engaged in writing to you, and yet I am so hurried always that I have never time to say all I wish to say, or to tell you how sincerely I love you; in fact how completely my affection for you is the passion of my life and how trifling every other feeling is in comparison with that; no human being ever loved a mother as much as I do you, but then no one ever had such a mother."[16]

Loving bonds also developed between women less closely related. For instance, in 1816 Louisa Payne wrote to her aunt Louisa Holmes of her strong feelings. "When I think that you have been away but one week," she wrote, "and that you intend to stay three or four weeks longer, I do not know how I shall stand it. I sit in your room all day long, as usual, but you are not there to talk to me, but still the room has charms to me because I know you loved it." [17]

Men's personal documents, like women's, were also rich with examples of lengthy and intimate relationships. Men remained in close contact with male kin and other male associates for decades, even lifetimes. Their writings, while not always as emotionally explicit as women's—there are fewer overt declarations of love, for example—nonetheless demonstrate sincere commitment, understanding, and caring. As would be expected, Virginia gentlemen discussed business, agriculture, and finances. Yet, in the same documents they also related bits of gossip, domestic news, and personal worries, as well as assertions of friendship and loyalty.

John Hartwell Cocke, for example, maintained many long-lived and vital relationships. As an influential leader of Virginia's antebellum gentry, Cocke kept extensive written records, and his personal papers contain a vast assortment of correspondence between himself and other landowners, businessmen, and professionals, many of which were maintained for years. One of his friendships was with Sally Kennon's fiancé, Captain Arthur Sinclair.[18]

Cocke's friendship clearly had an impact on Sinclair's life, ambitions, and marriage. Married several years and firmly established in domestic security, Cocke served as a model for Sinclair. In July 1809 Sinclair wrote, "It is my wish to marry and settle myself in the course of the coming winter, as I have no [interest in] those long engagements, where they can possibly be avoided." Sinclair, however, stressed the importance of locating a good home before taking a bride, a problem that appeared to be the major cause of delay. "There is no positive time fixed as yet," Sinclair wrote. "Sally has been generous enough to leave the time to me, so that you see I have some forbearance, or I should take the *bird* and look out for the *cage* afterwards." He elaborated on his desire for a proper home, declaring that "I wish my circumstances would admit of my settling to advantage near you, as I have more attachment to persons than places, and the charming girl to whom I am about to unite myself has declared her willingness to follow my interest where ever it may lead." [19]

In February 1810 Sinclair again wrote to Cocke of his desire for a home close to his friend. In phrases quite reminiscent of those found in women's letters, he wrote: "I yet look forward with pleasure my friend [to the time] when I may be settled near you and enjoy the peaceful and respectable life of a farmer. . . . I would give up all the society of this quarter, for that of your family alone, for we can be happier in the smallest circles of those we *love*, than in the midst of a city, where there is nothing like it."[20]

Harry St. George Tucker, another member of Cocke's close network of male friends, offered an excellent description of their relationship in an 1803 letter. "My dear friend," Tucker began, "whenever I sit down to write to my lowland acquaintances my heart sickens at the reflection that there is one among them so dear to me as yourself, whom I may have neglected." Tucker clearly cared for the man he addressed, apologizing for his neglect and noting that he wished for nothing to interfere with "the intercourse between men" so connected. These men, bound by "the strong ties of reciprocal esteem," found themselves longing to see those from whom they had been separated by other obligations. Tucker wrote: "Should my good fortune ever bring us together again I shall take great pleasure in talking over some happy moments we have spent in Williamsburg." "Forget not," he pleaded, "that you have a friend in this part of the world, whose solitary situation needs every comfort which the correspondence of old acquaintances can bestow."[21]

Men's ability to maintain correspondence, however, may have been hindered by the commitments and responsibilities of business, tasks quite different from those that occupied women. Their male role as provider and breadwinner likely cut into the amount of time available for personal letters, as an 1808 letter suggests. In apology for not writing more often, J. T. Barraud wrote: "The interests of my [friends] however, hold a place in my bosom, and tho' my attachments seldom are committed on paper, they are deeply engraved on my heart." He noted, however, that "perhaps this is too cold a state of love and requires to give it weight those marks which are generally adopted by society."[22]

Richard H. Lee eloquently described the bonds of friendship that early nineteenth-century men shared when he wrote, "I have received your last letter, and to let you into a secret, I began to be alarmed lest you should have forgotten that there was such a person in existence as your humble servant, and was the more so because I could not find an adequate apology for your long licence." Lee went on to reveal more than simple sadness at not hearing from his friend, John Hartwell Cocke, for a period of time. Lee appeared to fear rejection from a man he held dear. "You know Cocke," he wrote, "that to the male sex I never make professions of any kind, or at least your long acquaintance with me might have furnished you with the knowledge of this fact." He went on to explain, "This seeming reserve arises not from coldness of the heart or the want of sympathy or sensibility, for I look upon that man who can mingle and associate in society without some kindred sympathies and associations as a disgrace to the face of creation." Lee declared that instead, his "seeming reserve" came from "frequent disappointments in the choice of those persons to whom I have confided the [desire] to and [revealed] the overflowing of my heart. Too often I have been deceived not to be rendered cautious at this late day." Yet, he concluded, "even now at this late day in spite of the lessons which I ought to have learned from experience, my heart relies with confidence on some men whom I have met with, nor is the reliance and confidence the less for the want of professions."[23] One of the men whom Lee's "heart relied on" was John H. Cocke; they were both clearly capable of very strong attachments and vulnerable to the hurt of rejection.

Same-gender networks not only prepared antebellum men and women for the companionability and commitment of marriage but also served as a forum for reservations about the other gender. Between 1807 and 1809, for example, Sally and Mrs. Kennon's letters to the Mordecais exhibited a striking use of negative language regarding serious courting and relationships with men. Their words noticeably emphasized a sense of danger, conflict, and militaristic competition. In May 1808 Elizabeth commented to her friend Rachel, "Mercy me, how lucky it is for me that I am so old as to be impenetrable, and that I can stand all the artillery of brilliant eyes, charming shaggy whiskers, white teeth, hair put up in proper order, and all the etc. of a modern fine gentleman without receiving the least injury." In December 1807 she commented on her daughter's flirtations. "Sally says if she returns to Carolina without a wound she shall think herself invulnerable," she wrote, "for she sees so many charming he creatures that nothing else can preserve her, and she is now an inmate in the same house with two fascinating objects who do all in their power to make her happy, however she declares she is safe yet, but how long she will continue so she cannot tell . . . she cannot flatter herself with escaping unhurt, but she will not anticipate misfortune."[24]

Mrs. Kennon wrote often of her fear that Sally might enter marriage at too young an age, prematurely sacrificing her girlhood to the responsibilities of marriage. In February 1808 she wrote: "I should be afraid one or another of the charming fellows would steal her heart, if I did not observe, that they are only like meteors with her; they blaze for a short time but leave no impression, they are quickly forgotten, for after she loses sight of them she seems never to trouble her head about them again." Of the men who distracted Sally, she wrote: "They have very short reigns, for they are scarcely crowned before they are dethroned, indeed she declared to me the other day on her honor, that she never had in her life seen a man she would like to marry." Elizabeth concluded by revealing that Sally's "declaration, I assure you, gave me great pleasure for I should be very sorry if she was to think of involving herself in all the cares, all the troubles of married life at present." Three months later she displayed a similar attitude, writing that "Sally boasts of her freedom and says her heart is her own" and commenting, "I sincerely wish she may continue in her present situation some years longer, for I have no desire to see her shackled yet; as I am satisfied she never will be as happy when she has the care of a family as she is now." [25] Elizabeth feared the consequences of marriage, associating it with specters of danger, pain, injury, and punishment. It was a care-filled state, to be postponed if not avoided.

Sally also experienced worries over marriage, much like those articulated by her mother. In July 1809 she wrote to Ellen announcing her engagement, but she seemed to fear disapproval. "What will my Ellen say," she wondered, "when I tell her that I have actually determined to commence a matron and give up beaux and conquests." Dreading an end to her girlish frivolity, she tried to reason, "I do all this without one pang of regret, for believe me, I think his heart vastly preferable to half a score of those flutterers who are constantly buzzing about our ears, and only tend to produce confusion, without in reality being any kind of use in this world." Sally repeatedly asked Ellen to visit soon, as if she needed reassurance that their relationship would not end with Sally's engagement. "So you must positively come over," she wrote; "cannot you come before that great and important day, big with the fate of Arthur and Sally; you and my sweet dear Rachel certainly can, if it is only for a few days at the time I am noosed." [26] Sally was worried about the coming transformation, about the loss of her youth, with its rounds of visits, exciting beaux, and loving ties between girlfriends. She saw only the fearsome side, actually referring to it in terms of a deadly inflicted punishment ("noosed") and perceived the impact it would have on her young woman's network as well as the work and responsibility it would bring.

Just as Sally and Mrs. Kennon anticipated, one of the major drawbacks of marriage was that it inevitably led to an increase in worries and obligations. Marriage transformed carefree girlhood into anxious maturity as wife and, almost assuredly, as mother very soon after. [27] An 1816 letter from Mrs. L. Flintham to Louisa Holmes eloquently summarized this point. "I only am surprised," she wrote, "that you (do not be offended) have been privileged to remain so long in this character," that is, unmarried. She continued, "but be wise and retain your Independence, let no man lord it over you, for no woman can be free that has a Husband even if he were the best that Imagination can paint." As a married woman she spoke from experience; in August she told her dear friend: "If I should live to see myself free from a young child, or children, and the S. Boat continues to run, or any other Boat, I cannot realize how Big a pleasure I promise myself—seeing you all once more."[28]

Marriage was truly a passage from one way of life into another, as a woman left her family and childhood friends to become a young wife. In February 1808 Mrs. Kennon humorously commented on the notion of not relinquishing her Sally. "If Mr. Faulcon guesses right," she wrote to Rachel, "I ought to endeavor to keep her single for he says he is certain I will sleep with her the first night she is married, as he is convinced I will never trust her to any man's care." Suggesting the bonds between mother and daughter, as well as between Sally and Ellen, Mrs. Kennon continued: "And as to my suffering her to be in such a perilous situation without me, he is sure it is out of the question, for he knows I shall be apprehensive her husband will be rude to her unless I am there to prevent it. . . . Ask Ellen how she would like my situation was that the case."[29] Not only was she worried about Sally's entrance into the woman's world of marriage, but she suggested that Sally might find safer companionship with a woman—a role she and Ellen would willingly fill. Moreover, her description of the wedding night as "a perilous situation," while perhaps only playful, may also reflect the worry associated with initiation into sexual activity, bringing with it the fear and dangers of inevitable and frequent pregnancy.[30]

As Sally Kennon's 1809 letters to Ellen suggest, women also faced marriage with anxiety and sadness because they feared the impact that relocating and undertaking many taxing new duties would have on their treasured female friendships. Sally at first neglected the correspondence with her dear friend Ellen when the cares of a new marriage began to fill her time. Ten months after her wedding, troubled by sickness and back pain from her first pregnancy, she wrote to Ellen, "I did hope you would not have stood on ceremony with an old friend; particularly as you know my situation." Mrs. Kennon had told Ellen of Sally's sickness and pregnancy in an earlier letter, yet apparently Ellen still waited to hear from Sally before writing. Sally continued, "it was not inclination but necessity that withheld my pen," and requested "should any unforeseen event prevent my writing to you for the next two or three months promise that you will not again treat me as a stranger but will write as often as you can, and I give you my word, I will pay you with interest, as soon as it is in my power to scribble."[31] Sally needed assurance that Ellen still loved her, even though she was now a troubled and busy married woman.

Just as women feared the disruption of their friendly networks, they also grew anxious and melancholy over leaving the home of their parents and siblings, as an 1803 letter from the newlywed eighteen-year-old Nancy Barraud Cocke to her Norfolk family reveals. "I cannot enter upon a just description of my thoughts and feelings when I left my fond Parent's and Brother's arms," she told them, "without distressing you as well as myself." She went on to explain, "while your child lives she can never forget how much she owes her doting Parents, tho' I have the kindest of Husbands and one who does everything to make me happy and who I shall be happy with, I am sure, as long as I live." But the new Mrs. John Hartwell Cocke continued, "yet it will take me some time to be weaned from you enough to be happy without you, but as long as I live I shall be always more delighted and contented when I have my Parents and Brothers with me."[32] The safe, familiar security of her immediate family looked remarkably attractive to this new bride, despite her confidence in her husband.

Some of the antebellum apprehension over marriage may thus have been sadness over leaving familiar surroundings and loved ones, rather than an indication of deep problems between the sexes. And while women sometimes expressed their worries and fears concerning marriage within their world of female ties, it is clear that women needed both worlds to be happy. In December 1816 Mary Brown wrote her close friend Louisa Holmes of her recent engagement. She was careful to emphasize her happiness, perhaps even to overemphasize it.[33] "Since last I wrote," she announced, "I have voluntarily entered into a most solemn and serious engagement which takes such entire possession of my mind that I can neither think or write of anything else." The use of the term "voluntary" suggests that her friend might think otherwise and must have been intended to quell any doubts. She went on in a similar tone: "The amiable qualities as well as the ardent and steady attachment which this captivating youth professes to feel for your friend will, I am confident, ensure her lasting happiness."

In fact, Mary may not have been entirely sure about the power of her intended to guarantee her future happiness, for she seemed to need Louisa's reassurance that they would remain friends. "You see my Dear Louisa," she wrote, "what unlimited confidence I place in you; it is because I know your affectionate heart will participate in a sincere friend's happiness, and sympathize in their sorrows. I trust in the omnipotent God that nothing will result from this engagement that will oblige me to call on my sweet friend for her sympathy."[34] Mary obviously needed both worlds, that of women friends and that of husband, to be completely happy. She emphasized the importance she placed on the friendship and tried to remind Louisa that she expected her longtime friend to support her even after her marriage, much as Sally Kennon Sinclair begged her friend Ellen for continued support.

New brides were not the only ones troubled by the changes marriage precipitated. Those left behind also struggled to reconcile their feelings. Virginia Randolph Trist expressed fear in 1825 that her sister Ellen's marriage would result in the neglect of their close and loving relationship. She missed her sister deeply and craved a reunion, yet she realized that marriage and the changes it brought to their sisterly love were necessary. "Nevertheless," she told Ellen, "I wish nothing undone which has occasioned this separation; I am not so selfish as to wish to see your happiness sacrificed to save me a sacrifice, and I love Mr. Coolidge dearly and believe he can do more to make you happy than anyone in the world." Virginia acknowledged to Ellen that "you will have many things to occupy both your thoughts and time now that you have not had hitherto," but she longed for reassurance: "When ever my turn comes to engross you, let it be ever so short a time, write to me as you would speak if we were together my own dearly loved sister." She eloquently summarized the duality of their emotional lives, writing, "besides, I do not feel Jealous of him either, because my own heart shows me that perfect love for our husbands and sisters may exist together, and never clash one with the other." She closed this lovely letter: "Be then what you ever have been to me, dear, dear, Sister and I ask no more." [35]

Despite such fears of the unknown world of marriage and homesickness for the family of youth, we know that many women went on to enjoy deep and loving relationships with their husbands. An 1809 letter from Nancy Cocke expressed her feelings toward her husband and showed the development of their relationship since her 1803 letter longing for home. "William Skipwith has just returned; he tells me he left you in fine spirits," she wrote to John; "may you continue with such my husband, and return to the bosom of your wife with such feelings as welcome you here." Her words became increasingly intimate:

> Take care of yourself, my dearest soul, I will make myself happy until you return. My darling John and Louisa shall comfort me in your absence [and] another little cherub too will gladden my heart every now and then [referring to her pregnancy] and render a recollection of its father still dearer to my heart. Do not say I am saucy. I do not like to be thought so, you know. If I am, who made me so but yourself? . . . Heaven bless you my Husband and return you safely to me . . . may we dream of each other tonight and be as happy in our dreams as we might be in each other's arms. [36]

Other seemingly ideal marriages emerge from the writings of elite Virginians, marriages that lack any trace of antagonism or distance. Writing from Richmond in November 1812, William Daniel, for example, thanked his wife for her most recent letter but noted, "what makes your letter of infinite more value to me is that it gives an account of yourself and your health—subjects which take the lead in all the feelings and sympathies of my heart." He continued with emotion, "Oh my dear Margaret if you [could only] know, if you would believe, how much and how sincerely I feel on your account; how ardently and anxiously I wish to see you happily dwell; and how much I suffer to see you otherwise." His declarations went on, as he seemed quite worried for his pregnant wife's health. "For every tender feeling of my heart which ever led me to the preference of one female over another," he wrote, "still rest upon you, and you alone, my ever dear Peggy, can make those feelings a source of pain or of pleasure to me, as you are well in health, and appear to be happy in receiving that preference which they have bestowed upon you, or otherwise."[37] Daniel wanted his ill wife to know he still cared for her above all others and he needed to know that she was healthy and happy to accept his declarations.

William cautioned Margaret not to give too much to others and to reserve some time to care for her own and their family's needs. "My dear Margaret," he urged, "remember that you do not live for yourself alone—the happiness of a husband who loves you most truly, and the well being of our children rest upon your shoulders. Take care of yourself, nurse the means of restoring and preserving your health, and in making us all happy you cannot fail to be happy yourself in the end. . . . Do not permit your charity and sympathy for others [to] induce you to expose yourself all night—charity should begin at home."[38]

Sally Kennon Sinclair wrote of her love for her husband in 1809. "I can with truth say," she wrote to Ellen Mordecai, "I have loved Captain Sinclair from the very first moment I beheld him."[39] An 1811 letter from Sally's mother described her daughter and son-in-law's marriage in this way: "Her good man exceeds me so far in care, solicitude, and apprehensions about [Sally]," she reported, "that I cannot help laughing at him frequently for his needless fears; for he is always like a tender mother, fancying everything will hurt her, and trying to guard her from danger. . . . I witness so many proofs of his ardent love, and am convinced from every action of hers that it is reciprocal." She concluded, "I may truly say of them . . . sure this is bliss if bliss on earth there be, for never did I see two people more devoted to each other."[40]

Sinclair's long and esteemed career in the navy, however, must have added its own pressures and stresses to the Sinclairs' wedded "bliss." He was frequently away from home and often in danger. In January 1812 he was away at sea, active in the war with Britain, and Sally was pregnant. Sally's mother wrote of her concern for Sally's health and her worry over Captain Sinclair. "I dread the effect it [Sinclair's possible loss at sea] may have on her," Elizabeth fretted, "for so entirely is her whole heart devoted to him . . . I should greatly fear for her at anytime, but particularly in the interesting situation she is in at present."[41]

Women had reason to be concerned over pregnancy and childbirth, even under the best of circumstances. The state of medicine in the nineteenth century meant the experience was fearsome, painful, and overwhelmingly life-threatening, facts women lived with throughout their marriages. Not surprisingly, Sally's earlier letters also demonstrated deep concern over these dangers. In the July 1809 letter to Ellen announcing her engagement, Sally wrote, "Nancy Kennon [her sister-in-law] is in a fair way to present her lord and master with an heir; when I saw her last, which was about a fortnight or three weeks ago, she just began to show that her form would very soon be spoiled." The use of the term "spoiled" suggests her negative attitude toward the realities of pregnancy. She continued, describing her brother as "more delighted than I ever saw a man creature in my life; only hint at it and he is in a broad grin directly; plague take these men; I almost hate them all sometimes and determine not to marry." She continued in a similar vein a few months later. "Mrs. Lucy Nelson on Wednesday last presented her lord and master with a third daughter," she told Ellen, "and is, as the old women say on such occasions, as well as could be expected." Updating Ellen about Nancy Kennon, she wrote, "Nancy expects to bring forth in January; she is extremely large," and observed that "Robert who married Miss Wilson of this county will increase and multiply also in a few months, or rather he will make her do so."[42] Before her own marriage, Sally blamed men for this travail they visited upon women.

Sally eventually found herself in situations remarkably similar to those she feared, but she did not blame her husband. In March 1812 Mrs. Kennon wrote to Rachel Mordecai of Sally's health: "She is still in a very precarious situation; were you to see her you would scarcely recognize your gay, healthy, laughing, blooming, friend in the pale, emaciated, serious Mrs. Sinclair." Elizabeth anxiously continued, "she is at present in a way to increase her family, which may perhaps be one cause of her indisposition but she has complaints which do not proceed from pregnancy. . . . [I fear she is] in danger of a consumption, she has a constant cough, with frequent pains in her breast, these you know are two symptoms of that disorder."[43] In July she commented again on Sally's health, as well as her unique position as a naval officer's wife. "Here is your poor friend Sally," she wrote, "who used to be one of the liveliest of our set, now prey to conjugal and maternal uneasiness, for her husband is on the boundless ocean, she knows not where." Elizabeth went on sadly, "she expects to bring into the world a little innocent who may perhaps be fated never to see its father. These are melancholy thoughts, independent of her situation, and believe me my dear girl, a woman who is in daily expectation of enduring the pains and perils of childbirth needs no additional cause to increase her otherwise unhappy state of mind, but when added to her dread for herself to reflect on the dangers her husband is exposed to [only adds to her burden]."[44]

Sally's ill health and numerous pregnancies undoubtedly contributed to a stark contrast between her girlhood and her married life, a contrast on which her mother frequently commented.[45] In July 1810 Elizabeth wrote to Ellen, "Oh matrimony, matrimony, what a great metamorphoser art thou." She went on: "Did you ever think Sally Kennon, the wild, giddy, thoughtless, lively, rattlebrained Sally Kennon would become a real, down-right loving wife? But so it is, I give you my word. Why Ellen my dear, perhaps you may depreciate as much if you ever meet with a he creature who gets an entire possession of your heart, as the sailor has of hers, how differently will you both think then from what you did in the year eighteen hundred and six."[46] Despite the troubles nineteenth-century marriage brought—frequent and often complicated pregnancies, constant separations from traveling husbands, physical distance from girlhood networks—husbands and wives like the Sinclairs arrived at loving, loyal marriages.

The harsh biological realities of the time, not problems of cultural pathology, caused these couples their largest marital hardships. Mortality, not gender division, presented the greatest peril to marriage. While traditions of honor and patriarchy may have contributed to the frequency of pregnancies, these Virginia gentlemen were not distant or unconcerned for their mates' woes. If women sought the comfort and expertise of other women concerning their fears about childbearing, with convention excluding men from most aspects of the trying event, antebellum men expressed great concern and anxiety over their wives' condition and relied on their own male world of friendship to quell their fears.[47]

Sally's husband, for example, appeared naive about women's health concerns in a July 1810 account. Sinclair's mother-in-law wrote to Ellen Mordecai that Sally, the "poor old matron madame Sinclair," had been extremely sick with "ague and fever" as well as "a matrimonial complaint." Sally was, in fact, so sick that her husband had been prompted to write her mother. Elizabeth recounted the letter for Ellen, writing, "as he was convinced she was not able to write, and knew my anxiety about her, he took that task on himself and has from time to time informed me of her situation; in his last letter he says Sally is better." Mrs. Kennon quoted Sinclair, " 'She has I assure you been extremely sick, she is very much reduced, and yet, she is also quite fat; can you solve this enigma?' " Elizabeth, of course, knew what was behind this. "I think I can," she told Ellen; "I am an old experienced dame and can therefore guess these difficult things, although it does appear rather paradoxical." She teased the younger Ellen, "but you are such an ignorant inexperienced innocent creature that you cannot expound the riddle I am sure; I will take pity on you then, and explain this matter to you. Know then she is actually in the situation in which Lady Randolph, I believe it is, says 'women like to be who love their Lords.' " "Will it not appear strange to you my dear girl," she concluded, "to see her a mother?" [48]

While Elizabeth's tale makes Sinclair appear childishly unsure of his wife's condition, an April 1810 letter offers a different picture, suggesting that men shared a certain knowledge between themselves about the mysterious health problems suffered by their wives. On 10 April 1810 Sinclair wrote to his old friend John Hartwell Cocke that "my dear Sally and myself have at last sheltered ourselves under our own roof, you may be assured I am rejoiced at the circumstance." He went on to tell Cocke news about the various friends they shared, noting that "Mrs. Barraud complains a little, but nothing serious is the matter: perhaps *like my Sally*, the expiration of a certain number of months will produce a cure—poor dear girl, she gets up every morning with a very sick stomach, eats a hearty breakfast, and then grows dull and sleepy; it is about ten in the morning and she is nodding along side of me." [49] Sinclair apparently felt more at ease in discussing such a topic with his male friend than with his mother-in-law.

In the same letter, Sinclair revealed his attitude toward marriage in general. "I am much pleased at the prospect of this friend of mine getting married," he told Cocke, "as he is [miser]able, and I think, at least if I judge from self, it will add much to his future happiness in life." Much later in the year Sinclair wrote, "I am now enjoying all the happiness afforded by a comfortable home, and the company of an excellent wife after my long absence and hardships . . . my dear wife has gotten over her sick stomaches and is in as fine plump order as *a body could wish*." [50] Marriage was security, happiness, and comfort. It brought routine and satisfaction to this man's life. Even pregnancy could be viewed without fear and more as a symbol of domestic bliss, fostering feelings of pride and fulfillment.

Yet Sinclair could also show a more protective instinct toward his wife and seemed to experience uniquely male fears over her health. Sinclair and Cocke wrote about these feelings many times over the years. In 1816, for instance, Sinclair wrote, "I learn with regret that your wife is in bad health, but confidently hope it is only temporary, occasioned by her late confinement. . . . My beloved wife has given me another son, and *'is as well as can be expected,'* tho her health is extremely delicate. I wish to heaven she could cease breeding, at least until her health was better able to bear it. . . . I am in hopes I shall be ordered to the Mediterranean before I have it in my power to do more mischief in this way."[51] Sinclair's concerns suggest a sense of guilt which was likely shared by both men, perceiving their wives' troubles as caused by their "mischief." What impact did such feelings have in a time when men watched wives suffer, and often die, through childbirth?

Margaret Daniel attempted to allay her husband's worries when she wrote to him in April 1822. "I am happy to tell you, my dear Mr. Daniel, what I know will afford you pleasure to hear, that I am in better health than I have been for many months, indeed I believe I may say years." She then offered some details. "I have a fine appetite and my spirits are much better," she wrote. She then expressed her desire for his return, since William, a judge, was away at court at the time. "I have had a dream lately," she wrote, "which has delighted me very much, and I fondly hope it will come true, [but] if you do not chop the Cumberland people off with at least half of their fine chance of long speeches I fear it will happen before you get back and that would be distressing to me." She went on: "Besides [it would] change the fate of my dream, for I thought you [were] present when I had one of the largest and most lovely Boys I ever beheld, and the best part of it was [that it] was without any pain. So you see, your having another son depends on your coming home as soon as you can."[52] Her letter illustrates the value placed on the birth of a son in the nineteenth century, as well as the fear of pain in childbirth, but more importantly it shows that this couple shared their feelings in this matter. Mrs. Daniel desperately wanted her husband home, even as she tried to assuage his fears over her health and responded to the concern and devotion he had expressed in letters to her. Despite antebellum limitations against male participation in childbirth, the Daniels strived to share their concerns and distribute the burdens.

Like the Daniels and Sinclairs, the Cockes developed an emotionally satisfying marriage, even while they struggled with the realities of early

Fig 1.1. An idealized antebellum portrayal of Bremo, the home of Nancy and John Hartwell Cocke. (Original oil painting owned by John Page Elliott. Courtesy of the Manuscripts Division, Special Collections, University of Virginia Library)

nineteenth-century worries. Throughout their marriage they remained surrounded by a world of loving friends and associates, relationships that gave them strength and served as standards for their own union.

Entries from the closing months of 1816 in John Hartwell Cocke's extensive journal reveal the kind of life the Cockes made for themselves at Bremo (fig 1.1).[53] In late 1816 he began to record more than farm business and weather, turning to the solace of pen and paper to make sense of Nancy's persistent illness after the birth of their fifth child. Her slow decline deeply troubled her husband, and this record of their last days together suggests that their marriage was tender and loving and that it existed in tandem with both a female world of rich and loving bonds and a complex and emotional network of male associations.

Nancy Cocke's slow deterioration provided the opportunity to make known her final wishes and to express her emotions at the prospect she faced. She was, Cocke wrote, "all that I could have hoped for in a wife, or expected in a woman." Of her commitment to their family, he stated that "she again repeated that she loved us all too much, and was too deeply interested in the welfare of her children to wish to leave us; but as it pleased God to decree otherwise, she felt no dread at obeying the summons." Such resignation to God's will and deep religious faith offered comfort to the dying and to those left behind. Nancy's untimely departure may have even strengthened the faith of her widowed husband. As John C. Willis's chapter in this volume suggests, Cocke's religious convictions appeared to grow in the years after Nancy's death, as he built chapels on the property and pursued a religious mission to proselytize his slaves.

Nancy's lengthy illness also allowed her to plan for the future of the children she would be forced to leave behind. She told Cocke that she wanted her daughters to remain at home, not be sent to boarding school, living together under the supervision of their own father. In a show of deep respect and love, she entrusted "her faithful and well tried friend, Nancy Moreland," with the task of assisting John with this all-important task.

Cocke's diary included a description of a final meeting between Nancy and several of her "faithful and well tried" friends. He wrote of the scene, "addressing Mrs. E. Cary, [Nancy] begged that she and her other female friends would visit and console her friend [Nancy Moreland] for she knew her grief would be long and would prey upon her." Listing his wife's closest associates, Cocke wrote, "of her most particular friends, Mrs. Randolph Harrison, Miss Jane Harrison, Miss Virginia Cary, Mrs. Carle, Mrs. E. Cary and my sister Faulcon, she spoke in the most affectionate terms, and desired that certain presents should be made them in her name as mementos of her regards. . . . Then taking off her rings," Cocke recounted, "she gave one to Mrs. E. Cary and one to her friend Nancy Moreland, desiring them to wear them for her sake. Lastly, she took off her wedding ring, and presenting it to me, said 'you must have this, it has never been off before.'"

Cocke's diary goes on to relate the sad and final goodbyes between Nancy and her loved ones. Cocke recorded that her last words to their son, the youngest John Hartwell, were rich with "all the fervor of maternal tenderness," reducing the young John to tears, at which time Nancy also lost her composure. "Her fortitude and resignation, great as it was," Cocke touchingly wrote, "yielded to the feelings of nature. The Saint, for a moment, gave way to the mother, and she wept." Cocke stressed the important role played by Nancy's women friends at this most trying time. "Upon Mrs. Randolph Harrison's arrival to visit her," Cocke wrote, "she expressed the greatest satisfaction. To her she repeated all her hopes and described all her feelings in relation to the awful change she was about to undergo, and after private conference with this pious and excellent friend, she assured me it had resulted in strengthening her faith and assuring her confidence."

Nancy Cocke clearly maintained vital and meaningful relationships with a number of her female associates after her wedding and until the very moment of her death. The account of Nancy's last days even shows a similarity between the bonds of matrimony and loving friendships, symbolized in the giving of her rings. These relationships provided a model of love and understanding which she had applied to her marriage. Cocke's words reveal a strong and happy marriage thriving alongside Nancy's involvement in a cluster of intense friendships. "On the night of Monday, the twenty-third," Cocke wrote, "she again thought she would not live to see the morning. This was one of the nights when I alone performed the sacred duty of watching by her bedside. After our exhausted friends had retired to rest, she desired me to place a glass of wine and water on a stand near the bedside and to lie down on the bed by her . . . requesting that I would raise her up and give her the wine and water whenever the fits of coughing came on, saying that all she prayed for now was that she might die without a painful struggle." Cocke's words show a gentle kindness born of genuine love between man and wife. "On Wednesday the twenty-fifth [of December]," he continued, "the agonizing trial was carried to the last excess. It was the [fourteenth] anniversary of our marriage," and in a loving, romantic gesture, Nancy "said she could not as well commemorate this day as by bestowing her blessings upon the pledges of our love. The infant [whose birth sadly appears to have caused the fatal illness] and our younger children were carried to her and received her last embrace." Finally, on Friday, the twenty-seventh, Cocke wrote of his wife's "last ebb of life" as she died grasping the hands of both her adoring husband and her dear old friend Mary W. Cabell.

Polly Cabell wrote of the event to her husband Joseph. "I arrived just in time to bid a long adieu to the friend of my bosom," she told him, "and to witness the last sad scene, a scene which, altho' it tore my heart with anguish, I shall ever derive the sweetest consolation from having witnessed." She went on to tell Joseph that "my departed darling had often wished for me. That very morning she said again and again to Nancy Moreland, 'Oh Nancy, if I could see my dear Polly I could go perfectly satisfied.'" Mrs. Cabell wrote that a weary Nancy, upon hearing the carriage arrive, feared it was only just leaving to retrieve her friend and told Nancy Moreland to inform Polly that "I love her but I can wait no longer for her." Mrs. Cabell wrote to her husband that "Mr. Cocke came out to me, and throwing his arms around my neck and sobbing aloud, said that I had arrived just in time to see an angel die." Both husband and friend shared in Nancy's last moments as the "celestial being" turned "a look of affection" upon Polly "and held out her hand" to her cherished friend as well as to her beloved spouse. "Oh, who could paint the wild grief of her husband," Polly Cabell wrote, when he gazed upon his wife's "lovely but lifeless form."[54] At Nancy Cocke's deathbed, the reinforcing bonds of love and friendship completely intertwined.

The manuscripts of early antebellum Virginia reveal a complex picture. Deep emotional ties flourished between women, friends, sisters, mothers, and daughters. Women depended upon each other from girlhood to death for support and love. They shared girlish secrets, relayed gossip, discussed domestic matters, and explained their feelings about men, marriage, and childbearing. And just as women inhabited a loving world of same-sex friendships, men maintained similar ties. The letters of these Virginia gentlemen reveal that they were immersed in their own version of the "female world of love and ritual."[55] The same circumstances that drew women together—shared gender experience and regulated contact with the opposite sex—also stimulated bonds between men.

While the lives of prominent Virginia couples were filled with trials, responsibilities, and burdens, the roles of Southern lady and male patriarch clearly did not hinder the development of deep bonds between many husbands and wives. These women, unlike those described as helpless victims buffeted about by a brutal antebellum Southern culture, doomed to matches with rigid, uncompromising, honorific men, apparently made lasting and satisfying matches with caring mates. Marriage for Southern ladies was not an ordeal of "outward submission to male will" survived only by "inner constraint and hardihood" and dependence on "conventional illusions . . . designed to make the unbearable somewhat less frightening."[56] For Sally Kennon and other Virginia women like her, life was not one of misery, circumscribed by painful, insensitive tyranny. She had her trials, but they did not lead to a pathological emotional strain between husband and wife. While the youthful Sally clearly chafed at the prospect of being "noosed" in the presumed yoke of marriage, we know that the eventual reality of her life was more complex. The mature Sally loved her husband with great sentiment and accepted his absence at sea and the health problems that accompanied her childbearing years as an unavoidable price worth paying. Like Nancy Cocke and Margaret Daniel, she did not blame her husband or a Southern way of life for her troubles. Their struggles were more a result of the nineteenth-century lack of reproductive freedom and poor maternal health care than of cruel or distant marriages.

Companionate marriage did not "have to await changes in women's property rights, prospects of decent employment for wives and mothers, and a culture devoted to egalitarian principles generally."[57] It existed as part of the early nineteenth-century world of these white Virginians, a world that allowed for close, intimate ties between members of the same gender—ties that fostered the development of similarly loyal, concerned, and loving bonds between husband and wife.

Antebellum Virginia was necessarily one of the first places in the South to see the growth of these types of relationships. Had these people lived in a more rural or frontier section of the South, lacking a well-established mail and roadway system, communication between kin would have been more difficult. Had these elite men and women not been spared mundane work by the enforced labor of their slaves, they would have lacked the time to maintain connections to friends and family. And if the gentry had found themselves in economic trouble or in need of new land to make their way, wives would have been much more far removed from the networks of their youth and felt far more isolated and alone, perhaps bitter and resentful of husbands and the separation that marriage entailed.[58]

For Virginia's antebellum elite, the worlds of family and friends stayed well connected and closely bound. Here the genteel life-style fostered a variety of rich and loving relations for both men and women, relations to be depended on from youth through death, where the love for sisters and brothers, friends and family, clearly coexisted with the love of husbands and wives. Friendship and love flourished alongside and enriched the marriages of these Virginia couples, the two kinds of bonds enriching and reinforcing, "never clashing, one with the other."[59]

NOTES

I would like to thank the fine mentors I found at Carnegie-Mellon University. I am also grateful to the Department of History at the University of Virginia, most especially to Cindy S. Aron for her patient and much-appreciated guidance of my graduate studies. Thanks also to D. Alan Williams who helped with the original essay and to Edward Ayers for his thoughtful comments. Careful readings by Ron Atwater, Laura Lapins, and Nadine Marti were most helpful. With his skilled editing and friendly advice, John Willis's help was invaluable, and the time he invested improved this effort greatly. Finally, special thanks to Arnis and my parents for their ambitions for my success.

1   S. S. Kennon to Ellen Mordecai, 12 Nov. 1809, Kennon Letters, in the Whittle Family Collection, Acc. 7973, Manuscripts Division, Special Collections Department, Univ. of Virginia Library. All of the manuscript collections cited in this chapter are at this repository.

2   Barbara Welter, *Dimity Convictions: The American Woman in the Nineteenth Century* (Athens: Ohio Univ. Press, 1976); Nancy F. Cott, *The Bonds of Womanhood: Women's Sphere in New England, 1780–1835* (New Haven: Yale Univ. Press, 1977), and "Passionlessness: An Interpretation of Victorian Sexual Ideology, 1790–1850," *Signs* 4 (1978): 219–36; Kathryn Kish Sklar, *Catherine Beecher: A Study in American Domesticity* (New Haven: Yale Univ. Press, 1973); Anne Firor Scott, "Women's Perspective on the Patriarchy in the 1850s," *Journal of Southern History* 61 (1974): 52–64; Mary P. Ryan, *The Empire of the Mother: American Writing about Domesticity, 1830–1860* (New York: Haworth, 1982); Suzanne Lebsock, *The Free Women of Petersburg: Status and Culture in a Southern Town, 1784–1860* (New York: Norton, 1984); Elizabeth Fox-Genovese, *Within the Plantation Household: Black and White Women of the Old South* (Chapel Hill: Univ. of North Carolina Press, 1988). It is generally accepted that nineteenth-century ideals saw women's character as built on four cardinal virtues—piety, purity, submissiveness, and domesticity. Women were believed pious and pure, possessing virtue to be guarded at all times, while men were expected to respect women and to remain aloof and in control of their baser instincts. A wide variety of interpretations has been offered on the overall effect and results of such norms on women's position and status in society.

3   This first pole of scholarship is best represented by Bertram Wyatt-Brown, *Southern Honor: Ethics and Behavior in the Old South* (New York: Oxford Univ. Press, 1982), esp. pp. 226–53, and Catherine Clinton, *The Plantation Mistress: Women's World in the Old South* (New York: Pantheon, 1982).

4   This other perspective is most clearly stated in Jane Censer's *North Carolina Planters and Their Children, 1800–1860* (Baton Rouge: Louisiana State Univ. Press, 1984) and Jan Lewis's *The Pursuit of Happiness: Family and Values in Jefferson's Virginia* (New York: Cambridge Univ. Press, 1983).

5   Carroll Smith-Rosenberg's "The Female World of Love and Ritual: Relations between Women in Nineteenth-Century America," appearing in the first issue of *Signs: A Journal of Women in Culture and Society* 1 (Aug. 1975): 1–29, recreated a "female subculture" based in "long-lived, intimate, loving friendship" between women. Emphasizing the importance of avoiding the application of twentieth-century norms of intimacy to the past and arguing for the normalcy of such relations between women, Smith-Rosenberg vividly described how nineteenth-century women often turned to each other for emotionally satisfying supportive bonds. Such relationships existed as an antidote to the "severe social restrictions on intimacy between young women and men," and "devotion to and love of other women became a plausible and socially accepted form of human interaction." Women's complex networks of "deeply felt, same-sex friendships," she argued, "were casually accepted in American society." A "female world of varied and yet highly structured relationships appears to have been an essential aspect of American society," where "relationships between men and women differed in both texture and frequency from those between women." The lives of nineteenth-century women, bounded by the demands of domesticity and

separate spheres, were enriched by the rituals of varied and rewarding bonds with other women, creating, she maintained, "a world in which men made but a shadowy appearance."

See chapter 10 below, by Angie Parrott, for more on women's networks and the organization of a formal association of women in Richmond's United Daughters of the Confederacy.

6 Smith-Rosenberg has maintained that "American society between the mid-eighteenth and mid-nineteenth centuries fostered the emotional segregation of women and men." Same-sex friendships were easier to attain, she wrote, in part due to the "rigid gender-role differentiation within the family and within society as a whole," as well as "the biological realities" common to women—"frequent pregnancies, childbirth, nursing, and menopause"—which served to bring women together in "physical and emotional intimacy." Moreover, Nancy F. Cott has stated in *The Bonds of Womanhood* that women may have been more easily drawn to other women for love and tenderness because those qualities were perceived as foreign to men. Emotions of "the heart," she wrote, were reserved primarily for women, and women could find "truly reciprocal interpersonal relationships only with other women" because men were presumed incapable of such "sensibilities" and "sympathies." Women could turn to other women in gestures of love characterized by complete equality. Unlike relationships with men, same-sex friendships were not steeped in female subordination or disparagement. Women turned to each other for unique sensitive emotional bonding fostered by common experiences and a joint sense of inequality to men.

7 The phrase "companionate marriage" refers to an increased emphasis on notions of love, romance, and partnership as a new nineteenth-century ideal. As Suzanne Lebsock noted, "the standard formula for successful marriage" was once based on "concrete, calculable assets—property, earning capacity, social standing"; but in the nineteenth century, emphasis on romantic love began to obscure "the workings of money and power." During the 1800s "emotion moved to the center; mutual affection and respect replaced the call of duty and pressure from the community as the main ties that . . . bound husbands and wives together" (Lebsock, *Free Women of Petersburg*, 16–17). Jane Censer's *North Carolina Planters and Their Children, 1800–1860* and Jan Lewis's *The Pursuit of Happiness, Family and Values in Jefferson's Virginia* argue that the modern sentimental family existed in the eighteenth and nineteenth centuries, and they found evidence for companionate marriages in both Virginia and North Carolina. Lebsock has described the existence of this ideal in "a Southern town." She maintained that "the evidence from Petersburg suggests that marriage was fundamentally asymmetrical . . . mixed with the new ideal of mutual affection and respect were substantial elements of male dominance and coercion." The two patterns, she argued, existed (if only uneasily) alongside each other in Petersburg (Lebsock, *Free Women of Petersburg*, 17–18, 28–35). Elizabeth Fox-Genovese has argued similarly in *Within the Plantation Household*, particularly in the prologue, where she asserted that nineteenth-century marriage could be built on "respect, companionship, intimacy, shared values, humor, and all the elements of that deep love which stands the test of time, proximity, and separation" (p. 8) even while in many ways "the relations between men and women remained unequal" (p. 9).

8 The term "cultural elite" is found in Lewis's *The Pursuit of Happiness*, xv. On the use of personal documents left behind by these people, Lewis com-

mented, "there is no better source for uncovering the feelings of the past" (p. 280).

Of the Virginians discussed here, the Cocke and Kennon families were linked by bonds of marriage dating back to the eighteenth century when John Hartwell Cocke the elder (1749–1791) married Elizabeth Kennon (1755–1791). The families remained in close association and were bound through marriage again on 21 Jan. 1810 when Arthur Sinclair, John Hartwell Cocke's (1780–1866) close friend, first married to Cocke's sister Elizabeth (from 29 May 1801 to her death in 1803), married Sarah Skipwith ("Sally Short") Kennon. Sally's father, Richard Kennon, was the brother of Elizabeth Kennon Cocke, John Hartwell Cocke's mother. Sinclair thus married Cocke's cousin and maintained the family relation to his friend. Sally's mother, Elizabeth Beverly Munford Kennon, was the widow of the esteemed General Richard Kennon, who pursued a long and successful career in the Virginia military. Sinclair embarked on an equally long and distinguished career in the navy in 1798 until his death on 6 Feb. 1831. John Hartwell Cocke was also a general in the Virginia militia and a prominent leader of his state, closely allied with Thomas Jefferson, James Madison, and General Lafayette. He served as one of the founding members of the University of Virginia's Board of Visitors, serving from 1816 to 1852. William Daniel was a member of Virginia's judiciary, and his son, William Daniel, Jr., became an honored veteran and politician.

While this chapter discusses the personal relations among the white elite of antebellum Virginia, chapter 5 by Gregg Michel offers more about the economic world of this class.

9   After the death of Sarah Skipwith Kennon's father, General Richard Kennon, her mother, Elizabeth Beverly Munford Kennon, was faced with financial setbacks and took her family from Richland, their estate in Mecklenburg County, Virginia, to Warrenton, North Carolina, between 1805 and 1806. There they met and grew close to the Mordecai family, known for their contribution to North Carolina's education system. Sally was close to the second daughter in the Mordecai family, Ellen, her peer in age. Mrs. Kennon maintained a long friendship with Rachel Mordecai, the oldest daughter, who likely served as the mistress of the Mordecai home after the 1796 death of her own mother.

10   S. S. Kennon to Ellen Mordecai, 5 March, 9 July 1809, Acc. 7973.

11   S. S. Kennon to Ellen Mordecai, 25 Sept. 1808, ibid.

12   Mary Walker Carter to Ann Blaus Barraud, 11 July 1802, the Cocke Deposit, Acc. 640.

13   Margaret Baldwin Daniel to Mary Baldwin, 5 Nov. 1817, John Warwick Daniel Papers, Acc. 158.

14   Margaret Daniel to William Daniel, 25 Aug., 10 Sept. 1822, ibid.

15   Virginia Randolph Trist to Ellen Randolph Coolidge, 27 June 1825, Ellen Wayles Coolidge Correspondence, Acc. 9090.

16   Ellen Wayles Randolph to Martha Jefferson Randolph, 30 March 1814, ibid.

17   Louisa M. Payne to Louisa M. Holmes, 22 Aug. 1816, Acc. 640.

18   The rich and extensive archives of the Cocke family also inform chapter 2 by John C. Willis. Arthur Sinclair lost his first wife, Elizabeth Cocke Sinclair,

John Hartwell Cocke's sister, in 1803. Their two children, twins named Robert Carter Nicholas and Augusta, also died before his remarriage. Sinclair, a career naval officer, remained a close friend and associate of John Hartwell Cocke after Elizabeth's death and often wrote to Cocke of his desire to settle near his friend and pursue a fulfilling life as agrarian, husband, and father.

19 Arthur Sinclair to John Hartwell Cocke, July 1809, Acc. 640.

20 Ibid., 17 Feb. 1810.

21 H. St. George Tucker to John H. Cocke, 16 Feb. 1803, John Hartwell Cocke Papers, the Moore Collection, Acc. 3604. Apparently the two men attended the College of William and Mary together.

22 J. T. Barraud to J. H. Cocke, 16 March 1808, Acc. 640.

23 Richard H. Lee to John H. Cocke, 3 Sept. 1802, Acc. 3604.

24 E. B. Kennon to Rachel Mordecai, 10 May 1808, 3 Dec. 1807, Acc. 7973.

25 E. B. Kennon to Rachel Mordecai, 12 Feb., 10 May 1807, ibid.

26 S. S. Kennon to Ellen Mordecai, 9 July 1809, ibid.

27 Barbara Welter, in the first chapter of *Dimity Convictions*, explored in detail the stark contrast between the "light heartedness of girlhood" and "the weighty cares of domesticity and maternity." Elizabeth Fox-Genovese discussed the effects of the "protected girlhood" and the "unpreparedness" of the typical white elite girl to assume the role of household mistress in *Within the Plantation Household*, 109–16.

28 Mrs. L. Flintham to Louisa M. Holmes, 12 Sept. 1816, 13 Aug. 1817, Acc. 640.

29 E. B. Kennon to Rachel Mordecai, 12 Feb. 1808, Acc. 7973.

30 In addition to worries over pregnancy, Barbara Welter has pointed out that the nineteenth century was a time that valued purity in women very highly, purity standing as one of the four virtues that made up the essence of true womanhood. The loss of a new bride's virginity stood as "the single most important event in a young woman's life, when she bestowed her greatest treasure upon her husband, and from that time on was completely dependent upon him, an empty vessel, without legal or emotional existence of her own." Welter commented on a dilemma many young brides must have experienced: "woman must preserve her virtue until marriage, and marriage was necessary for her happiness. Yet, marriage was, literally an end of innocence. She was told not to question the dilemma, but simply to accept it" (Welter, *Dimity Convictions*, 24–27).

31 S. S. Sinclair to Ellen Mordecai, 5 Nov. 1810, Acc. 7973.

32 Ann Blaus ("Nancy") Barraud Cocke to the Barrauds, 1 May 1803, Acc. 640.

33 This may simply have been her usual writing style, but Nancy Cott has noted that weighty and important considerations often affected the way nineteenth-century women approached marriage (*Bonds*, 78–83). "The canon of domesticity and its enveloping social circumstances," she wrote, "freighted women's marriage choice with unprecedented meaning. Marrying meant beginning a vocation imbued with significance for society, as well as fitting one's neck to a 'yoke' that could not be broken (in accord with conventional propriety); and the separation of the home from 'the world' isolated women in their roles as wives and mothers. All this followed the

'romantic' acceptance of a husband. Young women's awareness of the conflict between romantic and economic elements in the marriage choice, and
the heavy social consequences of marriage (probably compounded by the
contrast between single and married women's lives), seems to have resulted
in an emotional reaction or 'marriage trauma' in the minds of some by the
1820s and 1830s" (p. 80).

34 Mary Brown to Louisa M. Holmes Cocke, 16 Dec. 1804, Acc. 640.

35 Virginia Randolph Trist to Ellen Randolph Coolidge, 27 June 1825, Acc.
    9090.

36 Ann B. ("Nancy") Cocke to J. H. Cocke, 21 Jan. 1809, Acc. 640.

37 William Daniel to Margaret Daniel, 22 Nov. 1821, Acc. 158.

38 Ibid.

39 S. S. Kennon to Ellen Mordecai, 9 July 1809, Acc. 7973.

40 E. B. Kennon to Rachel Mordecai, 1811, ibid.

41 E. B. Kennon to Samuel Mordecai, 14 Jan. 1812, ibid.

42 S. S. Kennon to Ellen Mordecai, 9 July, 12 Nov. 1809, ibid.

43 E. B. Kennon to Rachel Mordecai, 15 March 1812, ibid.

44 Ibid., 5 July 1812.

45 Sally gave birth to seven children in the seventeen years between her wed-
    ding (21 Jan. 1810) and her death (21 Aug. 1827), at the age of thirty-six.

46 E. B. Kennon to Ellen Mordecai, 9 July 1810, Acc. 7973.

47 Childbirth in the nineteenth century was clearly a frightening experience
    for women. As Suzanne Lebsock has pointed out in *"A Share of Honour":
    Virginia Women, 1600–1945* (Richmond: Virginia State Library, 1987), 74,
    while motherhood was glorified and idealized, "in reality, physical discom-
    fort and fears of death in childbirth clouded many women's pregnancies."
    Childbirth was "a fearsome ordeal" firmly steeped in anxiety, discomfort,
    and the very real possibility of death. Moreover, as Lebsock noted, "if all
    went well during the delivery, the mother was then free to begin worrying
    about the continued health of her child. She had good reason to worry. Every
    mother could expect to lose at least one of her children." These horrifying
    circumstances are explored in detail in *Motherhood in the Old South: Preg-
    nancy, Childbirth, and Infant Rearing* by Sally G. McMillan (Baton Rouge:
    Louisiana State Univ. Press, 1990). McMillan has shown that antebellum
    Southern women gave birth more frequently, lost more children, suffered
    poorer medical treatment, and died in childbirth more often than North-
    ern women of their time. Such fears and anxiety tended to draw women
    closer together. Judith W. Leavitt and Whitney Walton have pointed out in
    their article, " 'Down to Death's Door': Women's Perceptions of Childbirth
    in America," in *Women and Health in America*, ed. Judith Walzer Leavitt
    (Madison: Univ. of Wisconsin Press, 1984), 155–65, that women depended
    upon each other for help, advice, and expertise. Leavitt and Walton showed
    that "when other women, especially close friends and relatives could be
    secured, parturients felt more relaxed and in control of the situation." The
    help and comfort of other women "was important," they wrote, "because
    women perceived birth as part of women's sphere but also because women
    so commonly feared their birthings. Women were afraid of pain and suf-
    fering of birth, afraid of developing agonizing gynecologic problems that
    would be with them the rest of their lives." Barbara Welter wrote that

"the condition of pregnancy was treated as the most important state of a woman's life." Yet, she noted, it was also "a woman's event," which drew women together "in part because of society's separation of the sexes into sex-determined roles and spheres," as well as because "the fears and joys of childbirth could be best understood by other women" (Walter, *Dimity Convictions*, 67). Nineteenth-century men, hindered by a limited understanding of women's concerns and women's bodies, could not easily share in the experience.

48 E. B. Kennon to Ellen Mordecai, 9 July 1810, Acc. 7973.

49 Arthur Sinclair to John Hartwell Cocke, 10 April 1810, Acc. 640.

50 Ibid. and 15 Oct. 1810.

51 Ibid., 7 Oct. 1816. Sinclair did not know she would never recover from the delivery.

52 Margaret Daniel to William Daniel, 8 April 1822, Acc. 158.

53 Diary of John Hartwell Cocke, 26 Nov. 1816–1 Jan. 1817, Acc. 640.

54 Mary W. ("Polly") Cabell to Joseph C. Cabell, 29 Dec. 1816, Cocke Family Papers, Acc. 5213-A.

55 These are Smith-Rosenberg's terms.

56 Wyatt-Brown, *Southern Honor*, 22–53.

57 Ibid.

58 Elizabeth Fox-Genovese discussed the effects of movement to the Southern frontier on genteel Southern women in the early chapters of *Within the Plantation Household*.

59 Virginia Randolph Trist to Ellen Randolph Coolidge, 27 June 1825, Acc. 9090.

2

JOHN C. WILLIS

From the Dictates of
Pride to the Paths of
Righteousness: Slave Honor
and Christianity in
Antebellum Virginia

IN THE MID-1830S FLUVANNA COUNTY PLANTER JOHN HART-
well Cocke instructed a trusted house slave, Lucy Nicholas, to poll
his bondsmen on their attitudes toward religion. Cocke was specifically interested in which slaves professed Christianity. In the aftermath
of Nat Turner's 1831 millennialist slave rebellion, many Virginia slaveholders had ambivalent feelings about their servants' world views, particularly Christianity.[1] But fear of a slave uprising inspired by vengeful
Old Testament prophets was the least cause of Cocke's survey. Having
recently constructed a church for his bondsmen and employed missionar-
ies among them, Cocke was understandably curious about Christianity's
reception in the slave quarters. What Nicholas, a Christian herself, reported to Cocke must have pleased neither slave nor master.[2] Her find-
ings also challenge deeply entrenched ideas about religion's historic importance in African-American culture.

Contemporary Americans, mindful of the important contributions of
Christian leadership in the civil rights movement, assume that preach-
ers, and by extension, Christianity, have always been catalysts in the
black community. Historians writing during and after the movement
have also stressed the importance of Christianity and religious leaders
among blacks all the way back to slave times. By the 1970s most scholars
agreed that "the true shepherd of the black flock was the slave preacher."
Recent events and respected historiography suggest that because Christianity is and has been important in the lives of African-Americans, it
must also have been widespread.[3]

But Lucy Nicholas's report was this: despite Cocke's efforts and encouragement, a majority of his slaves did not profess Christianity. Nearly

three-fifths of the bondsmen publicly disclaimed the religion, despite the possible consequences of offending their Christian master.[4] And the slaves on Cocke's plantations may have been far more Christian than the average. Indeed, it is likely that as few as one-sixth, and no more than one-quarter, of adult slaves in the American South were Christians by the end of the antebellum era.[5]

If Christianity appealed to only a minority, what was the perspective of the non-Christian majority of slaves on Cocke's plantations and in the rest of antebellum Virginia? The "Schedule of General Cocke's Servants" holds the first clue. The survey shows that most of the slaves denying Christianity shared two striking characteristics: generation and gender. The young were the group most united by disbelief. Ninety-four percent of working slaves below marriageable age rejected the Christian message. These youths were not simply beyond the reach or attention of the Christian messengers: the twin facts that some working adolescents professed Christianity and that Lucy Nicholas questioned the young about their faith show they were encouraged to convert. And it was not only the young who eschewed faith. A majority of adult slaves from roughly eighteen to forty years old also turned away from Christianity. Fifty-five percent of the largest group on Cocke's plantations identified themselves as nonbelievers. Indeed, the only predominantly Christian generation was the elderly. On the Sabbath most nonelderly slaves on Cocke's plantations were part of the "large numbers of adults" who, one missionary confessed, "remain at home or spend the day in visiting or in ways still more exceptional."[6] The majority of slaves on the plantation of this Christian master only professed the faith in their last years before death.

Gender also influenced faith. Most of the female slaves on Cocke's plantations were Christian, but no generation of male slaves contained a majority of believers. Moreover, the values of male and female slaves increasingly diverged as they grew older. While a margin of 15 percent separated male and female Christians in their middle years, the split widened to 50 percent by the time they became grandparents. In the generation with the highest percentage of the faithful, the elderly, only half the men were Christian, while all elderly females professed Christianity. Men and women in the slave community approached the issue of faith very differently, and this separation became more pronounced with age.[7]

Not only were most slaves between their mid-teens and early thirties unconverted, they exhibited a host of aggressive and irreligious acts. Statistical analysis reveals that they were the slaves most likely to be whipped, to fight with their peers, and to rebel against chattel existence. A recent study of slaves' treatment in Virginia's criminal justice system shows that bondsmen of this age swelled the ranks of the law-breaking far beyond their portion of the slave population. Young slaves also dominated the ranks of Virginia's runaway bondsmen in the antebellum period, and as Gregg Michel's chapter suggests, young males were the slaves most eager to flee bondage when the Civil War reached Hickory Hill plantation.[8] Despite a few exceptions like Nat Turner's rebellion, this non-Christian majority of Virginia slaves resisted bondage individually and without divine inspiration.

Although the majority of slaves disavowed or ignored Christianity, their actions suggest adherence to another influential creed—honor. When they were threatened with dishonor, the behavioral patterns of enslaved and free Virginians were often comparable, despite the inevitable limits bondage placed on slave precedence. While Christianity often dulled the impact of the code of honor among older whites, younger Southern ladies and gentlemen (peers of the irreligious slave majority) were acutely aware of their reputations.[9] Historians have established that white Southerners' fixation on honor can be held accountable for much of the region's curious polarity of mood and behavior, but they have not yet examined honor's importance to antebellum slaves. White Southerners' social schizophrenia sprang from their fealty to honor—from their prickliness at perceived insults to their reputation for expansive hospitality; from their rigid class relations to their professed fondness for yeoman democracy; from their dueling to their decorousness. The honorific white South's self-concern and absence of social privacy heightened the importance of every inflection, glance, and touch. Honor undergirded the "ethical patterns that gave coherence to the region's culture," giving white Southerners a common outlook. The aggrandizement of slaveholding only strengthened honor's pervasiveness among whites of the region.[10] The significant ramifications of their honor culture for white actions makes the lack of inquiry into slaves' similar behavior problematic.

Antebellum white Southerners did not live in the world's only honorific culture, and scholars from a variety of disciplines have distilled a theory of honor by examining these societies. Like Christianity, honor relates the ideal values of a society to its actual social structure and conditions, reconciling the world as it is with the way its members would see it. To be honored is to be temporarily distinguished among persons sharing common values and concerns. Conversely, to be denied honor or to be shamed is an accusation of aberrance and an assertion of inferiority. One's self-perceived balance of honor and shame "is not only the internalization of the values of society in the individual but the externalization of his self-image in the world." A society's code of honor thus acts to guide, sanction, and reward the behavior of its members and illustrates, for outsiders, the culture's values at work.[11]

Honor is not confined to any rank of society, and we know that honor was a potent creed among postbellum blacks. Demeaned by past and present white injustice, many freedmen demanded unquestioning respect from their peers. Indeed, honor may have been even more lethal in the postwar black community than among antebellum whites.[12] Much as antebellum Southern aristocrats placed themselves above the law in their frequent resort to honor, so too did postwar blacks obey honor's dictates.

While slave honor cannot be proved merely by the subsequent strength of principles of black honor, it is unlikely that postwar black honor sprang from nowhere. If "poverty and degradation often raise the stakes of honor," poor and degraded slaves would be as likely as their emancipated descendants to know "the hurt that honor feels."[13] The crucial difference was the freedmen's greater ability to act on the bruised honor they often masked as slaves. It was fealty to this honor that drove young Virginia slaves to desperate acts and made so many of Cocke's bondsmen disavow Christianity.

The individual's worthiness is honor's focus, but that judgment is only rendered in the arena of a common culture. Despite slavery's threat of "social death" and the isolating implications of slaveholders' paternalism, it is clear that the lives of Virginia slaves were shaped by their fellow slaves as well as by their masters. Although bound to labor for their master by force, law, and incentive, many slaves—especially in Virginia —had freedom in the work they performed. Nowhere in America was slavery more diverse, more ubiquitous than in Virginia. Like their Deep South brethren, some slaves in southeast Virginia worked in the cotton fields. But Virginia slaves also forged iron, harvested shellfish, mined coal, salt, and gold, grew wheat, piloted canalboats, tended tobacco, and manufactured consumer goods. The widespread practice of allowing slaves to hire themselves out to the employer of their choice fostered this diversity and allowed slaves an avenue for occupational autonomy.[14] In their nonworking hours, Virginia slaves enjoyed even greater autonomy. On special occasions and in frequent social activities with other bondsmen, slaves combined African traditions and aspects of American culture within the crucible of enslavement, generating the myths, tales, songs, and expectations that mark a distinct culture. These cultural characteristics served a dual purpose, in both Africa and Virginia, of "not only preserving communal values and solidarity but also providing occasions for the individual to transcend, at least symbolically, the inevitable restrictions of his environment."[15] Virginia slavery's myriad permutations—its multiple adaptations in a society devoted to both agriculture and industry—were at the heart of the state's ambivalent stance on the edge of the South. And Virginia's multifaceted slave system, with individual incentives and frequent freedom from the overseer's watchful eyes, may partially account for the strength of honor among slaves in the Old Dominion.

Slaves' community of shared values was most evident in their loyalty to one another. As one white missionary wrote, "The Negroes are a distinct class in community, and keep themselves very much to themselves. They are one thing before the whites, and another before their own color." One ex-slave interpreted this loyalty among slaves as "respect." She recalled that "the real character of a slave was brought out by the respect they had for each other." Slaves expressed this respect in their willingness to hide unknown runaways and their refusal to betray a fellow slave. Another ex-slave claimed that slaves who wished to remain in the community "never tole on each other." Many whites attested to slaves' solidarity. As attorney C. W. Gooch wrote in a prizewinning antebellum essay on Virginia agriculture, "The vice which they hold in the greatest abhorrence is that of telling upon one another."[16]

Violent punishment of traitors reflected slaves' intense dedication to their community. One Sunday in 1856, planter John Marshall returned from church to find that "some of my negroe men had taken Billy [a slave] and stripped and whipt him." Marshall was "much distressed" that slaves he considered obedient ("none but one of them had received a stripe for many years") had not brought their grievance against Billy to his attention. Marshall did not realize how superfluous his slaves considered him when communal solidarity was at stake. But Billy seems to have learned the lesson of slave loyalty. He offered no contradictory explanations for his conduct and did not deny his punishers' accusation.[17] This errant slave encountered dramatic proof of the slave community's power, and he emerged with a renewed understanding of the importance of steadfastness to his fellow bondsmen.

Slaves also demonstrated their communal strength with the variety of warnings they carried to one another. The phrase "weevils [or bugs] in the wheat" was used by bondsmen to warn each other that whites had learned of a planned nocturnal meeting of slaves and to announce that the occasion was postponed. Ishrael Massie recalled that when house slaves told field workers that "Massa an' Missus been talkin' 'bout money," everyone understood that "dey gonna sell some slaves to de nex' nigger-trader dat come 'roun'." Warnings were also carried in song. George

White remembered how his mother, a leader among the slaves on their plantation, urged other slaves to finish their work to avoid punishment:

> Keep yo' eye on de sun,
> See how she run,
> Don't let her catch you with your work undone,
> I'm a trouble, I'm a trouble.
> Trouble don' las' always.[18]

In addition to warnings, there were other ways slaves cooperated to frustrate the intentions of whites and confirm slave loyalty. Masters often left whipping duties to overseers or black foremen. One such foreman, Gabe, "didn't like dat whippin' business, but he couldn't hep himself. When Marsa was dere, he would lay it on 'cause he had to. But when ole Marsa warn't lookin', he never would beat dem slaves. Would tie de slave up to one post an' lash another one.'Cose de slave would scream an' yell to satisfy Marsa, but he wasn't gettin' no lashin'. After while Gabe would come out de barn an' ast Marsa if dat was enough. 'Sho, dat's plenty,' say Marsa."[19] Although he risked beating and loss of his privileged position, Gabe remained loyal to the slave community. In their warnings to each other (in code, word, and song), their vengeance against traitors to the slave community, and their cooperation against whites, Virginia slaves of both genders and all generations displayed a strong communal loyalty which was the foundation of their honor culture.[20] And it was this slave community that judged a slave's honor in the many potentially shameful trials of his bondage.

Both male and female slaves obeyed the dictates of pride, and three types of behavior bespoke their adherence to honor: refusal to be dishonored, vengeance, and display. Of these, display was the most obvious and least hazardous badge of honor.

Virginia bondsmen were unable to indulge in their masters' level of ostentatious display, just as slavery prevented them from responding to dishonor according to the code duello, but slaves were vitally concerned with how their appearance reflected (or belied) their honor. This attention, especially to dress, often caused slaves much extra work. Ex-slave Fanny Berry remembered that although she and other female slaves received only two new dresses each year, they were proud and careful of their appearance. She described how slaves washed their clothes at night, the only time available to them, rather than wear dirty garments. Berry also recalled the importance of dressing festively for special occasions. "Gals would put on dey spare dress ef dey had one, an' men would put a clean shirt on. Gals always tried to fix up fo' partyin', even ef dey ain't got nothin' but a piece of ribbon to tie in dey hair." Decades after her emancipation, Nancy Williams recalled sewing quilts to make money for shoes and cloth. Other slaves also did extra work to earn money to buy clothes, and many recalled with surprising specificity occasions when they received new attire. Slaveholders sometimes used the bondsman's desire for finery against him; Cocke's slaves competed for the fine great-coats he awarded to his black foremen. While not as sartorially splendid as their masters, slaves' display served to proclaim their honor and deny psychological bondage. In the words of one white minister, "with a passion for dress, they frequently spend all they make . . . in fine clothes; their appearance on the Sabbath and on public days . . . is anything else but an index of their fortunes and comfort at home."[21]

Another indication of honor in the slave quarters was bondsmen's refusal to be dishonored, either by other slaves or by whites. Despite the strength of community among slaves, honor led some to pursue precedence over their fellows as an exclamation of individual worth. William S. Brown, clerk of King George County, recorded in his diary how one male slave shot and killed another in their master's dining room. Brown believed the culprit had been affronted by his victim and predicted the murderer would likely hang for his "jealousy." Another observer described "rivalries and ill-feeling" among slaves and attributed this competitiveness to "ambition" for precedence and distinction. It was obvious to an experienced itinerant that slave "families grow jealous and envious of their neighbors; some essay to be *leading* families." Plantation mistress Nancy Cocke observed this same self-assertiveness among the slaves on her Fluvanna County plantations. Without the firm hand of a master's discipline, she wrote, "a plantation . . . is a place of purgatory." This need to prevent his slaves' honor from disrupting plantation affairs led her husband to compose a volume of rules and advice for his overseers. Acknowledging the potency of honor among slaves, Cocke instructed his foremen that "quarrelling or vexatious and insulting language from one to another, and especially from a younger to an older negro, should be strictly forbidden." A contemporary outlined the dangers in allowing slave honor to run unchecked, declaring "where no decisive measures are taken to suppress these practices, plantations sometimes become intolerable, might gives right; the strong oppress the weak."[22]

Although dishonor at the hands of another slave affected a bondsman's reputation among his peers, the most striking accounts of slaves acting on honor came in their relations with whites. Usually in the name of discipline, but sometimes for even less explicable purposes, whites abused

slaves with verbal and physical insults. Most instances of slaves refusing to be dishonored arose, not surprisingly, in response to threats of
violence—to prevent the beating or raping of themselves or a member
of their family. Numerous bondsmen would not submit to any whipping. Some slaves even made known their refusal to be beaten before
there was any danger of dishonor.[23]

While slaves probably wished to avoid the pain of lashing as much as
the dishonor involved, the ways they denied whites this means of discipline and their pride in the accomplishment indicate a strong motive of
honor. A slave's first refusal to be physically dishonored by a beating was
a strong, and hazardous, statement against white control. By refusing his
master or overseer the ability to degrade him, the slave asserted his will
above that of his owner; he denied he was a mere chattel, an object, an
item of intelligent livestock. And if his courage failed to win him exemption, he knew that he might be beaten even more severely for this rebelliousness.

Significantly, many of the slaves who escaped the dishonor of beatings
already occupied important positions; they were the slave foremen, the
strongest slaves, and the slave artisans. These slaves used the advantages
afforded by their economic importance to prevent dishonor. Success in
refusing dishonor reinforced the slave's privileged position and elevated
him above those not beyond the lash. More than simply an escape from
pain, this behavior displayed privileged slaves' awareness of their importance; these acts were viewed honorably by other slaves and were recalled
decades later as significant accomplishments.

Many slaves, prominent for their skills or personality, claimed special
treatment. Ex-slave Frank Bell recalled that his Uncle Moses, a frequent
runaway and the plantation overseer, was never beaten. "If it had been
any other slave [the master] give him a good whipping, but not Uncle
Moses. Just wasn't going to whip him. Don't know why, ah guess he was
a little bit skeered to whip dat big man. Everybody else was skeered of
him too." Another slave told his enraged master, "I'll die before I let you
beat me!" Some female slaves also refused to be beaten. Ex-slave Eliza
Robinson later recalled that her cousin "Jane Minor was so unruly and
mean dat marse couldn't beat her like de t'other slaves." On one plantation, where the master had never beaten his slaves, a new overseer tried
"to beat de slaves, but he got beat hissef." Nor were rural slaves alone in
refusing to submit to whippings. One Rockbridge County ironworker is
said to have hurled himself into a furnace rather than be beaten. And the
father of ex-slave Sister Harrison would "go to the hiring grounds an'

tell the man who bought his services that he'd run away an' leave him if he tried to beat him during the year." [24]

Some otherwise obedient slaves eventually reacted violently to accumulated dishonor. The Reverend W. P. Jacobs's Uncle Charlie "made up his mind he wouldn't stand it any longer, so he jumped on the nigger-driver." Many slaves even refused verbal dishonor, fighting those who insulted them. Ex-slave Nancy Williams remembered how an overseer "got mad an' cuss my pappy, den is de time dat ole po' white trash got jumped." Another slave told of an overseer who "cursed this particular nigger because he wasn't working to suit him. The nigger jumped on the overseer to fight him." In a slight variation, one female slave "would say whatever she thought. Den de mistress would beat her." [25] Just as white Virginians were careful of their reputations, a slave might also loathe to be physically or verbally dishonored and fight to prevent it.

Vengeance was the third characteristic of slave honor. Slaves' retribution, a reaction to the shame of dishonor, was never as formally developed as that of whites. White Virginians might duel at twenty paces, but their bondsmen had no such leisure in redressing dishonor. Still, slaves' actions expressed both aggrieved honor and innovative methods of vengeance for the many sources of their shame.

Patrollers—the white night riders responsible for preventing illicit slave meetings and capturing runaways—frequently inflicted dishonor upon Virginia slaves and were thus prime targets for vengeance. Patrollers were pushed into rivers, showered with hot coals, tripped by vines pulled taut across paths, and sometimes found their horses' throats cut. Overseers, another source of slave dishonor, were also frequent targets for retribution. Ex-slaves reported that cruel overseers were beaten and pushed into fires. Masters, like overseers and patrollers, were remembered vengefully by Virginia's former bondsmen. Fanny Berry's mistress sometimes amused guests by having her pet dog bite the slave's younger brother. To retaliate for their "playin' wid my brother dis way an' call it 'musement," she lured the dog into the nearby woods and hanged it. [26] These acts of vengeance reflected and reinforced slave honor.

If degradations could not be avoided, they were usually borne with patience. Slaves understood that although slavery was not a "total institution," it had more insults than any one man or woman could prevent. Eugene Genovese, the most thorough student of antebellum slavery, has correctly observed that "the plantation contained many slaves who gave little or no indication of rebelliousness and dutifully accepted their subservient roles but who nonetheless did not surrender their will or their honor."[27] This seeming paradox of outward subservience and internal rebelliousness lies at the heart of slave honor.

Many slaves endured degradation by denying that acts against them could breach their honor. Instances of oppression, rather than causing shame, were selectively regarded as unpreventable. Dishonor unacknowledged was dishonor unfelt and required no redress. As ex-slave Jordan Johnson recalled, slave husbands often "went to de woods when dey know de wives was due fo' a whippin', but in de fiel' dey dare not leave. Had to stay dere, not darin' even look like dey didn't like it. . . . Charlie he jus' stood dere hearin' his wife scream an' astarin' at de sky, not darin' to look at her or even say a word."[28] Denying or ignoring dishonor removed the obligation to seek redress and was the safest way to reconcile honor and degradation.

Honor was important to many Virginia slaves. Through display, refusal to be dishonored, and vengeance, these men and women stood up— often at great peril—against slavery's dehumanization. But honor's attractiveness faded as slaves aged and realized both the enduring strength of the slave system and the danger of opposing their subjugation. In their middle years, Virginia slaves increasingly left worldly honor behind for the assurances of Christianity. Scenes from one life reveal both the significance of honor for younger slaves and how this reactive creed might give way to evangelical faith.

When Fields Cook was born in 1814, the son of an enslaved cook on a small plantation in eastern Virginia, there was little to distinguish him from others of his generation. In 1847, however, he did an unusual thing for a slave: he wrote a memoir of his life.[29] Cook did not focus on the evils of slavery or urge readers to abolish the "peculiar institution," as did a growing number of runaway slaves writing outside the South. Instead, he focused on the intimate victories and disappointments of his life, concerned more with recording his experiences than in claiming victimization. Cook did not enjoy enslavement and chafed at racial prejudice, but he understood that short of flight, suicide, or a miracle, he had little hope of escaping bondage. He knew he was one "of that colore . . . which . . . is thought . . . not entitle to much favour being shown us."[30] The tension of a proud man living despised in an honorific society underlies much of his autobiography, revealing more about the secular and religious values of Virginia slaves.

Cook grew up playing with the planter's son, a boy his age for whom he felt great friendship. The son of a privileged house slave and the companion of his master's son, Cook was partially sheltered from the cruelties of slavery as an adolescent. "I never knew what the yoke of oppression was in the early part of my life," he wrote.[31]

Cook did, however, have early exposure to evangelical Christianity. A revival caught the imaginations of the young boys, and they grew earnest for their souls. Although impressed with the importance of religion, Cook did not convert as a young man, remaining "ignorant of the ways of the lord." But his young master accepted Christ wholeheartedly and began fruitless witnessing to Cook. Instead of winning Cook to the Lord, the persistent messenger only angered his friend. Upset with his own inability to experience conversion and his friend's frequent admonitions, Cook grew "really agravated with god himself."[32] Like the young slaves on Cocke's plantations, Fields Cook felt no personal tie to Christianity.

Cook's growing realization of the limits bondage placed on his life exacerbated his anxiety over religion. He was becoming ever more familiar with his circumscribed future as a slave, for the previous year he had begun work in the fields while his friend was sent away to school. And he held God responsible for this hardship, feeling himself personally betrayed into slavery. "I had done all that I had a right to do for [God,] and . . . he had not done his part toward me." Cook became openly anti-Christian in his disappointment, hoping to "insult [God] by every wicked action that I could think of." Expressing a strikingly honor-conscious attitude, Cook "thought by so doing I should spite the great god of heaven and make him bow to my own will."[33]

He may have taken his lead from his boyhood friend, who about this time began "to feel some what a man and like a peafowl in the mist of a brude of chickens he began to raise his feathers and boast of the superiority which he had over me." Caught between the increasing oppression of slavery and his unfulfilled desire for faith, Cook focused on what secular honor he could claim for himself. Cook, much like his young master, became preoccupied with his reputation for dominance. Other slaves knew he was "so proud they had to be on their peas and qs or else I'd be insulted."[34]

Like many other antebellum Virginia slaves, display was the most visible manifestation of Cook's sense of honor. One such exhibition of his status, however, went dangerously awry. Instead of driving his old plow horse on an errand one day, Cook decided to take his master's flashy but only partially harness-trained colt. To heighten the effect, Cook hitched the horse to a light carriage and appropriated his master's fine long whip. He later recalled that the borrowed equipage "made me look very grand," and he set out "with all the pride of a general." Driving through town Cook saw "the people all looking at my fine horse and gig and to make the thing show better I thought I would show my whip." Any conveyance-proud Southern white male would have done the same. But when Cook gave the horse "one very good rap" to make him prance, the result was not very flattering. The touch of the whip put the high-strung animal "in a fret over which he did not get reconciled for some time." Indeed, in the ensuing mad dash the colt carried Cook, the gig, and the plow he was taking to be repaired out of the town and more than half a mile down the road. His life in peril, Cook leapt from the vehicle. He later realized how lucky he was to escape with only two sprained ankles and a bruised reputation.[35]

His near-fatal accident did not dampen Cook's penchant for display or move him closer to the Christian faith. At age twenty the slave moved to Richmond, either relocated by his master or hiring himself out in the city, and continued his quest for exalting accoutrements. He gave particular attention to his attire. Where once Cook had been content to go barefoot and wear ragged pants, he now became quite concerned with clothes. The presence of appealing and eligible young women intensified his need to appear of honorable means. Now he must "dress myself in my best."[36]

Cook eventually found a wife in Richmond. Romantic success made the slave less insecure for his reputation, and Cook once again grew concerned at his lack of faith. During their engagement his owner dispatched him to the western part of the state for three months. Before departing, Fields promised his fiancée Mary that he would pray for conversion. But when he returned, still an unbeliever, he was ashamed to find she had converted in his absence. Her example helped Cook become a Christian three years later, but like the slaves on John Hartwell Cocke's plantations, it was the female who moved first to faith.[37]

Fields Cook continued to forsake honor for the Christian faith. When he penned his memoir at age thirty-three, he recounted his pursuits of honor as headstrong foibles and stressed the strength he now found in otherworldly support. Looking back on honor's importance in his life, Cook realized he "was very proud when a boy, although I had nothing to be proud of." In concluding his autobiography the Christian slave left no doubt that he now abjured both the prideful attitude and quick-tempered expression of honor. Cook especially abhorred Christian slaves who employed the violent tactics he associated with honor. He never approved of Nat Turner's rebellion, despite its attempted overthrow of slavery and Turner's widely expressed, if explosive, Christian inspiration. Turner's violence, like that of honor-conscious slaves, was anathema to Cook. As a Christian slave he felt Nat Turner would have been "better never born than to have left such a curse upon his nation."[38]

Fields Cook was not born a Christian. Bondage slowed his long and painful spiritual journey even as it made faith's goal more enticing. Cook adopted the attitudes of honor in his search for a way to express his individuality, but he soon discovered the dangers of the creed. He continued to follow honor's dictates even after his desire for status led him to a humiliating brush with death. Cook could only divorce himself from the expectations of the honorific when he found happiness in his personal life. Like John Hartwell Cocke's slaves, Fields Cook knew that no matter how great a bondsman's need for solace or redemption or explanation of his fate, Christianity was not an automatic relief. Slaves came to the crossroads of honor and Christianity early in life, and many found the self-abnegating demands of Christ's teachings too much to bear. Others left the path of righteousness at times of great trouble or temptation, feeling they could only proceed on the trail of honor. For Fields Cook and the minority of Christian slaves the journey of faith was difficult but the destination worthy.

Our understanding of slavery has too long been clouded by explanations claiming that all slaves were either infantilized "sambos," glowering rebels, or great-souled Christians.[39] It is time to admit the complexity of slaves' lives and longings, a complexity manifested in Fields Cook's years of ambivalence. Despite the appeal of Christian missions, he was honor's captive during his youth and early adult years. The prickly, self-conscious, reactive individualism of honor appealed to Cook and other young slaves because it explained the impotence they felt as chattel. Shame permeated slave society, and slaves—the targets of that shame—felt honor's allure with peculiar intensity. Just as bondage limited slaves' ability to preserve their dignity, it also heightened honor's importance, making any distinction all the more precious. Not surprisingly, most Virginia slaves spent much of their lives honor-bound, only coming to evangelical religion after years of fruitlessly pitting their self-esteem against the power of the Southern slave system.

Yet Virginia's converted slaves may have found a stronger foundation for self-esteem than did those who clung to honor. For the context of divine authority placed the limited authority of masters and overseers in perspective. As Fields Cook discovered, the assurances of Christ brought faithful slaves a "space of meaning, freedom, and transcendence" that even the most prickly, honor-conscious bondsman could not claim.[40]

Whether in honor-driven reaction to chattel status or in Christian expectation of the promised equity of Judgment Day, Virginia slaves did
not surrender their souls to bondage.

NOTES

Much of this chapter's coherence flows from the kind efforts of friends
and colleagues. I must thank Edward L. Ayers for his patience and good-
humored suggestions; he encouraged me to pursue the notion of honor
among slaves despite its counterintuitive implications and has been an invaluable coconspirator in bringing this volume to life. I have too frequently
availed myself of D. Alan Williams's encyclopedic knowledge of Virginia
history—he introduced me to Fields Cook—and deeply appreciate his many
careful readings of the M.A. thesis from which this chapter is adapted.
John K. Brown took time out of his own research to read and critique this
piece: as always, I appreciate his thoroughness, good advice, and support.
Several of my fellow contributors to this volume have also given me helpful
insights. But Laura M. Lapins has my greatest gratitude. Her patience has
made this and many other "harebrained schemes" possible, and her friendship makes it all worthwhile. This chapter is adapted from my "Behind
'Their Black Masks': Slave Honor in Antebellum Virginia" (M.A. thesis,
Univ. of Virginia, 1987).

1   In 1831 Southampton County slave preacher Nat Turner led dozens of slaves
    in an uprising which left almost sixty whites dead in its wake. He was later
    captured and executed, but the rebellion reminded Virginia slaveholders
    that while Jesus predicted that the meek shall inherit the Earth, the Bible
    also contained examples of God aiding the wronged in battles against their
    oppressors. The Richmond *Enquirer* later admonished whites: "The case
    of Nat Turner warns us. No black-man ought to be permitted to turn a
    Preacher through the country" (quoted in George Washington Williams,
    History of the Negro Race in America, 2 vols. [New York: Putnam's, 1882],
    2:90). Thomas L. Webber examined masters' largely unsuccessful attempts
    to shape slaves' values in *Deep like the Rivers: Education in the Slave Quar-
    ter Community, 1831–1865* (New York: Norton, 1978).

2   "Schedule of General Cocke's Servants," Cocke Family Papers, Acc. 640,
    MSS Div., Special Colls. Dept., Univ. of Virginia Library (UVA Lib.). Cocke
    had a combination school and chapel constructed of brick for his slaves in
    1826, and a freestanding slave church was built in 1835. Cocke began manu-
    mitting deserving Christian slaves in 1832, an additional incentive for belief
    among his bondsmen and a possible motivation for the survey (see M. Boyd
    Coyner, Jr., "John Hartwell Cocke of Bremo: Agriculture and Slavery in the
    Ante-Bellum South" [Ph.D. diss., Univ. of Virginia, 1961], 325–34, 88–89,
    352–56).

3   John W. Blassingame, *The Slave Community: Plantation Life in the Ante-
    bellum South* (New York: Oxford Univ. Press, 1972, rev. ed., 1979), 131.
    This view echoes the sentiment expressed by a federal official in Alexan-
    dria, Virginia, who described one slave preacher in 1863: "This old negro
    has more influence over the blacks, and does more good among them,
    than all the missionaries and chaplains who have been sent here" (H. G.

Spaulding, "Under the Palmetto," *Continental Monthly* 4 [1863]: 196–200, quoted in Lawrence W. Levine, *Black Culture and Black Consciousness: Afro-American Folk Thought from Slavery to Freedom* [New York: Oxford Univ. Press, 1977], 47). August Meier and Elliott Rudwick have written that "the appearance of Blassingame's volume [*The Slave Community*] signaled the entry of the culture-and-community perspective [with emphasis on slave Christianity] into the mainstream of historical interpretation" (*Black History and the Historical Profession, 1915–1980* [Urbana: Univ. of Illinois Press, 1986], 267). Their chapter 4, "The Historiography of Slavery: An Inquiry into Paradigm-making and Scholarly Interaction," 239–76, explores this question at length.

4   Even slaves of Christian masters feared violent treatment. Jasper, a nineteen-year-old slave on Cocke's Bremo Recess plantation, was caught attempting to escape to freedom in the North. He was beaten so severely that despite Cocke's desire to sell him off the plantation, he was "under the Doctor's hand" for almost three months and was too debilitated to offer for sale for another four months (Cocke Family Papers).

5   The "Schedule of General Cocke's Servants" surveys the family structures, occupations, places of residence, and religious beliefs of Cocke's over 200 slaves. Only Cocke's 108 "working slaves" were questioned regarding whether they professed Christianity. On Cocke's plantations, black males and females worked as young as age fourteen: all of Cocke's slaves worked full time by age sixteen ("Schedule of General Cocke's Servants," ibid.; Coyner, "John Hartwell Cocke of Bremo," 81, 93). Eugene Genovese cited "W. E. B. DuBois and other scholars" to support the possibility that only one-sixth of adult slaves were Christian (*Roll, Jordan, Roll: The World the Slaves Made* [New York: Random House, 1974], 184). In *The Negro Church*, DuBois noted that there were 468,000 black church members in the South in 1859. Allowing a 3 percent increase in that figure by 1860 (the increase from 1844 to 1859 among Methodists, one of the most popular denominations with slaves, averaged between 2 and 3 percent), there were roughly 482,040 Southern black Christians in the last antebellum year. And one may estimate that half the 3,838,765 black Southerners in 1860 (1,919,383) were adult slaves. Dividing the number of Christians (482,040) by the estimated number of adult slaves (1,919,383) reveals that Christians probably accounted for about one-quarter of adult slaves. Since my estimate inflates the number of church members while restricting the ratio of adults among slaves to only half, this 25 percent figure probably expresses the maximum proportion of the South's Christian adult slaves (figures derived from W. E. B. DuBois, ed., *The Negro Church* [Atlanta: Atlanta Univ. Press, 1903], 29; Donald G. Mathews, *Slavery and Methodism: A Chapter in American Morality, 1780–1845* [Princeton, N.J.: Princeton Univ. Press, 1965], 66; U.S. Bureau of the Census, *Negro Population in the United States, 1790–1915* [Washington, D.C.: GPO, 1918], 55).

6   "Schedule of General Cocke's Servants," Cocke Family Papers; Coyner, "John Hartwell Cocke of Bremo," 81, 93; Charles C. Jones, *The Religious Instruction of the Negroes in the United States* (Savannah: Thomas Purse, 1842), 118. While Jones was devoted to spreading Christianity among Southern blacks, he admitted that at the beginning of the antebellum era "but a minority of the Negroes, and that a small one, attended regularly the house of God, and taking them as a class, their religious instruction was exten-

sively and most seriously neglected" (ibid., 64). Cocke seems to have deemed slaves marriageable after a few years' full-time work (see note 5, above).

7   "Schedule of General Cocke's Servants," Cocke Family Papers.

8   Stephen C. Crawford, "Quantified Memory: A Study of the W.P.A. and Fisk University Slave Narrative Collections" (Ph.D. diss., Univ. of Chicago, 1980), 96–110; Philip J. Schwarz, *Twice Condemned: Slaves and the Criminal Laws of Virginia, 1705–1865* (Baton Rouge: Louisiana State Univ. Press, 1988), 212 and n., 217, 283–84; Gregg Michel, chapter 5 below. Crawford's regionwide examination of younger slaves' resistance to the degradations of the system is corroborated for Virginia by records of the Richmond police, which list a large majority of antebellum slave runaways among this same age group (Richmond Police Daybook, 1834–43, Acc. 1481, UVA Lib.). Research by Mechal Sobel suggests this pattern of pronounced aggression in the late teen through early adult years was a pattern among Virginia slaves as early as the eighteenth century. She has written that "youth often found [slaves] rebellious" and argued that "some found their sense of self by opposing masters and slave-breakers" (Sobel, *The World They Made Together: Black and White Values in Eighteenth-Century Virginia* [Princeton, N.J.: Princeton Univ. Press, 1987], 41).

9   "The Schedule of General Cocke's Servants" confirms that most slaves, like their masters, converted to Christianity later in life. And for both races, organized religion was dominated by females and older males (Donald G. Mathews, *Religion in the Old South* [Chicago: Univ. of Chicago Press, 1977]). Bertram Wyatt-Brown probed the ambiguous tensions within the white South's marriage of honor and Christianity, "gentility," in his "God and Honor in the Old South," *Southern Review* 25 (April 1989): 283–96, and *Southern Honor: Ethics and Behavior in the Old South* (New York: Oxford Univ. Press, 1982), 88–114.

10 Wyatt-Brown, *Southern Honor*, xvi. As Edward L. Ayers has shown, "honor would have died in the South without the hothouse atmosphere provided for that culture by slavery" (Ayers, *Vengeance and Justice: Crime and Punishment in the 19th-Century American South* [New York: Oxford Univ. Press, 1984], 26).

11 Julian Pitt-Rivers, "Honor," in David Sills, ed., *The International Encyclopedia of the Social Sciences* (New York: Macmillan, 1968), 510, 503–5.

12 Wyatt-Brown, *Southern Honor*, xv; Ayers, *Vengeance and Justice*, 234–35.

13 Ayers, *Vengeance and Justice*, 235, 274–76.

14 A number of historians have addressed the diversity of slavery in Virginia. See Charles B. Dew, *Ironmaker to the Confederacy: Joseph R. Anderson and the Tredegar Iron Works* (New Haven: Yale Univ. Press, 1966), "Disciplining Slave Ironworkers in the Antebellum South: Coercion, Conciliation, and Accommodation," *American Historical Review* 70 (April 1974): 393–418, and "Sam Williams, Forgeman: The Life of an Industrial Slave in the Old South," in J. Morgan Kousser and James M. McPherson, eds., *Region, Race, and Reconstruction: Essays in Honor of C. Vann Woodward* (New York: Oxford Univ. Press, 1982), 199–239; Ronald L. Lewis, *Coal, Iron, and Slaves: Industrial Slavery in Maryland and Virginia, 1715–1865* (Westport, Conn.: Greenwood, 1979); Suzanne Lebsock, *The Free Women of Petersburg: Status and Culture in a Southern Town, 1784–1860* (New York: Norton, 1984); S. Sydney Bradford, "The Negro Ironworker in Ante

Bellum Virginia," *Journal of Southern History* 25 (May 1959): 194–206; Fletcher M. Green, "Gold Mining in Ante-Bellum Virginia," *Virginia Magazine of History and Biography* 45 (July, Oct. 1937): 227–35, 357–66; John Edmond Stealey III, "Slavery and the Western Virginia Salt Industry," *Journal of Negro History* 59 (April 1976): 105–31; John T. O'Brien, "Factory, Church, and Community: Blacks in Ante-bellum Richmond," *Journal of Southern History* 44 (Nov. 1978): 509–36; Robert S. Starobin, *Industrial Slavery in the Old South* (New York: Oxford Univ. Press, 1970); Richard C. Wade, *Slavery in the Cities: The South, 1820–1860* (New York: Oxford Univ. Press, 1964); Clement Eaton, "Slave-Hiring in the Upper South: A Step toward Freedom," *Mississippi Valley Historical Review* 46 (March 1960): 663–79. Philip J. Schwarz examined the historiography of free and enslaved black Virginians in his "'A Sense of Their Own Power': Black Virginians, 1619–1989," *Virginia Magazine of History and Biography* 97 (July 1989): 279–310. Maryland's slave system, where bondage was almost as multifaceted, is Barbara Jeanne Fields's subject in *Slavery and Freedom on the Middle Ground: Maryland during the Nineteenth Century* (New Haven: Yale Univ. Press, 1985). Lawrence Hartzell's chapter 6 below explores the postbellum implications of Petersburg's large hired slave and free black community.

15 Levine, *Black Culture and Black Consciousness*, 4–19, 24, 30; Blassingame, *The Slave Community*, 105–6. For a contrasting view, see sociologist Orlando Patterson's *Slavery and Social Death: A Comparative Study* (Cambridge: Harvard Univ. Press, 1982).

16 Jones, *Religious Instruction*, 110, 114; Charles L. Perdue, Jr., Thomas E. Barden, and Robert K. Phillips, eds., *Weevils in the Wheat: Interviews with Virginia Ex-Slaves* (Charlottesville: Univ. Press of Virginia, 1976), 235, 219–20.

17 Captain John Marshall Journal, Marshall-Gaines Collection, Acc. 2425, UVA Lib. Marshall did not appreciate the irony of Billy's punishment: he was disciplined by his fellow slaves in the same fashion that whites usually punished their chattels.

18 Perdue et al., *Weevils in the Wheat*, 299, 211, 309–10, 88.

19 Ibid., 290–91. Ex-slave West Turner, who related Gabe's solidarity, also pointed out the risks of aiding fellow slaves: "Once ole Gabe was beatin' de post so hard an' de slave was yellin' so dat Marsa call out to Gabe, "Quit beatin' dat nigger, Gabe. What you tryin' to do, kill him?" Slave come runnin' out screamin' wid berry wine rubbed all over his back an' Marsa tole Gabe if he didn't stop beatin' his slaves so hard, he gonna git a lashin' hisself."

20 Peter Kolchin's recent comparison of slavery in the American South and serfdom in czarist Russia places "community" among unfree laborers in broader perspective. Kolchin contrasted slaves' broad sense of brotherhood in grievance (which was often displayed in individual action) with serfs' collective patterns of resistance, revealing the pitfalls of exaggerating slaves' community. See his *Unfree Labor: American Slavery and Russian Serfdom* (Cambridge: Belknap Press of Harvard Univ. Press, 1987). The concept of honor is one way to reconcile slaves' incipient community with their habitually individualistic acts of resistance.

21 Perdue et al., *Weevils in the Wheat*, 32, 49, 316–17; Coyner, "John Hartwell Cocke of Bremo," 133; Jones, *Religious Instruction*, 145–46. For fur-

ther examples of slaves' penchant for display, see Perdue et al., *Weevils in the Wheat*, 66, 148, 210, 212, 277, 333, and Deborah Gray White, *"Ar'n't I A Woman?": Female Slaves in the Plantation South* (New York: Norton, 1985), 143.

22 William S. Brown Diary, 17 Jan. 1844, Brown-Hunter Family Papers, Acc. 4492, UVA Lib.; D. R. Hundley, *Social Relations in Our Southern States* (New York: Henry B. Price, 1860; rept. New York: Arno, 1973), 352; Jones, *Religious Instruction*, 136; Coyner, "John Hartwell Cocke of Bremo," 54; "Regulations for Overseers, 1816, Copied 1828," and "Standing Rules for the Government of Slaves on a Virginia Plantation, with Notes and Observations," Cocke Family Papers. For further examples of slaves' refusal to be dishonored by other slaves, see Schwarz, *Twice Condemned*, 250–52.

23 Genovese, *Roll, Jordan, Roll*, 619.

24 Perdue et al., *Weevils in the Wheat*, 26–27, 84, 238, 52, 135; Bradford, "The Negro Ironworker," 203–4. For other examples of Virginia slaves' refusal to be dishonored, see Perdue et al., *Weevils in the Wheat*, 324; Norman R. Yetman, ed., *Life under the "Peculiar Institution": Selections from the Slave Narrative Collections* (New York: Holt, Rinehart & Winston, 1970), 11–12, 88–91; John W. Blassingame, ed., *Slave Testimony: Two Centuries of Letters, Speeches, Interviews, and Autobiographies* (Baton Rouge: Louisiana State Univ. Press, 1977), 170, 419–20, 441–42.

25 Perdue et al., *Weevils in the Wheat*, 156, 317, 255, 309.

26 Ibid., 214–15, 180, 93, 241, 52, 96–97, 347, 162, 194, 45–48. For other examples of slave vengeance, see Schwarz, *Twice Condemned*, 238–40. Sometimes the need for vengeance did not end with slavery. Anna Harris was unable to forget the indignities of bondage. "No white man ever been in my house," she declared. "Don't 'low it. Dey sole my sister Kate. I saw it wid dese here eyes. Sole her in 1860, and I ain't seed nor heard of her since. Folks say white folks is all right dese days. Maybe dey is, maybe dey isn't. But I can't stand to see 'em. Not on my place" (Perdue et al., *Weevils in the Wheat*, 128).

27 Genovese, *Roll, Jordan, Roll*, 617.

28 Perdue et al., *Weevils in the Wheat*, 160. For other examples of slaves denying dishonor, see ibid., 206, 300–301.

29 Fields Cook's Memoir, box 2, Black History Miscellany, Library of Congress. The memoir was transcribed and edited by Mary J. Bratton and published as "Fields's Observations: The Slave Narrative of a Nineteenth-Century Virginian," *Virginia Magazine of History and Biography* 88 (Jan. 1980): 75–93. Cook's words are quoted here as transcribed by Bratton. Citations refer to page numbers in the published version. The memoir was obviously not penned for publication, and it is only through Bratton's thoughtful research that we know Fields Cook as the likely author. Cook's autobiography is important for locating the roots of black honor in the antebellum era. Ex-slaves might exaggerate their fearlessness to conform to the strong expectations of the postbellum honor culture described by Ayers in *Vengeance and Justice*. But Fields Cook's description of the slavery period both confirms the plausibility of the W.P.A. narratives and helps explain Cocke's survey.

30 Ibid., 78.

31 Ibid.

32   Ibid., 80.

33   Ibid., 80–82.

34   Ibid., 78, 88.

35   Ibid., 85–86.

36   Ibid., 87–88.

37   Ibid., 88–93.

38   Ibid. Even more than most Virginia slaves, Fields Cook left honor for Christianity: he later became a minister (ibid., 77).

39   Bertram Wyatt-Brown recently attempted to combine several such generalizations into a supertypology. See "The Mask of Obedience: Male Slave Psychology in the Old South," *American Historical Review* 93 (Dec. 1988): 1228–52.

40   Albert J. Raboteau, *Slave Religion: The "Invisible Institution" in the Antebellum South* (New York: Oxford Univ. Press, 1978), 318.

3

T. LLOYD BENSON

The Plain Folk of Orange: Land, Work, and Society on the Eve of the Civil War

ONE DAY IN THE EARLY SUMMER OF 1860 A MIDDLE-AGED man set out on a journey across Orange County, Virginia. The man was a farmer by trade, but on this day he was beginning a more uncommon job. The traveler was John F. Taliaferro, scion of a distinguished county family and the person selected by the federal government to enumerate the Orange County portion of the 1860 census. He headed first to the home of the local tax collector, Richard Richards, a man who knew the county's households better than any other citizen of Orange. Each year the tax collectors provided the state with much the same sort of information that the census obtained every ten years. It was therefore logical for Taliaferro to start his enumeration with such an experienced hand.

Taliaferro crisscrossed the county all that summer, starting in the small farm and scrubwoods district later renowned to the world as the grisly Wilderness battlefield, circling his way gradually west through rolling farmlands and the bustling railroad village of Gordonsville, finally sweeping back east through Orange Court House and the area around his own farm. When finished he had visited almost nine hundred households and compiled records on more than ten thousand people. While Taliaferro missed some people, counted others twice, and did not always record census items thoroughly, his efforts resulted in a remarkable document mirroring the vitality and diversity of local life in Orange on the eve of the Civil War.[1]

A number of Southern historians have used manuscript census and tax records of the type collected by Taliaferro and Richards to draw important conclusions about the nature of antebellum society, but the census and tax documents also have certain limitations unique to a largely rural and slave-oriented society. These limitations have helped make local histories of the South more abstract than comparable works in urban history based on similar sources. Since the street directories and census enumeration districts of big cities have few counterparts in rural counties, historians must generalize about Southern people from comparatively oversized units, thus losing the special character of each locale. Studies from such disparate states as Missouri, Texas, Virginia, and Georgia have a strange similarity, largely because they lack a concrete sense of place. Since no occupations were listed on slave schedules and a large majority of whites worked in agriculture, occupational studies of the South are by nature less informative than comparable studies of major cities. And, since the immigrant population of the rural South was so small, questions regarding the development of ethnic neighborhoods, the process of cultural assimilation, and the course of upward mobility that the census answers so well are not very important in Southern history.[2]

Instead of exploring immigration, assimilation, and spatial distribution, most Southern historians devote attention to abstract class structure and social relations. Economic democracy, the concentration of wealth, and the expansion of the market economy are the bread and butter of Southern local studies. Since land is the basis of agricultural societies such as the South, however, any study of local economic structures is incomplete without a complementary evaluation of local geography.

We do know that the planters made up the bulk of landowners in the rich river bottoms and deltas, while a much greater percentage of small farmers and stock herders were to be found in the backcountry and mountain highlands. Some historians argue that this pattern was the result of a gradual exclusion of smaller farms from the plantation regions as original settlers expanded their holdings or were bought out by more wealthy neighbors. The smallest farmers, these scholars suggest, were forced out of the rich delta bottoms by wealthy planters and could only find a homestead in the sand hills and piney woods or on cheap government lands where competition was less brutal. Other historians dispute this "exclusion thesis," citing evidence that large numbers of plain folk owned land in even the best districts and that these holdings were intermingled among the holdings of more wealthy planters. Advocates of the exclusion thesis have been quick to point out, however, that ownership in the same neighborhood did not necessarily imply that rich and poor held land of the same quality.[3]

In Orange County, both geography and social structure reflected the complex historical forces at work in antebellum Virginia. The tobacco slump following the panic of 1819, the rise of competition from planters in the western states, and an unstable fluctuation of tobacco prices and production led to hard times in the Virginia leaf districts in the three decades before 1850. Virginia farmers also faced extensive soil erosion

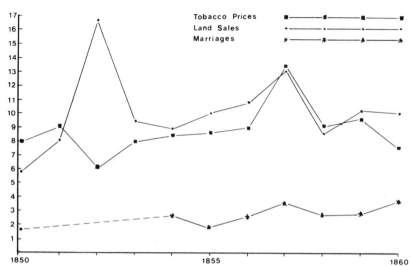

Fig 3.1. Tobacco prices, deeds, and marriages in Orange County, Virginia, 1850–60. Sources: Robert, *Tobacco Kingdom*, 133–34; General Index to Deeds, Orange County, vol. 3, 1848–90, and Auditor of Public Accounts, Land Books, Orange County, 1858–59, 1860–61, pp. 177, 497, VSL; U.S. Bureau of the Census, *The Seventh Census of the United States, 1850* Washington, D.C.: GPO, 1853), p. 260.

and a decline in productivity that made migration to cheap lands in the South and West very attractive. The residents of Orange County had endured the long depression by resorting to mixed agriculture, lower birthrates, and high out-migration, but important local and national changes during the decade before secession reversed the trend of these adaptations, particularly among the poorer elements of white society. High prices for staple crops and the improvement of transportation links with major markets caused an upturn in the local economy.[4]

The course of tobacco prices, land sales, and marriages during the 1850s is shown in figure 3.1. Except in 1852, the correspondence between land sales and tobacco prices is striking. The parallel is especially significant in 1857, when prices for wheat and corn went down, while both land sales and tobacco prices rose. Overall, the general upward trend of tobacco prices was sufficient cause of optimism among Virginia farmers. Average prices for middling leaf went below seven cents only twice in the 1850s, whereas they had only been above that level once in the previous ten years. Orange County farmers avidly bought and sold lands according to the tobacco markets; in 1860 alone, 12 percent of all tracts and town

Table 3.1. Occupational change in state and county, 1850–60

	1850 Census		1860 Census	
Virginia				
Farmers	106,807	(47%)	108,958	(36%)
Laborers	46,989	(21%)	44,041	(15%)
Orange County				
Farmers	429	(39%)	450	(53%)
Other agricultural	72	(7%)	61	(7%)
Unskilled laborers	190	(17%)	51	(6%)
Crafts and services	291	(26%)	221	(26%)
Civil or professional	65	(5%)	58	(7%)
Others	53	(5%)	12	(1%)
Total	1,099	(100%)	853	(100%)

Sources: U.S. Bureau of the Census, *The Seventh Census of the United States, 1850* (Washington, D.C.: GPO, 1853), 272; U.S. Bureau of the Census, *Eighth Census*, vol. 1, *Population*, 524–25; population schedules, 1850, 1860, NA.

lots exchanged hands, and transactions occurred even more briskly in 1852 and 1857. As conditions improved, farmers brought marginal fields into production, adding more than nineteen square miles to the county's improved acreage between 1849 and 1859. At the same time, there was a thirty-three-acre decline in average farm size between 1850 and 1860. The decade of 1850s, then, was a time of simultaneous expansion and deconcentration in landed wealth.[5]

Poor farm laborers benefited the most from these changes. Their improvement in status is mirrored in the changing distribution of occupations during the decade (table 3.1). While the absolute number of farmers increased by 2 percent in the state and 5 percent in the county, the number of laborers declined by 6 percent in the state and 73 percent in the county; many of the people who labored in 1850 had become landowning farmers by 1860. The poorer element of white society seems to have avidly seized the opportunities to buy land that arose in the 1850s. While the number of Virginians employed in nonagricultural pursuits exploded during the decade, the reverse was true in Orange County.

The draw of the land was due not only to improved tobacco prices but also to the development of railroad links to the county. These new links allowed residents for the first time to ship their products cheaply to lucrative markets in Richmond and Alexandria. The Louisa Railroad reached the village of Gordonsville in 1840, connecting with the Fredericksburg-Charlottesville stage line. This railroad, redubbed the Virginia Central in 1850, was joined at Gordonsville in 1854 by the Orange and Alexandria Railroad. These railroads brought a number of products to Orange, particularly dry goods, furniture, and commercial goods, and carried away

Table 3.2. Growth rates for selected male age groups: Orange and surrounding counties, 1850–60

County	Ages 15–19	Ages 20–29	Ages 30–39
Orange	5.6%	32.4%	18.0%
Spotsylvania	16.3	20.7	10.0
Greene	15.3	7.7	0.6
Louisa	0.0	− 9.4	− 7.9
Culpeper	6.9	−17.7	19.3
Madison	−17.4	−13.0	0.3
Albemarle	−18.8	−15.4	− 4.5

Sources: U.S. Bureau of the Census, *Seventh Census*, 242–45; U.S. Bureau of the Census, *Eighth Census*, vol. 1, *Population*, 500.

the rich agricultural harvest, while spurring village growth and adding to land values. The influence of the railroads on land sales is visible in figure 3.1, which shows that the number of transfers more than doubled in 1852 over the previous year. The Orange and Alexandria Railroad itself only purchased five tracts in 1852 for its right-of-way from Orange Court House to Gordonsville, but the general excitement over the new system generated a sudden land boom. Land sales were particularly brisk in Gordonsville, where the two railroads joined, but sales were up across the county.[6]

The good times brought by the railroads and high tobacco prices greatly increased the rewards of remaining in the county, especially for young men. There are no precise statistics, but the drop in out-migration can be inferred from population profiles. There was an unusual increase in the number of men aged twenty–twenty-nine and of children under ten in Orange during the 1850s (table 3.2). Meanwhile, there was a large increase in the number of marriages annually (see fig 3.1), which partly explains the sudden boom in the number of young children and provides further proof of the expanding opportunity and reduced out-migration characteristic of the state as a whole during this period.

This reduction in migration seems especially strong when Orange is compared to the surrounding counties. Not all of the upper Piedmont shared in the population expansion (see table 3.2). The combined figures for the seven counties surrounding Orange show a decrease from 1850 to 1860 in the number of free children under ten, suggesting that the boom of the 1850s depended on local circumstances. Only Orange, Spotsylvania, and to some extent Greene had important rail terminals or turnpikes and were located in the tobacco district. Culpeper was outside the tobacco-planting area, as was Madison County. Louisa County lacked any major railheads, despite the fact that the Virginia Central ran through the county, and the growth of nearby Richmond may have siphoned off many Louisa residents. Similarly, Albemarle's rail network was not completed until the late 1850s. Orange, which was in the tobacco district, lay on the only direct route from Alexandria to Richmond. Two turnpikes brought produce from the Shenandoah Valley east to the railroads. Orange's fortunate conditions were unique in this period.[7]

The strong local economy helped to expand opportunities for average people in Orange during the last decade of the antebellum era, but expansion is only part of their story. How did the common people or plain folk of the South fit into the rest of society? What was their position on the eve of the most crucial period in Southern history? These questions are particularly intriguing for a plantation county such as Orange. Slaves made up more than half of the population, and nearly half of all white households were slave-owning, yet the nonslaveholding whites hardly fit the stereotype of the "poor white." They were segregated neither by geography nor by a distinct cultural background. How these common people in the heart of plantation society stack up against the classical descriptions of nonplanter society put forth by historians and contemporary observers is still largely a mystery.[8]

Few people would claim that antebellum white society was devoid of distinct social groups. Attempts to divide this society into ranked social categories, however, have had ambiguous results. In the antebellum era, Hinton Helper, George Weston, and E. A. Seabrook were leading advocates of the thesis that the chief distinction in Southern white society resulted from ownership of property in slaves, and each lamented the degradation of other whites that they saw growing out of this sharp division. Their two broad categories, though, slaveholding and nonslaveholding, do not reflect the complexity and diversity of within each group. Daniel Hundley, writing in the 1850s, discerned at least seven different classes in the South, each based on behavioral characteristics rooted in heredity. His descriptions are an eloquent testimony to the rich texture of the South, but evidence about personality and behavior is scattered and hardly adequate for classifying all the members of a community. Furthermore, models based on genetic heredity have been discredited time and time again.[9]

Historians have held two opposing views about poor whites. One view, similar to Helper's, contends that poor whites lacked any economic, political, or social independence from the planters. The wealthy planter overawed his poor neighbors economically but kept their friendship and loyalty by hosting local barbeques and other entertainments. In short, the planters monopolized all the best resources of society, while leaving

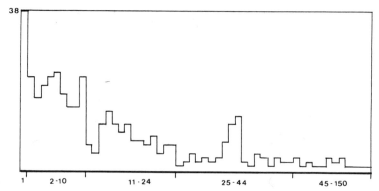

Fig 3.2. Profile of slave ownership in Orange County, Virginia,
1860. Sources: manuscript population schedules, free and slave
schedules, U.S. Census, 1860. Note: Figures are totals for each
household and do not correspond precisely to published totals
based on individual ownership.

the poor white to struggle on the hardscrabble soils of the backwoods.
The other view claims that poor whites suffered little under the plantation regime. They lived in the same districts as planters, in a kind of economic democracy. Moreover, the poor whites, through their large numbers and avid interest in politics, forced elected leaders to follow their
wishes.

The most satisfactory means of dividing society into groups lies between these two extremes and is based on a combination of property-
ownership and occupational rankings. Skill, authority, and wealth have
formed the basis of social rankings in many different cultures, and the
antebellum South was little different. Work and wealth give a good
notion of the social order among whites.[10]

Although ownership of slaves was a central characteristic of the South,
differences among slaveholders were great. Figure 3.2 shows the distribution of slaves among free households. Four obvious clusters stand out:
those holding one slave, those holding between two and ten slaves, and
those holding twenty-five or more slaves. The first group is worthy of
special attention because its members belonged to those households on
the margins of slave ownership. These 38 households have been joined
for analytical purposes with the 112 nonslaveholding households having
direct title to land within the county, another group on the margins of
ownership. The resulting classification of the county's households is summarized in table 3.3.

The data show that over half of all white households in Orange County

Table 3.3. Division of households in Orange County, 1860 (N = 870)

Ownership	Number	Percentage
25 + Slaves	68	(7.8%)
10–24 Slaves	112	(12.9%)
2–10 Slaves	175	(7.8%)
Land or 1 slave	150	(17.2%)
No land and no slaves	318	(36.6%)
Special cases*	47	(5.4%)

Sources: population schedules, 1860, NA; Auditor, Land Book, 1860, VSL.
*Includes 28 nonwhite, 13 illegible, and 6 duplicate households.

had at least one member who owned either land or slaves. Furthermore, about half of the propertyless households contained either craftsmen and service workers. The remaining households comprised the poor white class, with no property or skills, a rural proletariat entirely dependent on income from tenancy or manual labor. Evidence on the condition of these poor whites is scanty, but they should not be viewed collectively as mere ne'er-do-wells living in utter destitution and hopelessness. Given the high prices for all agricultural products in this period, and especially tobacco, farmers needed extra labor and offered high wages to those they hired. Tenancy was not the economic dead end it became after the Civil War. Recent studies of staple areas similar to Orange County show that where farmers raised crops requiring care during a large number of days during the course of a year, wage labor was lucrative. While slave labor had a competitive advantage in comparison to free labor on an annual basis, white manual labor proved quite valuable during the peak periods of planting, cultivation, and harvesting. As a consequence, wages for laborers were consistently high. The reduction in the manual labor force during the 1850s can only have raised wages higher. Finally, even the poorest Southerners could tap the bounty of the woods and streams. Orange County was by no means a howling wilderness on the eve of the war, but it had a considerable area in unimproved woodlands, particularly in the northeastern corner, and the county was also crisscrossed with streams. Fish and game, then, could have been found without much trouble by those in need.[11]

About half of the propertyless households contained artisans and service workers (table 3.4). The most striking thing about occupations in Orange, though, is that so many people from all ranks in society were craftsmen. Much has been made of the agricultural character of the South. The stereotypical poor white Southerner, in particular, has almost always been depicted as a tenant farmer or sharecropper. But the large percentage of Orange County residents employed in nonagri-

Table 3.4. Occupations in Orange County, Virginia, 1860

	Without property	Land or 1 slave	2–10 slaves	11–24 slaves	25 + slaves	Total
Farmers	82	80	125	98	65	450
Other agricultural	35	5	14	1	6	61
Unskilled	36	8	5	2	0	51
Crafts and services	110	56	43	10	2	221
Civil or professional	11	6	12	20	9	58
Other	3	2	5	0	2	12
Total	277	157	204	131	84	853

Sources: population schedules, 1860, NA; Auditor, Land Book, 1860, VSL.
Note: Table includes occupations of all white residents reporting work on census schedules.

cultural pursuits suggests that the county shared structural similarities with small-town communities throughout the United States. The wide wealth distribution of those employed in crafts and services also reflects the considerable range of success that people could attain in specific jobs. Merchants had an especially wide wealth distribution. German immigrant Bernard Bear, for example, had no real property, owning only a hog, a clock, and scattered other possessions for an inventory worth about $1,500. But another German merchant, Benjamin Rose, although approximately the same age as Bear, had accumulated nine slaves, owned two valuable lots in Orange Court House, and was about four times as wealthy as Bear. A third merchant, William J. Parrott, owned five slaves, three lots in Gordonsville, and personal property and inventory worth $78,000. A similar range of wealth prevailed for artisans; forty-one propertyless carpenters lived in the county, but there were also several skilled carpenters like Miles Lipscomb, with seven slaves aiding him in his craft. The number of merchants expanded more than the number of craftsmen during the 1850s, but combined employment in the two classes remained stable. The advent of the Orange and Alexandria Railroad meant that ready-made goods could be brought in cheaply from outside the county, resulting in a decline of artisans such as coopers and chairmakers between 1850 and 1860. But ready-made goods needed sales agents, and this fueled the corresponding increase in merchants over the same period.[12]

Land too was the object of commercial activity. Speculation in real property was the nineteenth-century equivalent of investment in the stock market. Some farmers in Orange bought and sold land frequently,

Table 3.5. Land distribution among social groups, Orange County,
Virginia, 1860

	Households		Total acreage		Avg. acres	Ave. assessment per acre
Land or 1 slave	123	(15%)	19,276	(9%)	157	$ 7.07
2–10 slaves:	104	(13%)	27,901	(13%)	268	9.69
11–24 slaves:	89	(11%)	39,040	(18%)	439	14.60
25+ slaves:	57	(7%)	49,439	(23%)	868	16.51
Other*	—	—	79,221	(37%)	370	12.70
Total	373	(45%)	214,939	(100%)	366	12.48

Sources: population schedules, 1860, NA; Auditor, Land Book, 1860, VSL.
*Includes indirect titleholders, unidentified holdings, and nonresident owners.

especially when tobacco prices were high. While the average number of
tracts per household was only 1.3, a few citizens in the county held as
many as ten parcels acquired at different times. Henry Hatch, for example, who lived near the hamlet of Verdiersville on the old turnpike
between Fredericksburg and Orange Court House, held eight separate
tracts in his neighborhood, only two of which were larger than a hundred
acres. Hatch's holdings were worth more than $5,600, however, and his
fourteen slaves tended 3 cows, 27 sheep, 17 hogs, and a few other head
of livestock while raising 150 bushels of wheat, 300 bushels of corn, 40
bushels of oats, 5,000 pounds of tobacco, 5 bushels of peas, 10 bushels
of potatoes, and 4 tons of hay. By any standard Hatch was a thriving
farmer, but not only rich farmers engaged in speculation. John Bledsoe,
for example, bought his first tract in 1838 when he was just twenty-two
years old. He sought two more pieces of land in the 1840s, then sold them
both in 1849. His transactions show the active participation of all kinds
of landowners in the real estate market.[13]

Despite the relative expansion and deconcentration of landholding in
the 1850s, the county's largest slaveholders still controlled a dispropor-
tionate share of acreage in 1860 (table 3.5). This concentration resulted
more from the potentially unlimited production capabilities of slavery
than from the atomization of nonslaveholder's lands. The average size
of holdings for those households with one or no slaves approached 150
acres, as much as a single family could cultivate without help. The few
households in this group that held more than 200 acres must have relied
on hired hands or slaves to work their crops and livestock. It is also likely
that many of these small landholders worked their farms with the aid of
tenants and nearby relatives. Caleb Smith, for example, farmed 58 acres
in the northeastern corner of the county with the aid of a single slave,

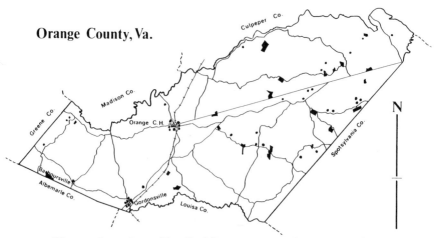

Orange County, Va.

Fig 3.3. Location of landholdings, owners of one or no slaves, Orange County, Virginia, 1860. (Traceable plots drawn to scale; dots represent probable locations of unplottable holdings.)

but it is likely that he could count on help from Walter Smith, a young man who lived just a few yards away, and perhaps from William Smith and his two sons, who farmed 197 acres just down the road. These labor exchanges were central to community life.[14]

Families with one or no slaves generally had enough acreage for household production, but their farms were much less valuable than those of the largest planters. The assessment values given in table 3.5 show that the lands of the largest slaveholders were worth more than twice that of the holdings of the smallest property owners. Three factors affected the assessment values: land quality, number and quality of buildings, and the distance to mills, markets, and towns. Of these, buildings added the most to the value of a holding. Elhanon Rowe, for example, owned a large work force of twenty-four slaves and held eight tracts in the Mine Run neighborhood. Seven of his tracts were worth less than $5 an acre, but his substantial farmstead of six buildings was assessed at $12 an acre. The solid homes of Orange planters were visible symbols of wealth and contributed significantly to assessment values, but these homes were also symbols of dead capital that could not be used to make more money. The small cabin, in contrast, represented a relatively efficient use of capital. Poverty might come knocking any time at the homes of small farmers who did not have the cushion of a few extra slaves to sell, so small cabins could mean survival and had the added benefit of being less expensive come tax time.[15]

Land quality—the fertility of soils, terrain, and drainage—also af-

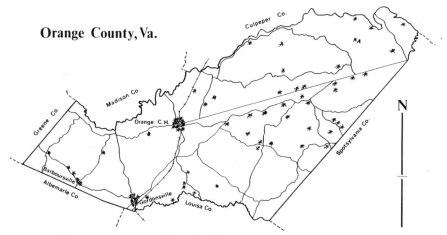

Fig 3.4. Location of landholdings, owners of 2 to 10 slaves, 1860, Orange County, Virginia.

fected assessments, but not as directly as some have claimed. Lewis C. Gray argued in the 1930s that the soils worn out by many years of tobacco planting were given over to subsistence farmers, as planters took up the most fertile bottomlands. His description, though, exaggerates the actual conditions of the plantation districts. Figures 3.3–3.6 illustrate the intermingled and scattered character of landholding among the four property-holding groups.[16] Many owners of one or no slaves were clustered in the eastern half of the county, especially in an oblong district between the Fredericksburg Turnpike and the border with Spotsylvania County, but they could also be found in the two major towns. The largest slaveholders were concentrated in the areas along the railroad, near the border with Louisa County, and around a crossroads hamlet known as Jackson's Shop. It is evident that some of the wealthy landowners resided in parts of Orange where few of the poorest landowners lived, but figures 3.3–3.6 show that none of the propertied groups was isolated residentially from the rest. Members of all four groups could be found in Gordonsville, around Orange Court House, and near Jackson's Shop, among other places. Furthermore, all four groups were intermingled on the vast medium-quality Nason-Tatum soil district which lay in the eastern half of the county.[17]

Within the Nason-Tatum district, owners of one or no slaves were found on precisely the same soils as their more wealthy neighbors. John Kube, for example, was a shoemaker and farmer who tended a large herd of sheep and hogs, as well as raising corn, wheat, rye, oats, tobacco, peas, potatoes, and hay, all without the help of slaves. Kube's farm was worth

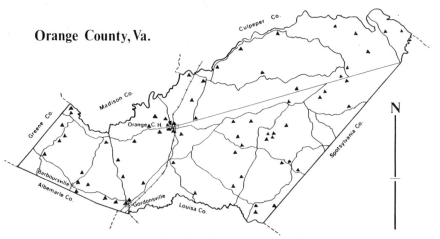

Fig 3.5. Location of landholdings, owners of 10 to 24 slaves, 1860, Orange County, Virginia.

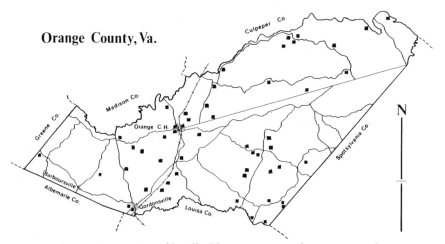

Fig 3.6. Location of landholdings, owners of 25 or more slaves, 1860, Orange County, Virginia.

about $4.50 an acre and was situated roughly a mile away from Elhanon Rowe's. Hugh Simpson's thirty-seven-acre farm was located on much the same type of land as Kube's. Simpson's plot, which the Irish carpenter, his wife, and three sons had farmed since 1846, was worth $2.97 an acre, not much more than contemporary rates for government lands in the West. Kube and Simpson probably lived in cabins, but they did not have to scrape an existence out of barren and hardscrabble soils.[18]

A final example from the same soil area shows the importance that the third factor—access to towns, markets, and transport facilities—had on land values. Robert Tear, a young blacksmith who hailed from Pennsylvania, bought 102 partly wooded acres bounded on one side by an unfinished railroad. Tear's property was located halfway between the Kube and Simpson farms and shared the same rolling terrain and soil types. At $6.97 an acre, however, Tear's land was twice as valuable as theirs, mostly because of the potential benefits the railroad would bring. On a larger scale, it is no coincidence that the area where the small landholders were most concentrated was also the part of the county farthest from the railroads and market towns. Simpson's farm was fourteen miles away from Orange, sixteen from Louisa, twenty from Fredericksburg, and eighteen from Culpeper. Assessments were relatively low in this part of the county because transportation costs were high, not because soils were inferior. The expense of shipping, though, did cause smaller farmers to be dependent on their richer neighbors for transportation and marketing services. At the same time, the planters relied on artisan-farmers like Kube, Simpson, and Tear for shoemaking, blacksmithing, carpentry, and a host of other services. Each group required the aid of the other, and the exchange worked to the benefit of both.[19]

In economic terms, then, there is scant evidence that one group of whites had predominance or preponderant influence over another or that invisible forces in society worked mostly for the benefit of planters. On the other hand, planters had more protection against bad times than the small farmers did; there is little evidence of an entirely self-reliant class of autonomous common people. Rather, the economic quilt in Orange was stitched tightly and made up of many different fabrics. Neither hegemony or autonomy can adequately describe the complexity of society in the plantation districts.

The Civil War provided the most crucial test of Southern white society and the link between planters and plain folk. The participation of nonslaveholders in a conflict fought ostensibly to preserve slavery is an apparent paradox. Yet two generations of fiery rhetoric had transformed a question of simple economic self-interest into a vital issue of ideology and survival. The actions of men in Orange County during the secession crisis and ensuing war illustrate the complex effects that both ideology and economic self-interest had on the common people and local society.[20]

Most white Southerners agreed that slavery should be preserved, but they agreed on little else. The presidential election of 1860 is a case in point (table 3.6). Party loyalty played a major role in the outcome of the election. Although a vote for Breckinridge was a vote for secession in many Southern states, in Virginia it probably represented loyalty to the

Table 3.6. Vote in presidential elections, Orange and surrounding counties, 1848–60

Year	Votes for Democratic candidate	Votes for opposition candidate	Total vote
	Orange County		
1848	281 (49%)	296 (51%)	577
1852	343 (54%)	290 (46%)	633
1856	437 (60%)	287 (40%)	724
→ 1860	475 (53%)	427 (47%)	902
	*Surrounding counties**		
1848	2,539 (52%)	2,335 (48%)	4,874
1852	3,699 (59%)	2,610 (41%)	6,309
1856	4,082 (64%)	3,385 (36%)	6,367
→ 1860	4,206 (60%)	3,088 (40%)	7,699

Sources: Richmond *Enquirer*, 17–24 Nov. 1848, 11 Nov. 1852, 18 Nov. 1856; Richmond *Daily Dispatch*, 11 Nov. 1856, 19 Nov. 1860.
*Albemarle, Culpeper, Greene, Louisa, Madison, and Spotsylvania.

Democratic party. On the other hand, a vote for Bell, the opposition candidate, was more clearly a vote for continued union. Supporting Breckinridge, according to one Richmond newspaper, was a manly avowal of resistance to Lincoln's inevitable election. Yet the paper also stressed that such a vote represented loyalty to the nation: "as you desire perpetuation of this Union, as you value your constitutional rights; as you love Virginia, do not fail to go to the polls next Tuesday."[21] While the majority of voters in the county went for Breckinridge on election Tuesday, Bell's camp also made a strong showing: the election was decided in the county by only forty-eight votes, with a 91 percent turnout of adult white males at the polling places.[22]

Lincoln's election was a foregone conclusion by October, and immediately after his victory became official, a campaign for delegates to the Virginia Secession Convention began. W. W. Scott, a young man of fifteen in the winter of secession, described the atmosphere of the campaign:

> After the election of Lincoln, which was followed so soon by the secession of South Carolina and the other Southern States, the Secessionists of the County grew bolder and more aggressive, and when the State Convention was called to determine the course of Virginia, party feeling became very tense. Rosettes of blue ribbon, called "cockades", appeared everywhere, even at the churches. Men, boys, and even girls, wore them. The Unionists were less demonstrative, but no less resolute. Candidates to represent the County were numerous and eager. Col. John Willis, Major John H. Lee, Hon. Jeremiah Morton and perhaps others, aspired to represent the seces-

sionists. The contest finally narrowed to Mr. Morton, on that side, and Mr. Lewis B. Williams, the elder, who had been attorney for the Commonwealth for thirty years, for the Unionists. . . . Mr. Morton was elected by a good majority.[23]

The convention avoided any action until after the firing on Fort Sumter in April. Once open hostilities began, however, they acted quickly, passing a secession ordinance on 17 April 1861. Though the actual ordinance did not become law until ratified by the people in the spring elections, everybody recognized that Virginia's secession was fact. Large numbers of men hurried to Gordonsville, Orange Court House, and Culpeper Court House to enlist in the Virginia militia on the night of 17 April, and residents of the county unanimously ratified the ordinance in the May election. The crowds and excitement generated by the preparations for war were so great that they became hazardous. In late May a crowd accidentally caused a troop train to collide with a passenger train, killing two men.

In the few weeks between the convention elections and the attack on Fort Sumter, the men of the county swallowed their doubts over secession and presented a virtually united front in defense of their homes. Theirs was an ideology of localism, fueled by many decades of sectional confrontation. It is unlikely that many men in the county were ardent Southern nationalists, but most viewed Lincoln's call for troops as a clear sign of Northern tyranny, and henceforth the issue was clear. Armed defense against oppression was the only logical alternative they saw available.[24]

When the time came to enlist in the Confederate army, though, individual economic circumstances tempered enthusiasm. Table 3.7 shows enlistments by members of the five social groups. Two things are striking about the county's enlistment figures: first, the eagerness of all social groups to join the fight, and second, the effect of employment on military service. Martial ardor ran high in the early days of the Confederacy, even among men with regular employment, but soldiering fever was especially strong among those young men who were without a trade. The sons of the large slaveholders could afford to leave home for the army because they contributed relatively little to the household economy. In contrast, men from propertyless households started making an economic contribution to their family purse at an early age, and by the time they reached their twenties were frequently heading their own households. Such men could ill afford to race across Virginia with Confederate generals J. E. B. Stuart or A. P. Hill. They were needed at home.

Only with the introduction of conscription in the winter of 1862 did

Table 3.7. Enlistment of Orange County residents, 1861–65

Year enlisted	Without property	Land or 1 slave	2–10 slaves	11–24 slaves	25+ slaves	Total
1861						
Had occupation	24 (28%)	16 (23%)	14 (16%)	13 (21%)	8 (15%)	75 (21%)
No occupation	24 (28%)	22 (32%)	38 (44%)	31 (49%)	32 (59%)	147 (51%)
1862–65						
Had occupation	23 (26%)	18 (26%)	14 (16%)	3 (5%)	4 (7%)	62 (17%)
No occupation	11 (13%)	8 (12%)	13 (15%)	12 (19%)	4 (7%)	48 (13%)
Under age in 1861*	5 (6%)	5 (7%)	7 (8%)	4 (6%)	6 (11%)	27 (8%)
Total	87	69	86	63	54	359

Sources: Compiled Service Records, NA; Green, *Orange in the Civil War*; Scott, *Orange County*.
*Men aged 12–17 on the 1860 census.

the Confederate government convince these men to join the war effort. Conscription had its biggest impact on Orange's employed men. While only 34 percent of those who signed up in 1861 had an occupation in the 1860 census, more than 56 percent of the adult enlistees after 1861 had an occupation. Thus the specific circumstances of each individual potential soldier determined the degree of participation in the Confederate war effort. The frequently repeated charge that the Civil War was a "rich man's war and a poor man's fight" is not borne out by the records of Orange. The figures show that even after 1862, when the grim realities of the conflict had replaced early enthusiasm for rebellion in Virginia, members of propertyless households and the most wealthy families continued to enlist at similar rates. Class consciousness certainly existed in the South at this time, but it played a small role in determining the participation of ordinary soldiers in the war.[25]

The plain folk of Orange do not fit neatly into the classic models of Southern white society. Rather, the people whom John Taliaferro recorded in his census were a diverse lot that defies easy description. Some of the propertyless and tradeless people in the county were obviously poor whites. But it is also clear that most of the other people in Orange were plain folk, much like their counterparts in small towns all over America. There is virtually no evidence to suggest that the institution of slavery created a society in which ordinary whites were uniquely oppressed. Nor were they the economic equals of the planters. Rather, it seems they faced the same structural handicaps of average citizens everywhere in the United States. Market facilities for many farmers were still distant, opportunities in the traditional crafts were shrinking, and commercial opportunities in the villages were just beginning to expand. Most of the planters and plain folk shared the same neighborhoods and the same soil types, fought for the same cause, and were linked by mutual social and economic bonds.

Yet plain folk were much more vulnerable to changing conditions than were planters. They lived in cabins and worked at home until conscripted because they had little economic breathing room. In this sense there was little economic democracy, since the burdens of society weighed most heavily on the shoulders of the least wealthy. The economic improvement of the 1850s, though, convinced many average citizens of Orange that they too could reap their society's rich harvest. The unanimity of Orange County on the eve of war is explained in part by this perception of the potential benefits that the plantation system could bring. Ordinary men believed that the slave system had something to offer them, and planters by necessity granted some sense of political equality to poorer members of their community. These shared concerns motivated both groups beyond simple economic self-interest and firmly tied the community of Orange to the Southern cause, for good or ill.

NOTES

1 Population schedules of the Eighth Census of the United States, 1860, Orange County, Va., National Archives (NA), microfilm.

2 For the classic study of Southern society based on manuscript census returns, see Frank L. Owsley, *Plain Folk of the Old South* (Baton Rouge: Louisiana State Univ. Press, 1949). Studies using Virginia tax returns include Luther Porter Jackson, *Free Negro Labor and Property Holding in Virginia, 1830–1860* (1942; rept. New York: Atheneum, 1969), and A. Jane Townes, "The Effect of Emancipation on Large Landholdings, Nelson and Goochland Counties, Virginia," *Journal of Southern History* 45 (Aug. 1979): 403–12. For the similarity of many local studies of the South, see, for example, Randall C. Manring, "Population and Agriculture in Nodaway County, Missouri, 1850 to 1860," *Missouri Historical Review* 30 (July 1978): 388–411; Randolph Campbell, "Planters and Plain Folk: Harrison County, Texas, as a Test Case," *Journal of Southern History* 40 (Aug. 1974): 369–98, and "Population Persistence and Social Change in Nineteenth Century Texas: Harrison County, 1850–1880," ibid., 48 (May 1982): 185–204; Townes, "Effect of Emancipation"; James C. Bonner, "Profile of a Late Antebellum Community," *American Historical Review* 49 (July 1944): 663–80.

3 Paul H. Buck, "The Poor Whites of the Ante-Bellum South," *American Historical Review* 31 (Oct. 1925): 41–54; U. B. Phillips, "The Origin and Growth of the Southern Black Belts," ibid., 9 (July 1906): 798–816; Lewis Cecil Gray, *History of Agriculture in the Southern United States to 1860* (Washington, D.C.: Carnegie Institution, 1933), 533–37; Owsley, *Plain Folk*, 76–89, 150–229; Fabian Linden, "Economic Democracy in the Slave South: An Appraisal of Some Recent Views," *Journal of Negro History* 31 (Jan. 1946): 140–89; Gavin Wright, *Political Economy of the Cotton South: Households, Markets, and Wealth in the Nineteenth Century* (New York: Norton, 1978), 24–42; Forrest McDonald and Grady McWhiney, "The Antebellum Southern Herdsman: A Reinterpretation," in Edward Magdol and Jon Wakelyn, *The Southern Common People: Studies in Nineteenth-Century Social History* (Westport, Conn.: Greenwood, 1980), 119–37, esp. pp. 125–28.

4 Joseph Clarke Robert, *The Tobacco Kingdom: Plantation, Market, and Factory in Virginia and North Carolina, 1800–1860* (Durham: Duke Univ. Press, 1938), 139–57; Avery O. Craven, *Soil Exhaustion as a Factor in the Agricultural History of Virginia and Maryland, 1606–1860*, University of Illinois Studies in Social Science, 13 (Urbana, 1925), 9–179, esp. pp. 122–61; John Thomas Schlotterbeck, "Plantation and Farm: Social and Economic Change in Orange and Greene Counties, Virginia, 1716 to 1860" (Ph.D. diss., Johns Hopkins Univ., 1980), esp. pp. 301–24.

5 See Gray, *History of Agriculture*, 1039; Douglass C. North, *The Economic Growth of the United States, 1790–1860* (New York: Norton, 1966), 204–

15; Robert, *Tobacco Kingdom*, 143–57. Land figures based on State of Virginia, *Biennial Report of the Auditor of Public Accounts, 1860–1861* (Richmond, 1861), 496, and Auditor of Public Accounts, Land Book, Orange County, Va., 1860, Virginia State Library (VSL). See also Schlotterbeck, "Plantation and Farm," 306. For land deconcentration with less favorable results, see Emmanual LeRoy Ladurie, *The Peasants of Languedoc*, trans. John Day (Urbana: Univ. of Illinois Press, 1974), 88–97.

6 Schlotterbeck, "Plantation and Farm," 302–5; William H. B. Thomas, *Gordonsville, Virginia: Historic Crossroads Town* (Verona, Va.: McClure, 1971), 12–17; John F. Stover, *Iron Roads to the West: American Railroads in the 1850s* (New York: Columbia Univ. Press, 1978), 60–66; Charles W. Turner, "Railroad Service to Virginia Farmers, 1828–1860," *Journal of Agricultural History* 22 (Jan. 1948): 245–47. For railroad purchases, see Auditor of Public Accounts, General Index to Deeds, Orange County, Va., vol. 3 (1848–1860), Orange County Clerk's Office.

7 For the long-term picture of migration in Orange and Greene counties, see Schlotterbeck, "Plantation and Farm," 121–36. For age-sex pyramids, see Roland Pressat, *Demographic Analysis: Methods, Results, Applications*, trans. Judas Matras, (Chicago: Aldine-Atherton, 1972), 263–82. Virginia figures from U.S. Bureau of the Census, *The Eighth Census of the United States, 1860, vol. 1, Population* (Washington, D.C.: GPO, 1864), xxxiii. For tobacco production, see Robert, *Tobacco Kingdom*, 151–57.

8 Literature on nonplanters includes Daniel R. Hundley, *Social Relations in Our Southern States* (1860; rept. Baton Rouge: Louisiana State Univ. Press, 1979); George M. Weston, *The Poor Whites of the South* (Washington, D.C.: Henry M. Price, 1856); Frederick Law Olmsted, *A Journey in the Seaboard Slave States in the Years 1853–54, with Remarks on Their Economy* (New York: Putnam's, 1904); Hinton Rowan Helper, *The Impending Crisis of the South: How to Meet It* (New York: Burdick Brothers, 1857); E. A. Seabrook, "The Poor Whites of the South," *Galaxy* 4 (Oct. 1867): 681–90; Phillips, "Black Belts"; Avery O. Craven, "Poor Whites and Negroes in the Antebellum South," *Journal of Negro History* 15 (Oct. 1920): 14–25; Buck, "Poor Whites"; A. N. J. Den Hollander, "The Tradition of Poor Whites," in W. T. Couch, ed., *Culture in the South* (Chapel Hill: Univ. of North Carolina Press, 1934), 402–31; Roger Shugg, *Origins of Class Struggle in Louisiana: A Social History of White Farmers and Laborers during Slavery and After, 1840–1875* (Baton Rouge: Louisiana State Univ. Press, 1939); Bonner, "Profile"; Robert R. Russell, "The Effects of Slavery upon Non-Slaveholders in the Ante-Bellum South," *Journal of Agricultural History* 15 (April 1941): 112–26; Blanche Henry Clark, *The Tennessee Yeoman, 1840–1860* (Nashville: Univ. of Tennessee Press, 1942); Herbert Weaver, *Mississippi Farmers, 1850–1860* (Nashville: Univ. of Tennessee Press, 1946); Linden, "Economic Democracy"; Owlsey, *Plain Folk*; Gavin Wright, "Economic Democracy and the Concentration of Agricultural Wealth in the Cotton South, 1850–1860," *Journal of Agricultural History* 44 (Jan. 1970): 63–94; Eugene D. Genovese, "Yeoman Farmers in a Slaveholder's Democracy," ibid., 49 (Jan. 1975): 331–42; Wright, *Political Economy*; McDonald and McWhiney, "Southern Herdsman"; Richard C. McMath and Orville Burton, eds., *Class, Conflict, and Consensus: Antebellum Community Studies* (Westport, Conn.: Greenwood, 1981).

9 Helper, *Impending Crisis*; Weston, "Poor Whites"; Seabrook, "Poor Whites." On the diversity of the slaveholding and nonslaveholding cate-

gories, see Buck, "Poor Whites," 41–44, and James Oakes, *The Ruling Race: A History of American Slaveholders* (New York: Vintage, 1982); Hundley, *Social Relations,* esp. pp. 7–263.

10 Some qualifications about the use of occupation and wealth should be kept in mind as the scales are applied to Orange. Since Taliaferro applied the occupation of "farmer" equally to landless sheepherders like William Amos and renowned gentry planters like Benjamin J. Barbour, ownership of land or slaves is more important than occupation in the ranking of "farmers." Furthermore, since "ownership" in the largest sense also includes knowledge of crafts, trades, and skills, each wealth group has an implied subcategory. Finally, since Taliaferro's report of real and personal wealth is wildly different from the tax assessor's report, the census figures must be taken with a grain of salt. Taliaferro's numbers are most reliable on the number of slaveholders in the county, where he found 92 percent of Richards's count, so slaveholding is used here as the best index of wealth among county residents. For social rankings in several cultures, see Donald J. Treiman, "A Standard Occupational Prestige Scale for Use with Historical Data," *Journal of Interdisciplinary History* 7 (Autumn 1976): 283–304. For the difficulties of using occupational scales and discussion of current literature on the subject, see Olivier Zunz, *The Changing Face of Inequality: Urbanization, Industrial Development, and Immigrants in Detroit, 1880–1920.* (Chicago: Univ. of Chicago Press, 1982), esp. pp. 420–43. A classic study using both wealth and occupation is Bonner, "Profile," pp. 38–49. For the census and tax assessments, see U.S. Bureau of the Census, *Statistics of the United States (Including Mortality, Property, &c.,) in 1860, Compiled from the Original Returns and Being the Final Exhibit of the Eighth Census* (Washington, D.C.: GPO, 1866), 506; and Virginia Auditor, *Biennial Report, 1860–61,* 496, 265.

11 For a classic description of the lazy poor white, see Olmsted, *Seaboard States,* 78, 82–83, 96–97, 143, 165. On the costs of labor and the changes in tenancy, see Forrest McDonald and Grady McWhiney, "The South from Self-Sufficiency to Peonage: An Interpretation," *American Historical Review* 85 (Dec. 1980): 1095–1118; Carville Earle, "A Staple Interpretation of Slavery and Free Labor," *Geographical Review* 68 (Jan. 1978): 52–65; Carville Earle and Ronald Hoffman, "The Foundation of the Modern Economy: Agriculture and the Costs of Labor in the United States and England, 1800–1860," *American Historical Review* 85 (Dec. 1980): 1055–94. On hunting and fishing as part of the Southern diet, see Hundley, *Social Relations,* 261–62; Sam Bowers Hilliard, *Hogmeat and Hoecake: Food Supply in the Old South, 1840–1860* (Carbondale: Southern Illinois Univ. Press, 1972), 70–91. For the woodlands of the country in 1864, see "Chief Engineer's Office, Map of Orange, from Surveys and Reconnaisances by Walter Izard, 1st. Lt. Egrs. P.A.C.S.," in Library of Congress (Lib. Cong.) Map Collection. For drainage and waterways, see U.S. Department of Agriculture, Soil Conservation Service, Soil Survey, Orange County, Va. (Washington, D.C., 1971), 164, and map sheets 1–46; U.S. Department of Interior, Geological Survey, 7½ Minute Series Topographical Maps, Barboursville, Belmont, Chancellorsville, Culpeper, Germanna Bridge, Gordonsville, Lahore, Madison Mills, Mineral, Mine Run, Rapidan, Richardsville, Rochelle, Rockville, and Unionville, Virginia, quadrangles.

12 For scholarly recognition of nonagricultural employment in the antebellum South, see Ulrich Bonnell Phillips, *American Negro Slavery: A Survey of the*

Supply, Employment, and Control of Negro Labor as Determined by the Plantation Regime (1918; rept. Baton Rouge: Louisiana State Univ. Press, 1966), 336, 403; Shugg, *Origins*; Linden, "Economic Democracy," 142–46; Schlotterbeck, "Plantation and Farm," 237–39. On the range of taxable inventory carried by Orange merchants, see Virginia Auditor, *Biennial Report, 1858–1859* (Richmond, 1859), "Statistics of Orange County." County merchants paid a tax ranging from $20 to $96 on sales. Examples are drawn from population schedules and tax books.

13 Auditor, Land Book, 1860; Index to Deeds, vols. 1 and 2, VSL; manuscript population schedules, 1860, NA; agricultural schedules of the Eighth Census of the United States, 1860, Orange County, Va., VSL, microfilm; Auditor of Public Accounts, Personal Property Book, Orange County, Va., VSL; Margaret C. Klein, *Tombstone Inscriptions of Orange County, Virginia* (Baltimore: Genealogical Publishing Co., 1979).

14 On landholding concentration, see Jackson Turner Main, "Distributions of Property in Post-Revolutionary Virginia," *Mississippi Valley Historical Review* 41 (Sept. 1954), 244; Wright, *Political Economy*, 33; Schlotterbeck, "Plantation and Farm," 306. For the Smiths, see Auditor, Land Book, 1860; population schedules, 1860, Orange County, Va., NA.

15 On Rowe, see Auditor, Land Book, 1860; population schedules, 1860, NA; Alfred H. Guernsey and Henry M. Alden, *Harper's Pictorial History of the Civil War* (New York: Fairfax, 1977), 522, shows the Rowe farm at the center of the Confederate lines. For a description of some distinctive Orange County homes, see Scott, *Orange County*, 202–15.

16 Sources for figs. 3–6: population schedules, 1860, NA; Orange County, Va., Deed Books, 23–45 (1804–60), VSL; "Map of Orange," and "A Map of Orange and Spotsylvania, Va." (after the copy in the Military Papers of General R. E. Lee), Lib. Cong. Map Collection; Geological Survey, 7½ Minute Series; *The Official Atlas of the Civil War* (New York: T. Yoseloff, 1958), plates 44-3, 47-6, 55-1, 83-2, 87-1, 87-8, 96-1; William W. Scott, *A History of Orange County, Virginia* (Richmond: Everett Waddey, 1907), "A Map of Orange County, Virginia," Soil Conservation Service, Soil Survey, map sheets, 1–21, 23, 26–30, 33–46. Figures show 69 households (46 percent) with 2–10 slaves, 70 households (63 percent) with 11–24 slaves, 50 households (74 percent) with 25 or more slaves.

17 Gray, *Agriculture*, 452; Soil Conservation Service, Soil Survey, "General Soil Map."

18 For Kube, see Klein, *Inscriptions*, 42; Auditor, Land Book, 1860; population schedules, 1860, NA; Orange County Deed Books 40:19, 41:195; Soil Conservation Service, Soil Survey, map 13; agricultural schedules, 1860, VSL. On Simpson, see Auditor, Land Book, 1860; Orange County Deed Book 40:386; population schedules, 1860, NA. Simpson did not produce enough to be listed in the agricultural census. Note that both Kube and Simpson were craftsmen. For maps of their holdings, see T. Lloyd Benson "The Plain Folk of Orange County" (M.A. thesis, Univ. of Virginia, 1983).

19 On Tear, see Population Schedules, 1860, NA; Orange County Deed Book 44:43; Soil Conservation Service, Soil Survey, map 20. For the neighborhood relations, see Schlotterbeck, "Plantation and Farm," and Genovese, "Yeoman Farmers."

20 See especially William J. Cooper, *The South and the Politics of Slavery,* 𝓔

1828–1856 (Baton Rouge: Louisiana State Univ. Press, 1978); David M. Potter, *The Impending Crisis, 1848–1861* (New York: Harper Torchbooks, 1976); Michael F. Holt, *The Political Crisis of the 1850s* (New York: Wiley, 1978); Eric Foner, *Politics and Ideology in the Age of the Civil War* (Oxford: Oxford Univ. Press, 1980).

21 Scott, *Orange County*, 147–51; Henry T. Shanks, *The Secessionist Move-* ← *ment in Virginia* (1934; rept. New York: A.M.S., 1971), 112; Cooper, *Politics of Slavery.*

22 Richmond *Daily Enquirer*, 26 Oct., 2 Nov. 1860; Scott, *Orange County*, 148.

23 Scott, *Orange County*, 148–49.

24 Shanks, *Secession Movement*, 191–213; Scott, *Orange County*, 149; Compiled Service Records of Confederate Soldiers Who Served in Organizations from the State of Virginia, (Companies A, C, and F, 13th Virginia Infantry), M-382, NA. The referendum passed 853-0. See Richmond *Enquirer*, 4 June 1861. For the railroad accident, see *Annual Reports of the Rail Road Companies of the State of Virginia, Made to the Board of Public Works, for the Year Ending September 30, 1861* (Richmond, 1861), 57. See also chapter 4 by Kevin C. Ruffner below.

25 Discussion based on table 3.7. See also Benson, "Plain Folk," app. 2.

4

KEVIN CONLEY RUFFNER

Civil War Desertion
from a Black Belt Regiment:
An Examination of the
44th Virginia Infantry

DESERTION FROM THE CONFEDERATE ARMY WAS A COMPLEX
and controversial issue for Southern military and civilian leaders alike
during the American Civil War.[1] Debate over the role of desertion in the
Confederate defeat has raged among historians since Appomattox. Desertion of Confederate soldiers is variously interpreted as a sign of war
weariness, a lack of Southern tenacity or courage, an expression of class
conflict, frustration with harsh Confederate war measures, and an indication of stillborn Southern nationalism.[2] While observers generally
agree that "desertion lowered morale" throughout the South and fostered "a condition probably more disastrous to the Confederacy than
inferiority of numbers," there have been few studies at the regimental
level where desertion had its greatest impact on fighting spirit and combat effectiveness.[3]

This study of the 44th Virginia Infantry Regiment seeks to uncover the
causes and effects of desertion in a military organization which served
throughout the four years of war. It explores the role of age, occupation, ethnicity, military rank, marital status, slaveholding wealth, and
military experience in the desertion of regimental personnel. The 44th
Virginia drew its men from a part of the state where society depended
upon stable agricultural products and a viable slave economy, a society
which had many reasons to support the Confederacy. Yet the regiment
also recruited soldiers from the industrial city of Richmond and from a
rural yeoman class whose allegiance to the Southern cause was uncertain
in 1861. Was desertion from the 44th Virginia a result of the popular assertion that the Southern struggle for independence was "a rich man's
war, a poor man's fight"?

The 44th Virginia Infantry Regiment was typical of the volunteer units
raised in the Commonwealth of Virginia during the spring of 1861. The

regiment came from the Piedmont, which supplied the backbone of Virginia's infantry regiments during the first year of the war. The Piedmont, a region of rolling hills in central Virginia, straddles the Tidewater region in the east and the Blue Ridge Mountains in the west. Settled at the time of the American Revolution, by the mid-nineteenth century the Piedmont was a community of numerous small towns and farms.

Nine companies of the 44th Virginia came from the heart of the Piedmont in June 1861, with men hailing from Amelia, Appomattox, Buckingham, Charlotte, Fluvanna, Goochland, Louisa, and Prince Edward counties. An additional company was recruited among the residents of Richmond, Virginia's capital, which lay to the east of the Piedmont. The ten companies of the 44th Virginia had a total wartime strength of 936 officers and men.[4]

The Piedmont was the richest section of the state in terms of slave wealth and numbers and earned the distinction as Virginia's "Black Belt." The area's total white population of 37,000 contrasted with over 60,000 slaves and free blacks. Slaves were the Piedmont's most valuable commodity; the average slaveholder owned twelve slaves, three more than the state average. Louisa County, the home of Company D, was among Virginia's ten largest slave counties at the outbreak of the war.[5]

The Piedmont's agricultural production was made possible by the heavy investment in slavery. Tobacco served as the major cash crop, although farmers also raised corn and wheat in large quantities. While most white men were employed as farmers or farm laborers, large numbers earned a living as skilled craftsmen. Moreover, income generated from farming, particularly tobacco, supported the growth of urban centers throughout the Piedmont. The largest town in the 44th Virginia's segment of the Virginia Piedmont, Farmville in Prince Edward County, had 1,500 free and slave residents in 1860. There, farmers from the outlying counties brought tobacco and other produce to market, purchased store goods, and sought professional guidance for legal, educational, medical, or religious matters. Piedmont Virginia lay near larger towns and cities, including Richmond, Charlottesville, Lynchburg, and Petersburg. With the development of land transportation and better communications in the years before the war, the Piedmont became increasingly tied to the economic well-being of Richmond. Three railroads and one canal connected the rural counties of central Virginia with the state capital.[6]

While the neighboring Piedmont remained overwhelmingly native born, Richmond attracted many immigrants, mainly Irish and German, who composed 13 percent of the city's population of 38,000 in 1860. Richmond acted as the mercantile and banking center for the Piedmont, and much of the region's wheat and tobacco was processed and sold in Richmond. Additionally, Richmond had a thriving slave market selling surplus labor from Piedmont farms and plantations to dealers from the Deep South.[7]

The men who marched to war with the 44th Virginia in 1861 were statistically representative of the society they swore to defend.[8] The regiment was overwhelmingly of native stock, with only 3 percent of the soldiers born outside the United States, mostly in Ireland and Great Britain. Another 3 percent of the members of the 44th Virginia hailed from other states of the Union, scattered from Connecticut to Florida and Mississippi. The majority of these non-Virginians previously resided in Maryland or the District of Columbia and enlisted in Richmond's Company E after Union forces occupied the border areas. The outbreak of the fighting trapped a number of foreign and non-Virginian men in Richmond who enlisted in the 44th Virginia in a wave of enthusiasm. Several others returned to Virginia from elsewhere in the nation to enlist with former neighbors and family members. The regiment remained closely affiliated with the Piedmont throughout the war, and 94 percent of the 648 men with known birthplaces were native Virginians.

The 44th Virginia was a mixture of young men (in some cases merely boys) and older personnel. The median age at the time of enlistment was 24, while the single largest age group of enlistees was 19. The bulk of the regiment, 33 percent, ranged between the ages of 20 to 25 while another 29 percent joined the army at ages 26 to 35. Sixteen percent of the unit enlisted at age 18 or 19, and another 16 percent were over 36. A further 6 percent of the 710 men with known ages enlisted as minors under the age of 18; this percentage may actually have been greater given the lack of strict enlistment standards. The youngest soldier of the 44th Virginia enlisted at 14 in Company F during the spring of 1861. The oldest man in the regiment, age 65, enlisted at the same time in Company B.

An officer of the Richmond Zouaves, Company E of the 44th Virginia, noted the composition of his unit while training at Camp Lee in Richmond in 1861: "Yesterday I was making out the muster roll, and was struck with the various pursuits which our men had left to follow the drum. When I finished I could easily understand that the jargon of the Zouaves was technical language instead of slang phraseology. Theologians, lawyers, M.D.'s, artists, actors, privateersmen, clerks, laborers, and artisans all find a place side by side in the ranks."[9] A survey of the 534 members of the 44th Virginia whose antebellum occupation is known supplements the officer's observation. Laborers slightly outnumbered those soldiers who were listed as farmers, 96 to 91, although the "laboring" category included farm laborers as well as day and common laborers. An additional 11 men reported as farmhands in the 1860 census, while only one man (the lieutenant colonel of the regiment) was listed as a "planter." Four men made their living as tenant farmers, and another 67 worked as overseers or farm managers.

Unlike many areas of the Deep South, the Piedmont supported a wide range of occupations. This diversity was reflected in the ranks of the 44th Virginia. The regiment had 34 carpenters, 11 shoemakers, 9 bricklayers, 7 blacksmiths, 6 wheelwrights, 2 scythemakers, 2 cabinetmakers, and 2 coachmakers, among other men who worked as plowmakers, plasterers, turners, coopers, weavers, tailors, gunsmiths, or millwrights. The regiment also included 67 soldiers who were students when they enlisted and other young men who were apprentice mechanics, watchmen, cabinetmakers, and tinmakers. A professional core existed in the 44th Virginia with 13 clerks, 11 medical doctors, 10 merchants, 6 teachers, 5 lawyers, 2 ministers, and 1 judge, as well as several sheriffs or marshals. Among the less commonly held occupations were men who worked as actors, engineers, sailors, hotelkeepers, and one daguerreotypist. The 44th Virginia had a multitude of nineteenth-century occupations and was not simply a regiment of farmers, as is often assumed of Confederate units.[10]

The educational background of the members of the 44th Virginia was representative of the state's white men. Illiteracy was an endemic problem throughout the South, and the regiment had its share of men with little or no schooling. At least 72 men could not sign their names on army muster rolls and pay vouchers or were considered illiterate by census takers in 1860. This illiteracy rate of 8 percent corresponds to the state average for whites. Yet there were well-educated men in the 44th Virginia; at least 31 men had some college experience when they joined the regiment, with Hampden-Sydney College, the University of Virginia, and the Virginia Military Institute being the preeminent schools.[11]

Since the Piedmont lay in Virginia's "Black Belt," the men of the 44th Virginia had a direct investment in slavery. A survey of four companies of the regiment, representing Amelia, Appomattox, and Fluvanna counties, reveals that 51 percent of the soldiers were slaveholders or the sons of slaveholders. Another 10 percent of the men in these four companies worked as overseers or laborers on farms with slaves. While the number of slaves held by the average slaveholder in each company varied, slavery was an important aspect in the lives of most men in the 44th Virginia. One modern historian has noted that slavery in Louisa County was the backbone of that county's economy and that "no other property was so flexible—or so valuable." Eventually, most young nonslaveholders in the regiment, including overseers and laborers, could aspire to obtain slaves.[12]

Going to war meant several things for the men of the 44th Virginia. Obviously, the defense of Virginia and the "peculiar institution" ranked as crucial issues. The Piedmont overwhelmingly supported Virginia's ordinance of secession after the firing on Fort Sumter. While the region was not known for rabid secessionist fire-eaters, everyone recognized that emancipation would wreak economic havoc in the Piedmont and disrupt the social order.[13] Fearing that a war would be largely fought on Virginia's soil, the commonwealth was among the last states to withdraw from the Union and did so only when coerced by the actions of the Federal government. Once the state decided to join the Confederacy, most whites enthusiastically supported the war effort. Military service for Piedmont Virginians also had religious connotations. One soldier in Company F wrote home from Richmond after a few weeks of duty that "I feel quite cheerful and contented do not trust in my own strength or the strength of armies, but in the God of Battles feeling that we are in the right and will prevail. . . . I believe it is possible for one to serve their country and at the same time serve the Lord. Indeed I think he who puts his trust in Him is the only man who can serve his Country faithfully."[14]

For many reasons, then, white men of the Virginia Piedmont eagerly accepted the governor's call to defend the state. War fever struck both natives and immigrants, and in some cases more than one family member joined the 44th Virginia. Eight pairs of fathers and sons served together in the unit, and one father enlisted with his two sons. The regiment also had 43 sets of brothers and 12 cases where three brothers fought together. One family had four brothers in the ranks of the 44th Virginia. The men of the regiment went to war alongside family relations, neighbors, school friends, fellow churchgoers, and work partners from home. This communal war effort maintained the morale of the soldiers in the face of adversity.[15]

After a short period of training in Richmond, the unit left for western Virginia.[16] The unit participated in the frustrating engagements at Rich Mountain, Cheat Mountain, and Greenbrier River where Confederate forces met little success. The 44th Virginia remained there and spent the winter of 1861–62 on the now forgotten front. Combat losses were minimal, but disease and accidents caused havoc in the 44th Virginia and claimed the lives of at least fifty men. Following this dismal period, the regiment fought throughout the spring of 1862 in the Shenandoah Valley as part of Stonewall Jackson's "foot cavalry." The 44th Virginia served in every campaign with the Army of Northern Virginia from Gaines'

Mill in the summer of 1862 until Appomattox in the spring of 1865. The regiment suffered heavy losses at Second Manassas, Sharpsburg, Chancellorsville, and Gettysburg. At Chancellorsville, for example, the 44th Virginia played an active role in Jackson's flank attack and lost 81 killed, wounded, and missing from an estimated total of 150 officers and men. The 44th Virginia was virtually annihilated in the early morning hours of 12 May 1864, when over 150 men were captured at the "Mule Shoe" at Spotsylvania. From that time on, the regiment was a mere shadow of its former self and limped through the 1864 Shenandoah Valley campaign. The final blow to the 44th Virginia occurred with the debacle at Fort Stedman in March 1865 and the capitulation of most of the unit. The long march to Appomattox Court House (ironically, the home of the 44th's Company A) further weakened the regiment, and only 17 men of the 44th Virginia surrendered there on 9 April 1865.

The 44th Virginia Infantry Regiment lost 189 men to death from all causes during the course of the war. Ninety-two of this number died in battle or from wounds, while 69 died of disease or accident. Another 28 men succumbed to disease in Federal prisoner-of-war camps. Overall, death claimed some 20 percent of the men who served in the 44th Virginia. The chance of receiving a wound in battle was great, as at least 212 men were injured in the war; this figure does not include those men who died from their wounds and is probably on the low side. Among the survivors, at least 167 men were wounded once during the war; 38 were wounded twice; 5 men were wounded three times; and 2 soldiers were hit four times during the four years of fighting. The regiment lost a total of 225 men by capture, including two men who were taken prisoner by Union troops on three different occasions. While these battle losses affected the strength of the 44th Virginia, the impact of nonbattle losses—desertion, discharge from military service, resignation, and reassignment to other duties—was profound.

The question of desertion in the Confederate army is often regarded as an outward sign of the soldier's growing despair with the war and the problems of the homefront. Desertion as such is seen as a major problem in the Confederacy only after the twin defeats at Gettysburg and Vicksburg in 1863. While this is generally valid for the Confederacy as a whole, an examination of the 44th Virginia suggests that desertion patterns varied significantly among the regiments of the Army of Northern Virginia.[17]

Desertion plagued the 44th Virginia throughout the war and reached a crisis point within the first eighteen months of combat. Private William J. Shepherd of Company F acknowledged a potential weakness in his comrades while at Camp Lee. "Some men pretend to be very brave and make a great noise, but when the pinch comes they will shrink from duty." [18] Indeed, the regiment lost its first men to desertion while drilling at Richmond before leaving for western Virginia. Private Robert Redman, a twenty-four-year-old native of Wylliesburg in Charlotte County and a member of Company I, deserted on 24 June 1861. Redman was later arrested and returned to the company in September. Charles C. Lands, a private in Company E, deserted in early July and never returned to military service. [19]

Lands's desertion was quickly followed by that of Private Julian T. Mitchell of Company B. Mitchell, a young laborer from Goochland County, left on 1 July and remained absent until early December 1861. The long march from Staunton into western Virginia exhausted the troops of the 44th Virginia, many of whom had to drop out as stragglers, the first example of the problem that affected the regiment throughout the war. One of these men, Private Meredith M. Ogg of Louisa County's Company D, was sent to recuperate at his home in Frederick Hall on 5 July. Ogg, however, showed no inclination to rejoin the 44th Virginia and was arrested as a deserter in early 1863. Within the first two months after enlistment, twelve men were absent without leave from the 44th Virginia. Before the year was over, fifty members of the regiment had been listed as absent without leave.

The first case of "mass" desertion from the 44th Virginia occurred shortly after the debacle at Rich Mountain in July 1861. The captain of Company F wrote a friend after the Confederate defeat that "no doubt you have seen accounts of the retreat of the 44th Regt. It seems that the first thing we learned was to run well. . . . our retreat I fear had a bad effect on our regiment." [20] The defeat prompted at least four men of Company C to leave the regiment's camp at Monterey on 21 July and travel home to Buckingham County. The four soldiers were later arrested by the county sheriff and delivered to Captain Thomas R. Buckner in early August. [21]

The approach of winter increased the despair of the officers and men of the 44th Virginia at their forlorn post in western Virginia. The regiment's commander appealed to the secretary of war to transfer the 44th Virginia to Manassas or to the peninsula east of Richmond where the weather was "still mild & agreeable." Colonel William C. Scott noted that the 44th Virginia "had been decimated by disease generated by hardships & the vigor of the climate of North Western Virginia." Scott concluded his lengthy letter by reminding the War Department that "many[,] perhaps a large majority[,] of my men would reenlist next Spring if their lives should not be destroyed, or their ardour dampened by a winter campaign in the North West."[22]

Dissatisfaction with army life grew as the 44th Virginia remained in the cold mountainous region of the state. Henry M. Price, a private in Company K and a peacetime doctor from Fluvanna County, protested to the secretary of war about the treatment that soldiers received at the hands of army doctors and officers in western Virginia. Price in his letter of 24 September stated that "we object to the too frequent ignorance & neglect of the physicians & their carelessness in examining the sick. We object to the arbitrary manner in which the officers from General down, deal with men—their equals, frequently superior in social position—deal with all by rule & law. We object to officers cursing & swearing at men—while we are punished for the like."[23] Such treatment, resented by well-educated men such as Price, was also disliked by other enlisted men who often likened their positions to that of slaves.

The question of furloughs became the biggest issue in the minds of all soldiers of the 44th Virginia. Homesickness, boredom, and deprivation during the first winter led troops to long for home and family. When asked by his future wife about coming home, Lieutenant John M. Steptoe of Company A responded: "You spoke of my getting a furlough! They are among the things ranked impossibilities here." The army refused to grant healthy men leave to visit home because so many members of the regiment had been evacuated to hospitals or allowed to recover at home. While the regiment recorded only 15 men (including 1 officer) absent without leave in early November (2 percent of the regiment's total strength of 663), this number doubled during the next month as men disobeyed orders and left.[24]

That soldiers of the 44th Virginia grew increasingly impatient with military life during the winter is evident from the number of applications for discharge or transfer. As early as mid-July, Colonel Scott told the governor of Virginia that his regiment was greatly reduced by discharges of soldiers unfit for service in the field.[25] The poor condition of many soldiers, readily apparent when the regiment marched into western Virginia, grew worse when strange diseases struck the raw levies. A total of 130 soldiers were discharged from the 44th Virginia throughout the war, mostly for reasons of health or age. The majority of these discharges took place during the first months of war and were related to the poor physical condition of many men and their dissatisfaction with the army.

Requests for discharge came from all social classes in the 44th Virginia. Dr. Edward H. Allen of Dinwiddie County asked President Davis to discharge his son, Private Peter W. Allen, and Private Charles C. Carr of Company H so the two young soldiers could resume their studies at Hampden-Sydney College. Realizing that the two young soldiers had not accomplished much in western Virginia, Dr. Allen wrote that "time with them, at their age is precious, and perhaps it is important to train up our young men for usefulness—as that they shall be kept in service in the defense of their country."[26]

Orderly Sergeant Thomas C. Morgan of Company I faced a greater predicament when service in the west appeared futile. The forty-three-year-old Charlotte County farmer left his wife with five young children as well as an aged mother to run the farm with forty to fifty slaves in May 1861. Morgan's overseer also joined the army, leaving Mrs. Morgan as the sole manager of the estate. Morgan requested to be released from the army in August 1861, because of poor health and to supervise the crops and slaves. Morgan's wife wrote a long letter the following month, appealing for her husband's return. "I have bourne my loneliness without murmuring, but have wasted my strength to some extent, exposing myself to the sun & weather and now feel my task more than I can undergo."[27]

Another member of Company I requested his discharge two days before the regiment entered its first major battle in May 1862. Richard W. Lawson, a thirty-one-year-old private, had been absent without leave during the previous fall, and he appealed to the secretary of war for assistance: "I write you a few lines to find out if I cannot be taken from the armey and put to some other bisiness for I am so afflicted with rheumatism in my legs that I am scarsley ever fit for duty whitch my captain will sertify at any time I think that I could stand shuemakeing I can make a very good peg or sade shue if you can you will oblige me verry mutch P.S. Pleas let me no as soon as you can as I am willing to surv at any thing that I can do and I think I can stand that because I would not have to march[.]"[28]

The army did little to relieve the agony of the 44th Virginia and further hampered control of the regiment with the Bounty and Furlough Act, passed by the Confederate Congress at the end of 1861. The law, designed to maintain the volunteer Southern army after the expiration of its one-year enlistment, authorized a bounty of $50 and a sixty-day furlough for each soldier who reenlisted to serve for two more years of military service. Those soldiers who reenlisted were permitted to form new companies and to elect their own officers.[29] The Bounty and Furlough Act offered the men of the 44th Virginia an opportunity to escape from western Virginia and to improve their military situation.

Several officers of the 44th Virginia quickly recognized the value of the new law. The acting commander of Company C wrote to the secretary of war in December for permission to take his unit to Buckingham County to recruit because "many of the men have families which they have not seen since entering service: They have all been importuning me to allow them a short leave of absence to see their wives & children & make arrangements for another year." Other commanders, primarily those of Companies A, E, and F, attempted to transfer their companies to different units. Tired of infantry service and marching, the commander of Company F wrote that "very few will re-enlist if they are compelled to remain in the same company & Reg't., but all will if allowed to join wherever they wish." [30]

The transfer of Company A to the desirable duty of heavy artillery prompted extreme unrest within the 44th Virginia. The acting commander of the regiment never consented to the company's transfer in April 1862 and protested that "it has had a most unhappy effect upon this regiment. . . . This act of the Sec of War is taking one of the best companies in the whole service from my command, without supplying its place [and] has given the regiment a shock that it will never get over. Unless something is done to stop this state of things and prevent companies, and individuals from leaving this command and entering other corps . . . the regiment will be ruined." [31]

The Bounty and Furlough Act heightened dissatisfaction because only a few of the soldiers obtained transfers and even fewer received their reenlistment furlough. In addition, the Confederate government imposed conscription in April 1862, forcing most of the enlisted men to remain with the regiment. A twenty-four-year-old overseer from Appomattox County, Private William E. Isbell, summarized the general attitude of Company A in a letter to his father in March:

> I can not reenlist unconditionally, for I know very few if any of our company will, besides if I rightly understand the law on the subject if only one man reenlist in a company enough men will be drafted to fill the company & he compelled to remain in it, and officers be appointed over them. So that he might as well be in a militia company & moreover men of the lowest character may be associated with him. Now I can not consent to this, but I am very well satisfied that I am in for two years more for nearly all of our company have agreed to reenlist provided our Capt can get heavy artillery & we do not doubt his success.[32]

The election of company officers, which occurred simultaneously with the reenlistment of the 44th Virginia, further exposed a lack of unit cohesion and created more agitation and rivalry in the regiment. Sixteen company-grade officers in the 44th Virginia were denied their positions in the elections and replaced by new commanders, often elected directly from the enlisted ranks. Five soldiers of Company I disputed their company election on 1 May 1862 and applied for a transfer to the 56th Virginia because:

1st. That this company is composed of Rowdies, Drunkards, Thieves, Murderers, blackguards and every other kind of persons the world ever knew.

2nd. That in the elections which took place . . . some of the men who were elected were nothing but a set of whiskey sellers in camp and by this means got offices which they were totally unfit to fill. A few honorable exceptions with some who were elected.

3rd. That in Capt. Jeffress' company we have many friends & acquaintances with whom we wish to be during the war.

4th. That when the Company to which we now belong was made up we were acquainted with but few of them & in hopes we could remain with them 12 months. We have nearly done it & found them to prove worse than was ever anticipated by any person . . . for our reputation . . . grant [us] the much desired transfer.[33]

The 44th Virginia at the commencement of the spring 1862 campaign in the Shenandoah Valley was an untested but demoralized unit. The lack of worthwhile duty, agitation over transfers, extensive sickness, and the general unfitness of many men for military service affected the morale of the regiment. Desertion jumped dramatically in the 44th Virginia as 187 men were reported as absent without leave throughout 1862. Combined with straggling, discharges, battle losses, illness, military details, and other factors, the 44th Virginia mustered only a handful of men during some of the war's bloodiest battles. At the height of the Seven Days' battles in early July, the brigade commander of the 44th Virginia counted only 44 men present for duty in the regiment.[34]

Desertion reached enormous levels once the Valley campaign and the fighting around Richmond got underway. Ninety-one men broke ranks between May and July 1862, with the majority of desertions occurring in June. In fact, the largest, single "mass" desertion in the history of the 44th Virginia took place at Brown's Gap in a three-day period following the battle of Port Republic on June 9. At least twenty men took advantage of the lull to pass through the gap in the Blue Ridge Mountains and head to Charlottesville. From there, it was an easy journey to their homes in nearby counties. Such desertions, known as "French furloughs," were common throughout the Confederacy.[35] In the case of the 44th Virginia, this was the first time that the regiment had been in the vicinity of home in nearly twelve months. The men of the regiment felt that they had done their duty for the moment and that they deserved a break. Although several were still absent in 1863, most of the deserters returned to duty within a matter of weeks.

The soldiers of the 44th Virginia who deserted in 1862 came from all walks of life, although their median age, twenty-seven, was higher than that of the regiment as a whole. The vast majority who left the regiment that year were enlisted men, mainly privates. Only four officers of the regiment were listed as absent without leave during the second year of war. No single prewar occupation had a monopoly on desertion in the unit; rather, deserters were merchants as well as tenant farmers. Desertion was concentrated among five groups: in order of precedence, laborers, overseers, farmers, carpenters, and students. Every company in the 44th Virginia suffered from the problem of desertion, some to a greater extent than others. Company H from Amelia County had only five deserters in 1862, while Richmond's Company E accounted for nearly 30 percent of the regiment's total desertion that year.

Desertion in 1862 was related to two major shortcomings in the 44th Virginia: the poor condition of many soldiers and inadequate leadership. Older men, a relatively high number of whom served in the unit, were susceptible to desertion because of poor health or their inability to march long distances, survive in all sorts of climatic conditions, and then to engage in combat. Unlike most of their younger counterparts, older men also had responsibilities at home that prevented lengthy military service. Desertion, however, afflicted many teenage soldiers of the 44th Virginia; it was common for minors to leave the regiment and seek the shelter of home once active campaigning began. The optimal window for military service in the Confederacy were those young men between eighteen and about twenty-five; these men did not have medical, family, or employment reasons that spurred desertion.[36]

The regiment lacked a firm leadership base in the first eighteen months of the war, a deficiency which hindered the development of the chain of command and unit discipline. Field-grade officers were political appointees, and company officers generally had little previous military experience. Unit elections in both 1861 and 1862 disrupted the regiment and led to the elevation of unqualified officers.[37] The absence of many officers during the winter of 1861–62 as well as during the fighting in 1862 set a poor example for the troops. The regiment was nominally commanded by a colonel, yet inexperienced captains were often left in charge while Colonel Scott was either sick or attending to political duties in Richmond. Several company commanders left their units during the harsh winter in western Virginia and went home, forcing lieutenants and occasionally sergeants to take charge.[38]

Private John A. Garnett of Charlotte County described the situation in Company I in a letter to his uncle in January 1862: "We have sevean out of our Company that have gone home without Ferlows and it is thought they will dealt with very swiley [swiftly or severely?] when they return, but what more could be expected when Capt Marshall set the examples left heare about 10th of Oct, and have not bin seen since & drawing Capt wages and Wm Gilliam doing Capt buisiness and drawing Lieutenants wages but I understand he [Captain Marshall] has bin written to, to attend his Court Marshall, he has bin of but little service to the Southern Confederacy."[39] Similar incidents occurred in other companies of the 44th Virginia, giving a poor example to soldiers who were, only months before, civilians.

The manner in which officers treated enlisted men did little to foster confidence between the ranks. Captain James E. Robertson's Company A was the finest unit in the 44th Virginia because Robertson took care of his men; a low death rate from disease and the lack of any deserters from the company in 1861–62 attest to his success. The acting commander of the 44th Virginia acknowledged that Company A was "one of the best in the whole service" when the unit transferred to the artillery in the spring of 1862.[40] In contrast, Company E from Richmond had the highest desertion rate in the 44th Virginia. The company commander, while sick in Richmond in early 1862, was listed as absent without leave and dismissed from the service without court-martial. This left the unit's first lieutenant in command and he, too, was often absent. Company E, composed mostly of immigrants and nonnatives of Richmond, experienced a divisive unit election in 1862, and the former company commander claimed that the entire affair was illegal.[41] The new captain of the Richmond Zouaves managed to get his company briefly assigned to Richmond as a heavy artillery company in mid-1862. This posting did not help morale; rather, it detracted from effective control of the unit because the men soon left for vice dens in the capital. Five men deserted Company E on one day in July, and of the fifty men recruited as substitutes by Captain Edward M. Alfriend during the summer and fall of 1862, forty deserted.[42]

An examination of the service records of several deserters from the 44th Virginia illustrates the scope of the problem during the critical year of 1862. Private Samuel B. Glass, a Fluvanna County blacksmith born in 1818, enlisted in Company K in 1861. Present with the unit until the spring of 1862, Glass was listed as absent without leave from that time until the following spring. He returned to duty briefly and was subsequently discharged as overage in May 1863. Like many of the discharged members of the 44th Virginia, Glass continued to serve as a reservist in Fluvanna County.[43]

Private Edward D. Cottrell enlisted in June 1861 with Richmond's Company E, claiming to be eighteen though he was actually sixteen. He served with the company until October when he was sent to a hospital for typhoid fever. Cottrell's commander stated that the young soldier then deserted and remained away from Company E until March 1862. Cottrell fought with the 44th Virginia through the first month of the Shenandoah Valley campaign until he again deserted at the end of May. Captain Alfriend did not hear anything of Cottrell until the spring of 1863, when he learned that Cottrell had enlisted in the 10th Virginia Cavalry Regiment during the previous fall. Alfriend demanded that Cottrell be returned to Company E, and the delinquent soldier rejoined his original unit until officially transferred to the cavalry in September 1863.[44]

A third case involved a young soldier from Company C. Private Robert A. Taggart, a laborer in his father's blacksmith shop, enlisted in Buckingham County during the spring of 1861. Taggart served with the unit until he deserted at Brown's Gap on 11 June 1862. He remained absent until late August when he attempted to rejoin the 44th Virginia but was captured by Union troops near Manassas. Taggart spent a short time in a Federal prisoner-of-war camp but was exchanged soon afterwards. Without Company C's knowledge, the Confederate War Department detailed Taggart to work in Richmond's Tredegar Iron Works in October 1862. Taggart was thus absent without leave until the following August when his commander requested the soldier's return to the field.[45]

In most cases, regimental officers were helpless to prevent the desertion of unit personnel in 1862. Commanders were partially to blame because the officer corps of the 44th Virginia itself was plagued by absenteeism from illness, wounds, and other problems. The turnover in officers made it extremely difficult to maintain control of enlisted men. Officers, in turn, were handicapped by vague laws that blurred the differences between desertion and simple absence without leave. The difficulty in distinguishing between the two military crimes remained a serious problem throughout the war.[46] Officers also faced myriad obstacles in keeping track of company soldiers. Most of the military hospitals in Virginia were located in the hometowns of the soldiers of the 44th Virginia, and it was relatively easy for members of the regiment to obtain permission to perform duty at these hospitals even though they were physically capable of service in the field.[47]

Even when deserters were caught by government officials or returned voluntarily to the regiment, they faced minimal punishment at the beginning of the war. Most deserters were simply charged with absence without leave and forfeited pay for the number of days of unexcused absence. If the soldier served as a corporal or sergeant, he was usually reduced to the ranks. Advertisements for deserters published in Richmond newspapers during 1862 were generally ineffective despite monetary rewards. A handful of men were arrested in the capital and committed to various military prisons to await release by company officers, but their number was negligible. Thus, soldiers learned that the punishment for desertion was rarely harsh.[48]

Private John McIntyre of Company E is an example of the laxness of Confederate discipline. McIntyre joined the Richmond Zouaves in July 1861 when the seventeen-year-old sailor from Liverpool, England, was stranded in the South by the blockade. Like many of his comrades in Company E, McIntyre deserted in 1862, but he had the rare misfortune to be apprehended. At his court-martial in Richmond, the young Englishman introduced a statement made to a notary public claiming that he did not intend to establish domicile in the United States upon his arrival in 1860. Based on McIntyre's testimony, the court found him guilty of absence without leave, and he was sentenced to forfeit one month's pay and to serve one month at hard labor. McIntyre, however, was soon released from custody because he had already "been in confinement with ball and chain for a period of about three weeks." A few weeks later, McIntyre was discharged from Confederate service as a nonconscript.[49]

Only one member of the 44th Virginia was sentenced to death for desertion during the Civil War. A Richmond court-martial ordered on 28 October 1862 that Private John F. Parke of Company E "be shot to death with musketry" for desertion. Parke, a young resident of Petersburg, enlisted in Company E at the beginning of the war and deserted during the summer of 1862. From his prison cell at Castle Thunder in Richmond, Parke heard the court's verdict. A correspondent for the city's *Daily Dispatch* witnessed Parke's reaction. "The reading of the document had a visible effect on the condemned; his face became deadly pale, and he trembled like an aspen."[50]

Parke's influential acquaintances exerted pressure to save his life. Thomas Smythe of Petersburg wrote a lengthy letter to President Jefferson Davis asking for leniency because of Parke's family connections, overall good character, and youth. Smythe noted that Captain Alfriend believed that Parke "fell out of the ranks in a long march through weariness and sickness" and that a "wicked fellow" induced Parke to desert.

Smythe concluded that Parke had learned a valuable lesson and that he would never again desert. "It was so common a thing to desert, that its seriousness did not impress his feeble judgement." Smythe's petition, signed by ninety-nine other citizens of Petersburg, saved Parke's life. President Davis commuted the sentence and ordered the private to his regiment. Parke fell in battle six months later at Chancellorsville.[51]

By the fall of 1862, desertion had reached a point in the 44th Virginia where, combined with absences from wounds and illness, it gravely affected the regiment's combat effectiveness. The number of men absent without leave represented 10 percent of the unit's total strength and nearly a quarter of the regiment's effective, or present for duty, strength in October. This rate increased the next month with no sign of diminishing. Only with the cessation of active campaigning after mid-December could army leaders turn their attention to the pressing problems of desertion.[52]

General Jackson, corps commander of the 44th Virginia, was known for rigid adherence to military discipline, and he soon instituted new means to combat absenteeism and other crimes. Jackson authorized the dispatch of officers and men from each regiment in the corps to return home and arrest all absentees as well as recruit new volunteers. On 23 January nine officers and sergeants from the 44th Virginia left camp to travel to the Piedmont in accordance with Jackson's orders. One member of Company E was also sent to southwestern Virginia to arrest all deserters from that company who illegally joined partisan units or the Virginia State Line. Lieutenant Robert J. Shelton successfully netted three deserters in Louisa County. Meredith M. Ogg, one of the deserters, had been absent since July 1861, while the other two men had left the regiment at Brown's Gap the preceding summer.[53]

In addition to the increased pressure placed on deserters at home, the army enforced discipline among those men who returned to duty from desertion. General Jackson tried hundreds of men in his corps for desertion in the first months of 1863, and penalties were often severe. Lieutenant Thomas F. Boatwright of Company C wrote his wife about two men in his company undergoing court-martial:

> You wished to know if Joe had been court marshall. He has been and the sentence was twenty extra [days'] duties and one month's pay taken away from him which was hard. Joe takes it so. I am sorry it is so with him but they are serving others much worse. We have a court marshall going on now they have appoinded me Judg Advocate. We tried a case today and will try one tomorrow. I dislike it so much but cannot help myself. I dis-

like to sentence men to punishment but we are bound to obey orders here. W. P. Riddle will be tried by Brigade Court Marshall. I fear it will go very hard with Wat but I hope it may not but they are so very strict here that it seems they do not mind punishing men; to give you a case two men will be shot next Saturday at 12 o.c. for desertion so you see how hard they are on deserters.[54]

The enforcement of regulations in the Army of Northern Virginia combined with other factors to reduce desertion of soldiers from the 44th Virginia. Desertion, as a reflection of a breakdown of unit discipline, was resolved in the 44th Virginia during the first months of 1863 and never again reached its earlier level. At the beginning of January 1863, the number of men absent without leave from the regiment still hovered around 25 percent of the unit's effective strength. By the end of February, the absentee rate had been reduced to 14 percent.[55] All told, only 27 men deserted in 1863 as compared to 187 during the previous year.

The primary reason for this reduction was Conscription Act, initially enacted in April 1862. This act has been criticized for numerous shortcomings, including exemption and substitution, but it had a positive, if overlooked, attribute. The first Conscription Act permitted the discharge of soldiers over the age of thirty-five and under the age of eighteen as well as the release of foreign nationals or border-state residents who could prove that they never intended to establish permanent residence in either the then United States or the newly established Confederate States of America.[56] Under the guise of the Conscription Act, the 44th Virginia legally discharged those soldiers who were most prone to desertion: the regiment's older personnel who were physically incapable of performing military duty; the extremely young who were not psychologically prepared for war; and foreigners or non-Virginians who never fully supported the Southern cause.

The discharge of the least effective soldiers from the 44th Virginia and the detail of skilled men to war factories throughout the state left the regiment a smaller but better integrated unit after 1863. Soldiers, both officers and enlisted men, were now combat-hardened veterans who had survived pitched battles, hard marches, and the ravages of camp diseases. Officers had proved themselves worthy of command, and friction between the ranks diminished. The men, through their suffering, developed strong bonds as comrades, and the regiment was proud to serve under Jackson's command. Kinship ties further strengthened unit bonding because most of the soldiers were family members or had known each other before the war. In the words of one historian, "desertion did not simply mean desertion from some abstract entity called the Confederate States of America; it meant abandoning the men with whom one had fought." Lieutenant Boatwright, a former enlisted man, echoed this sentiment when he commented on the desertion of troops from another regiment in his brigade after Gettysburg: "Our cause looks down just now and I am sorry to say but it is so that the soldier thinks so and many of them are saying that let the war end no matter which way it goes this I am sorry to see for we few who suffered has much to give up now."[57]

Another, very different, element influenced the soldiers of the 44th Virginia during the winter of 1862–63. The wave of Christian revivals gave men renewed vigor to continue the struggle despite all odds. The 44th Virginia shared this spirit with its enthusiastic young chaplain. Robert Nelson, a Baptist, organized nightly prayer meetings and conducted two services on Sundays. Sergeant Reubin B. Hudgins of Company C wrote home that "the most pleasure I see on earth now is looking into the future for my present life is a very hard one. I enjoy myself very much at prayer meetings every night[;] they are increasing in interest daily. I do love our Chaplain he is . . . always ready to talk on the subject of Religion." Nelson's efforts attracted a number of officers and men of the regiment who had previously shown little regard for spiritual matters. These "sinners" were slowly becoming more "efficient" soldiers and less prone to desert the Southern Christian crusade.[58]

Finally, the good news of furloughs lifted the morale of the 44th Virginia. The simple granting of leave alleviated much of the pressure to desert during the dreary days in winter camp. Military leave, the army's punishment of deserters, the positive effects of the Conscription Act, the development of esprit de corps, and revivals all combined to create a new soldier in the 44th Virginia. Desertion from the regiment was never thoroughly eliminated, but it never again reached the proportions of 1862.[59]

The 44th Virginia, despite its almost total destruction in the spring of 1864, retained its fighting spirit until the surrender at Appomattox. The number of deserters from the regiment in 1863, only twenty-seven, reveals that desertion did not strike every Confederate unit equally after Gettysburg. The punishment of deserters from other Confederate units did, however, affect the morale of the men of the 44th Virginia. Lieutenant Boatwright witnessed the execution of North Carolina troops for desertion and murder in September: "Our Div. was called out to witness an *awful awful* sin—ten men tied to a stake and shot to death. They were [North] Carolinians. . . . we formed a square that all could see them; and after ward they were shot. We then marched by them. This was done to have a good effect on the men but I doubt its doing much good for our soldiers are hardened to such seens. And they all say that they ought to have been imprisoned and their worth saved for the Government—I think this would have been better myself." [60]

The ultimate test for the men of the 44th Virginia came when they were captured by the enemy. Only a handful of men are known to have deliberately surrendered to Union troops. The worst incident occurred in late March 1864 when four privates abandoned their picket posts and swam across the Rapidan River to give themselves up. The first man to desert, Private Amos P. Ellis, had joined Company H in August 1862. He had been captured in Maryland and returned to duty following his exchange. Ellis had no previous record of desertion and was described by his captors as an "intelligent man." Ellis took the oath of allegiance and was sent north to Philadelphia where he was released.[61]

Three days after Ellis deserted, privates William Buchanan of Company E and Robert Chandler and John M. Ladd of Company F swam across the river to the enemy. Buchanan, also an August 1862 enlistee, had been imprisoned at Castle Goodwin in Richmond for an earlier desertion. Chandler and Ladd joined Company F in Fluvanna County at the beginning of the war and were repeat offenders. Chandler, an illiterate farm laborer, had first deserted in the spring of 1862, and when he surrendered to Union troops he left his wife and three children in Fluvanna County. Ladd had deserted at least three times before the spring of 1864. He, too, abandoned his wife behind Confederate lines. The three deserters swore never to take arms against the Federal government and were released from captivity. Lieutenant Boatwright shared his thoughts with his wife: "We had the misfortune to lose four men while down there [on picket duty;] they went over to the enemy [,] it is the first time that any of our Regt. has left except while in Pa. Such things have a dreadful affect upon good soldiers[,] it makes them fear the success of our Cause. It makes me feel dispondent relative to our final Independence. Men are getting very tired of this war. And I sometimes fear that our soldiers will get so wearried that many of them will desert." [62]

Boatwright had reason for concern. Jones's Brigade, to which the 44th Virginia was attached during the spring of 1864, suffered a spate of desertions. While the 44th Virginia lost only four men to desertion, the brigade's five regiments had a total of fifty men who surrendered to the enemy in March and April. Lieutenant John D. Greever of the 50th Virginia wrote home that twelve men from his regiment deserted while on picket duty. Despite Boatwright's fear, desertion in the 44th Virginia was far below the average of other regiments in the brigade, with no apparent

Fig 4.1. Flag of the 44th Virginia Infantry Regiment, captured at Spotsylvania, 12 May 1864. (Courtesy of the Museum of the Confederacy, Richmond)

reason accounting for the difference. Overall, desertion remained light with only twenty-two soldiers (including the four men in March) leaving the unit in 1864.[63]

For those soldiers captured in battle by the enemy, especially at Spotsylvania in May 1864 (see fig 4.1), survival became a struggle. The poor health of many men, terrible prison conditions, and the lack of basic necessities tested the conviction of all Confederate soldiers. Two hundred and twenty-five officers and men of the 44th Virginia were prisoners of the enemy during the course of the war; twenty-eight members of the regiment died in captivity, and several others perished shortly after exchange. The Union army exerted considerable pressure on Rebel soldiers to take the oath of allegiance or to join the Federal cause as "Galvanized Yankees." Nearly one thousand Southerners accepted this offer at the Point Lookout, Maryland, prison camp during 1864–65, as did many others at camps throughout the North.

The temptation of food, shelter, and freedom attracted twelve members of the 44th Virginia to switch sides during the war. This number, only 5 percent of the total number of regimental personnel captured, is perhaps the best testimony of the loyalty of the 44th Virginia to the Southern cause. Corporal Wesley C. Hebard, a twenty-two-year-old plowmaker from Goochland County and a member of Company K, is evidence of this loyalty. Captured in the summer of 1864 and imprisoned at Point Lookout, Hebard received this letter from his sister living in New York:

> We are very sorry to hear that your health is so poor. I wish you were here with us. Uncle Henry says the only way for you to get out of prison is to take the oath of allegiance. That is the only help for you he says if you are willing to do that you must go to the Provost Marshal and tell him that you wish to take the oath of allegiance, and that you wish to come and he will send you right over. Uncle H. says if you will come over here, you are welcome to a home with him until you can get into business, he says he will do all he can to get you into business, he says the best thing you can do is to come on here, he think[s] it will be a good thing for you. I hope you will take his advice and come. We are strong Union people here but you just come and see us, and I will promise you will find kind friends. I am sure that you will like it here and not go back to Virginia, to live again for anything. I love my old native state just as well as I ever did, and love all my dear friends just the case I do not think I should be contented to live in VIRGINIA. I must say that the North has done a good deal for me. I have a great many kind friends here, and consequently the place seems very dear to me. . . . I know you must feel sad and lonely, particularly if you are not well. Now if you will only come over here we will do all we can to make you comfortable. There is not a day passes but what I think of you and pray for you.[64]

This letter clearly reveals the divisive nature of the war and the pressures that Confederate soldiers felt to abandon their cause and comrades while in prison. Nonetheless, Hebard refused to follow his sister's advice and remained a prisoner of war until his release in June 1865. While Hebard and many other prisoners of the 44th Virginia battled the terrors of captivity, a handful of soldiers of the regiment still fought the enemy. In early December the 44th Virginia transferred from the Shenandoah Valley to the Petersburg front. Passing through the home counties of the regiment on the Virginia Central Railroad, ten men of the 44th Virginia took "French furloughs." This lapse of discipline was short-lived, and nine of the delinquent soldiers returned to duty before the end of the month. The final strength report of the 44th Virginia (now consolidated into one company) showed that seventy-five officers and men were present for duty on 31 December. Another two dozen soldiers were absent from the unit as detailed or on furlough, while only two privates were carried as absent without leave. The 44th Virginia thus had a desertion rate of less than 3 percent of its effective strength at the end of 1864.[65]

This rate did not change greatly during the first months of 1865. The 44th Virginia was an exception to the massive desertion that afflicted other regiments in the Army of Northern Virginia. The 42d Virginia, in the same brigade as the 44th, reported the desertion of twenty-six soldiers to the Union army between May 1864 and March 1865. Twelve of those soldiers left the unit during the month of February. In contrast, there were only four men of the 44th Virginia absent without leave during 1865. One of those soldiers, Captain Alfriend of Company E, was cashiered from the army for longtime absence without leave and disobedience to orders.[66]

Two explanations may account for the cohesion of the 44th Virginia. The surviving veterans of the regiment now fought literally for the defense of their homes and families. The front at Petersburg was only a short distance from the farms and towns of the Piedmont. The regiment knew what lay in store for their families if the North defeated the Southern army, having witnessed Union terror at Fredericksburg and other locations throughout Virginia. Second, the regiment still had the moral and physical support of the folks at home. The commissary sergeant of the 44th Virginia acknowledged this support in early February 1865. "I feel under many obligations for the continued kindness of you all at home, but for it my sufferings in the Army would be greatly enhanced."[67] These twin factors, the responsibility to defend the home against the Yankee vandals and the support that homefolks provided the soldiers, kept the 44th Virginia in action until the bitter end.

In summary, desertion from the 44th Virginia Infantry Regiment was primarily a phenomenon of the early war period, a product of the recruitment of men unsuited for military life. When these soldiers fell out of the ranks, desertion reached a critical level in the 44th Virginia. The Conscription Act of 1862 discharged those men least fit for Southern military service and largely alleviated the problem of desertion in the 44th Virginia. In early 1863 the officer corps finally freed itself from the shackles of political appointees and the unit electoral system that had fostered poor leadership. The officers who remained by the midpoint of the war became professionals through the test of combat and higher standards, such as examination boards for officer competency. The veterans of the 44th Virginia developed an esprit de corps through combat, supplemented by renewed spiritual vigor. The support offered by families and friends at home boosted the morale of the soldiers through the darkest days of the struggle.

This study of desertion from the 44th Virginia suggests that desertion was not derived from lower-class disenchantment with "a rich man's war, poor man's fight." Rather, desertion afflicted all echelons of the 44th Virginia and was more closely allied to age, physical condition, and family responsibilities than economic or class factors. Deserters came from all walks of life and military ranks. Had the South recruited competent soldiers in 1861, desertion would not have been such a problem in 1862. The hasty organization of the Southern forces also handicapped the development of a proper military hierarchy necessary to administer a mass army. A quick victory eluded the South, frustrating its soldiers. Units, including the 44th Virginia, became bogged down in useless campaigns during the first year of the conflict, testing the patience of the troops and increasing the difficulties for many of the unit's unqualified soldiers.

Despite overwhelming odds during the war, the 44th Virginia remained a cohesive unit in support of the Southern cause. Desertion did hamper unit effectiveness, but losses from battle, disease, and capture proved more disastrous. The regiment reflected its roots as a white "band of brothers" from the Black Belt of Virginia. There were dozens of Black Belt units in the Southern army, including regiments from North and South Carolina, Georgia, Alabama, and Mississippi. Studies of their patterns of desertion might reveal patterns similar to those of Virginia's 44th, where desertion grew from factors other than those which afflicted regiments from the mountains and sand hills of the South, areas whose men never had a deep commitment to the Confederate cause. The Confederate army needs to be considered as a complex mosaic of diverse units, not an undifferentiated whole.

NOTES

I would like to express my gratitude to the editors for their assistance in transforming my thesis into a chapter. Robert H. Ruffner played a significant role in proofreading this chapter. Sonja Ruffner and Ed Collins rendered enormous help with text-processing. Dr. Richard J. Sommers of the United States Army Military History Institute was very helpful in finding new materials pertaining to the 44th Virginia. I would also like to thank the numerous individuals and institutions that assisted me as I researched the 44th Virginia for previous works and for this chapter.

1   These themes are discussed in Kevin Conley Ruffner, " 'A Dreadful Affect

upon Good Soldiers': A Study of Desertion in a Confederate Regiment"
(M.A. thesis, Univ. of Virginia, 1987).

2 See Richard H. Beringer et al., *Why the South Lost the Civil War* (Athens:
Univ. of Georgia Press, 1986); Paul D. Escott, *After Secession: Jefferson
Davis and the Failure of Confederate Nationalism* (Baton Rouge: Louisi-
ana State Univ. Press, 1978), and Escott, *Many Excellent People: Power and
Privilege in North Carolina, 1858–1900* (Chapel Hill: Univ. of North Caro-
lina Press, 1985); Steven Hahn, *The Roots of Southern Populism: Yeoman
Farmers and the Transformation of the Georgia Upcountry, 1850–1890*
(New York: Oxford Univ. Press, 1983); Gerald F. Linderman, *Embattled
Courage: The Experience of Combat in the American Civil War* (New York:
Century, 1987); Malcolm C. McMillan, *The Disintegration of a Confed-
erate State: Three Governors and Alabama's Wartime Home Front, 1861–
1865* (Macon, Ga.: Mercer Univ. Press, 1986); James M. McPherson, *Battle
Cry of Freedom: The Civil War Era* (New York: Oxford Univ. Press, 1988);
Grady McWhiney and Perry D. Jamieson, *Attack and Die: Civil War Mili-
tary Tactics and the Southern Heritage* (University: Univ. of Alabama Press,
1982); Bessie Martin, *Desertion of Alabama Troops from the Confederate
Army: A Study in Sectionalism* (New York: Columbia Univ., 1932); Reid
Mitchell, *Civil War Soldiers* (New York: Viking, 1988); Albert B. Moore,
Conscription and Conflict in the Confederacy (New York: Hilary House,
1963); Georgia Lee Tatum, *Disloyalty in the Confederacy* (Chapel Hill:
Univ. of North Carolina Press, 1934); Emory Thomas, *The Confederate
Nation* (Baton Rouge: Louisiana State Univ. Press, 1978); Bell Irvin Wiley,
The Life of Johnny Reb: The Common Soldier of the Confederacy (Baton
Rouge: Louisiana State Univ. Press, 1980).

3 Martin, *Desertion of Alabama Troops*, 258. Several articles study desertion
at the state level or from the perspective of the community: see Richard
Bardolph, "Confederate Dilemma: North Carolina Troops and the Deserter
Problem" *North Carolina Historical Review* 66 (Jan., April 1989): 61–86,
179–210, and "Inconstant Rebels: Desertion of North Carolina Troops in
the Civil War," ibid., 41 (April 1964): 163–89; Judith Lee Halleck, "The
Role of Community in Civil War Desertion," *Civil War History* 29 (June
1983): 123–34; Richard Reid, "A Test Case of the 'Crying Evil': Desertion
among North Carolina Troops during the Civil War," *North Carolina Historical Review* 58 (July 1981): 234–62; Maris A. Vinovskis, "Have Social
Historians Lost the Civil War? Some Preliminary Demographic Speculations," *Journal of American History* 76 (June 1989): 34–58.

4 Lee A. Wallace, Jr., *A Guide to Virginia Military Organizations 1861–
1865*, rev. 2d ed. (Lynchburg: H. E. Howard, 1986). A breakdown of
the regiments that formed in 1861 shows that the Piedmont provided
sixteen regiments, more than any other section of the state. Some regiments were composed of companies from different parts of the state. The
1860 presidential election returns were grouped into sections; according
to that grouping, the Piedmont section included the following counties:
Albemarle, Amelia, Amherst, Appomattox, Bedford, Brunswick, Buckingham, Campbell, Charlotte, Culpeper, Cumberland, Dinwiddie, Fauquier,
Franklin, Fluvanna, Greene, Goochland, Halifax, Loudoun, Louisa, Lunen-
burg, Madison, Mecklenburg, Nelson, Nottoway, Orange, Patrick, Pittsyl-
vania, Prince Edward, Powhatan, and Rappahannock (Richmond *Enquirer*,
25 Dec.1860).

5 Population and slave statistics derived from U.S. Bureau of the Census, *The Eighth Census of the United States, 1860* (Washington, D.C.: GPO, 1864), vol. 1, *Population*; ibid., *Agriculture*. For a study of Louisa County's economy, see Crandall A. Shifflett, *Patronage and Poverty in the Tobacco South: Louisa County, Virginia, 1860–1900* (Knoxville: Univ. of Tennessee Press, 1982).

6 The Virginia Central Railroad ran from Richmond through Louisa County to western Virginia. The Richmond and Danville Railroad bisected both Amelia and Charlotte counties, while the Southside Railroad, running from Petersburg to Lynchburg, passed through Prince Edward and Appomattox counties. The James River and Kanawha Canal pierced the heart of the Piedmont and prompted the growth of towns such as Columbia and Scottsville. For an example of such growth, see Virginia Moore, *Scottsville on the James: An Informal History* (Charlottesville: Jarman, 1969).

7 For further details on Richmond, see Michael B. Chesson, *Richmond after the War* (Richmond: Virginia State Library, 1981), 7–18.

8 The data presented here are based largely upon research conducted for my book, *44th Virginia Infantry* (Lynchburg: H. E. Howard, 1987). For specific details regarding two companies of the 44th Virginia, see Kevin Conley Ruffner, "Fluvanna Goes to War: The Experiences of Two Infantry Companies," *Bulletin of the Fluvanna County Historical Society* 47–48 (Fall 1989): 4–66. The roster used for the basis of this chapter was organized using Compiled Service Records of Confederate Soldiers Who Served in Organizations from the State of Virginia, Record Group 109, Microfilm 324, reels 877–83, National Archives (NA), and a variety of other sources, including the 1860 census and postwar Virginia pension records. A note on sources and methodology is located in my thesis as well as an introduction to the roster in *44th Virginia Infantry*, both of which go into detail regarding the preparation of the roster.

9 Richmond *Daily Whig*, 2 July 1861.

10 The occupational diversity of Confederate soldiers is shown in Wiley, *The Life of Johnny Reb*, 330.

11 Virginia had a white male illiteracy rate of 5.9 percent in 1860. During the same year 83,000 white males attended school in the state. U.S. Bureau of the Census, *Statistics of the United States (Including Mortality, Property, &c.) in 1860, Compiled from the Original Returns and Being the Final Exhibit of the Eighth Census* (Washington, D.C.:, 1866), 58, 507.

12 This survey is a comparison of names on company muster rolls with the slaveholders listed in the 1860 census. Slaveholding wealth varied within counties as seen in the two companies from Fluvanna County (Ruffner, "A Dreadful Affect," 7–8; Shifflett, *Patronage and Poverty*, 9–11).

13 Fluvanna County, for example, approved Virginia's act of secession by 877 votes to no opposition (Richmond *Daily Dispatch*, 30 May 1861). The Piedmont narrowly supported Democratic candidate Breckenridge for president in 1860. The eight-county region of the 44th Virginia voted in 1860: Breckenridge, 3,863; Bell, 3,069; Douglas, 200; Lincoln, 0 (Richmond *Enquirer*, 25 Dec. 1860).

14 William J. Shepherd to his family, 20 June 1861, Old Stone Jail Museum, Fluvanna County Historical Society, Palmyra.

15 The percentage of married men at the time of enlistment, about 16 percent, is admittedly low, considering the number of older men in the regiment. The marital status of soldiers was not often recorded in service records, and the census does not always reveal the relationships of members of the same household.

16 For a more complete history of the military activities of the 44th Virginia, see Ruffner, *44th Virginia Infantry.*

17 Wiley, *The Life of Johnny Reb,* 183. For a discussion of the role of women and desertion, see George C. Rable, *Civil Wars: Women and the Crisis of Southern Nationalism* (Urbana: Univ. of Illinois Press, 1989).

18 Shepherd to his family, 20 June 1861, Old Stone Jail Museum. This study of desertion counts all men who were absent without leave or considered deserters. The Confederate army never fully defined desertion as compared with absence without leave although the death sentence for desertion was amended to five years' imprisonment or hard labor in 1863 (Lonn, *Desertion during the Civil War,* 57). The modern U.S. Army definition of desertion is Article 85 of the *Manual for Courts-Marial,* which states that desertion is the act of leaving one's unit or military post with the intention to never return. The judge advocate must prove that the soldier intended to never return to military service and can do so by showing that the accused disposed of his uniforms, purchased tickets for travel, was arrested a great distance from his military assignment, made previous statements about deserting, or could have surrendered to military officials but did not. Joining another branch of service or a foreign army without permission is considered an act of desertion. The sentence for desertion in wartime is death. "Entries on documents, such as personnel accountability records, which administratively refer to the accused as a 'deserter' are not evidence of intent to desert." Conviction of soldiers for desertion is still difficult under these guidelines, and only one soldier in the American army was executed for desertion during World War II (U.S. Department of the Army, *Manual for Courts-Martial* [Washington, D.C.: GPO, 1984], 4:10–12). Confederate soldiers were classified as deserters or absent without leave by commanders for a number of reasons: absent sick at home or in hospitals away from the main army, detailed to extra duties by other commanders, home on furlough from hospitals without the knowledge of units, delayed in returning to duty by illness, weather, transportation problems, or enemy action, and soldiers joining other military units without the permission of their original unit. The Union army experienced similar difficulties, and a postwar report estimated that 25 percent of all Northern deserters were "unavoidably absent from various causes" (Reid, "A Test Case of the 'Crying Evil,'" 240–41).

19 All discussion of deserters, unless otherwise noted, is based on the roster in Ruffner, *44th Virginia Infantry.*

20 Captain Weisiger to Abram Shepherd, n.d., in David W. C. Bearr, "Palmyra Soldier: Diary and Letters of W. F. Shepherd," *Bulletin of the Fluvanna County Historical Society* 38 (Oct. 1984): 29.

21 Further discussion of the social characteristics of these deserters can be found in Ruffner, "A Dreadful Affect," 26–27.

22 Colonel Scott to Assistant Secretary of War, 14 Nov. 1861, Letter 7621-1861, Letters Received by the Confederate Secretary of War, RG 109, M437, NA (hereafter cited by letter number, date, and LSOW).

23 Letter 5882-1861, 24 Sept. 1861, ibid.

24 John M. Steptoe to Hamie Leftwich, 21 Oct. 1861, Steptoe Family Papers, Acc. 6515, MSS Div., Special Colls. Dept., Univ. of Virginia Library (UVA Lib.); morning report of the 44th Virginia, 8 Nov. 1861, File of the 44th Virginia, RG 109, NA.

25 Colonel Scott to Governor Letcher, 21 July 1861, Records of Virginia Forces, 1861, RG 109, M998, NA.

26 Letter 6210-1861, 2 Oct. 1861, LSOW.

27 Morgan to Secretary of War, 12 Aug. 1861, E. E. Morgan to Secretary of War, 22 Sept. 1861, Letter 5549-1861, ibid.

28 Letter 210-L-1862, 6 May 1862, ibid.

29 Douglas Southall Freeman, *Lee's Lieutenants: A Study in Command,* 1 (New York: Scribner's, 1942): 171.

30 Letter 8064-1861, 3 Dec. 1861, Letter 58-J-1862, 15 March 1862, LSOW.

31 Letter located in file of James E. Robertson, Compiled Service Records, 20th Virginia Heavy Artillery battalion, RG 109, M324, NA.

32 William E. Isbell to father, 10 March 1862, Lewis Leigh Collection, U.S. Army Military History Institute, Carlisle Barracks, Pa. (USAMHI).

33 Letter 358-H-1862, 1 May 1862, LSOW.

34 "Strength of Genl. Lee's Army during the Seven Days Battles," *Southern Historical Society Papers* 1 (1876): 419.

35 A good example of the common soldier's view toward "French furloughs" is in John O. Casler, *Four Years in the Stonewall Brigade* (Dayton, Ohio: Morningside, 1971), 49–50. Casler's regiment was in the same division and later brigade with the 44th Virginia from 1863 until the end of the war. Another view is stated by George C. Eggleston, a brother of a member of the 44th Virginia: "The men who volunteered went off to war of their own accord, and were wholly unaccustomed to acting on any other than their own notion." After a battle, Confederate soldiers would "cooly walk off home, under the impression that they had performed their share" (George C. Eggleston, *A Rebel's Recollections* [Bloomington: Univ. of Indiana Press, 1959], 70, quoted in Brian Holden Reid and John White, "'A Mob of Stragglers and Cowards': Desertion from the Union and Confederate Armies, 1861–65," *Journal of Strategic Studies* 8 [March 1985]: 67).

36 Wiley, *The Life of Johnny Reb,* 331.

37 Military leadership is a crucial element in the successful conduct of war. The principles of leadership include loyalty to the nation and unit, strong personal character traits, knowledge of human nature, and the ability to motivate men in the face of adversity (U.S. Department of the Army, *Military Leadership,* FM 22-100 [Washington, D.C.: GPO, 1983], 44). An example of the discontent aroused by the 1861 elections can be found in Bearr, "Palmyra Soldier," 22–23. For a discussion of the role of unit elections in the Confederate army, see David Donald, "The Confederate as Fighting Man," *Journal of Southern History* 25 (May 1959): 178–93.

38 Colonel Scott left the regiment in November 1861 to attend the Constitutional Convention in Richmond to rewrite Virginia's state constitution after its dissolution of ties with the Union. Returning to the unit briefly in January, Scott left for his home in Powhatan County on account of illness and

did not return until April 1862. Lieutenant Colonel Hubard was placed in acting command of the 44th Virginia although he, too, was ill during the winter and was forced to relinquish command to Captain Buckner of Company C. Major Alexander C. Jones of the 44th Virginia was rarely present as he was detailed to other duties.

39 John A. Garnett to William Gray, 19 Jan. 1862, William Gray Papers, box 3, Mssl G7952aFA2, Virginia Historical Society.

40 Robertson was later promoted to major in 1863. Company A maintained its good standing as a heavy artillery unit in Richmond and suffered minimal desertion. See Compiled Service Records, 20th Virginia Heavy Artillery Battalion, RG 109, NA; Letter 200 1/2-L-1863, Spring 1863, LSOW.

41 The dismissal of Captain Edward McConnell generated considerable letter writing by the former commander of Company E to the War Department. McConnell was finally reinstated in early 1863 but promptly resigned his commission. His initial dismissal appears to have been based on personal conflicts between the captain and regimental officers rather than McConnell's absence. "My long continuing absence was caused by having typhoid fever, the time of absence was six weeks, while I was sick and compelled to be away, there were officers in town who had been away three and four months from the Regiment, and one or two who were or had been absent six months, there has been no notice taken of their being away, but I am reported and made an example of while officers did it before and after me and were not noticed." Additionally, McConnell stated that "in reference to the reorganization there was no legal election, only two men in the company voting while there was between 45 and 50 men present. I was there and saw the election, the men refusing to vote and reenlist (those over 35 and under 18) because Genl. [Edward] Johnson refused to let me have the office of captain again" (Letter 532-C-1862, 26 May 1862, LSOW).

42 The only mention of the enlistment of these fifty substitutes and their subsequent desertion is found in Letter 324-V-1863, Nov. 1863, Letters Received by the Confederate Adjutant and Inspector General's Office, 1861–65, RG 109, M47, NA (hereafter cited as LAIGO). The names of most of these men are not listed in the Compiled Service Records because the original muster rolls of Company E for most of 1862 and 1863 were not available to postwar compilers. Only five muster rolls (covering two-month periods) survive from Company E, and three were indexed in the Compiled Service Records at the turn of the century. The other two muster rolls are located at the Library of Congress; information from these rolls is included in the roster (Ruffner, *44th Virginia Infantry*).

43 Glass died of disease in 1865 (Glass's service record at NA and his widow's pension application on 30 April 1888 at the Virginia State Library).

44 Edward D. Cottrell, Compiled Service Records, 10th Virginia Cavalry Regiment, RG 109, NA.

45 Robert A. Taggart, 44th Virginia Infantry Regiment, ibid.

46 A look at the military justice system and military police operations is found in William M. Robinson, *Justice in Grey: A History of the Judicial System of the Confederate States of America* (New York: Russell and Russell, 1968), 359–82, and Kenneth Radley, *Rebel Watchdog: The Confederate States Army Provost Guard* (Baton Rouge: Louisiana State Univ. Press, 1989), 102–63.

47 Major Confederate hospitals were located in Richmond, Petersburg, Charlottesville, Staunton, and Farmville while smaller hospitals were established at Columbia, Palmyra, and Scottsville. All of these hospitals were either in the hometowns of companies of the 44th Virginia or nearby. For a case of one such soldier, see Ruffner, "A Dreadful Affect," 46.

48 An example of a deserter notification issued by Captain Gilliam of Company I is in Richmond *Daily Dispatch*, 8 Aug. 1862. Lists of Confederate soldiers held by authorities at Castle Thunder and Castle Goodwin were published in Richmond papers during 1862. Most of the prisoners were accused of desertion (Richmond *Daily Examiner*, 2, 9 Sept. 1862).

49 John McIntyre, Compiled Service Records, 44th Virginia Infantry Regiment and 19th Virginia Heavy Artillery Battalion, RG 109, NA; Confederate States War Department, *Report of the Adjutant General's Office to the Honorable James A. Seddon, Secretary of War* (Richmond: J. W. Randolph, 1863), 16–17.

50 John F. Parke, RG 109, 44th Virginia Infantry Regiment and 19th Virginia Heavy Artillery Battalion, NA; Richmond *Daily Dispatch*, 31 Oct. 1862.

51 Letter 1997-W-1862, 3 Nov. 1862, LAIGO. Also included with Smythe's petition is a letter written by Parke while a prisoner at Castle Thunder to "Cooper," asking for help for a member of the "Ringgolds."

52 Regimental roll of the 44th Virginia for October and November 1862, File of the 44th Virginia, RG 109, NA.

53 Henry Kyd Douglass, *I Rode with Stonewall: The Experiences of the Youngest Member of Jackson's Staff* (Chapel Hill: Univ. of North Carolina, 1940), 213; Special Order 22, paragraph 9, 22 Jan. 1863, Army of Northern Virginia and arrest documents found in Robert J. Shelton, Compiled Service records, 44th Virginia Infantry Regiment, RG 109, NA.

54 Thomas F. Boatwright to wife, 27 Jan. 1863, Boatwright Papers, MS 73, Southern Historical Collection. Univ. of North Carolina at Chapel Hill (SHC, UNC). For more discussion of these deserters, see Ruffner, "A Dreadful Affect," 51–52.

55 Jones's Brigade morning report for 10 Jan. 1863, William B. Taliaferro Papers, Museum of the Confederacy, Richmond; compilation of personnel on Jan.–Feb. 1863 company muster rolls (with exception of Company K), dated 28 Feb. 1863, File of the 44th Virginia, RG 109, NA.

56 For more details on the various conscription acts and exemption/substitution, see Moore, *Conscription and Conflict in the Confederacy*.

57 Reid Mitchell, "The Creation of Confederate Loyalties," in *New Perspectives on Race and Slavery in America: Essays in Honor of Kenneth M. Stammp*, ed. Robert H. Abzug and Stephen E. Maizlish (Lexington: Univ. Press of Kentucky, 1986), 99; Thomas F. Boatwright to wife, Aug. 1863, Boatwright Papers, SHC, UNC.

58 Reubin B. Hudgins to cousin, 31 March 1863, Boatwright Papers, SHC, UNC, For an example of a converted soldier, see ibid. The role of religion and its reinforcement of military discipline is discussed in Drew Gilpin Faust, "Christian Soldiers: The Meaning of Revivalism in the Confederate Army," *Journal of Southern History* 53 (Feb. 1987): 63–90. According to Faust, religious fervor helped Southerners adjust to the emerging industrial concept of time, including "discipline, regularity, and subordination." Evan-

gelicalism promoted "efficiency" in the ranks and, as one observer noted, supposedly eliminated the "greatest evil of our army, in a military point of view . . . that of straggling" (ibid., 74–77).

59 Thomas F. Boatwright to wife, Feb. 1863, Boatwright Papers, SHC, UNC.

60 Thomas F. Boatwright to uncle, 25 Sept. 1863, ibid.

61 For more information on these individuals, see roster entries in Ruffner, *44th Virginia Infantry.*

62 Thomas F. Boatwright to wife, 28 March 1864, Boatwright Papers, SHC, UNC. Boatwright may have been referring to the disappearance of Private John D. Perrow of his company during the Gettysburg campaign. Perrow later joined a Union cavalry regiment in September 1863.

63 John D. Greever to "Miss Mollie," 17 April 1864, Greever Family Papers in private collection of T. C. Greever. It is interesting to compare Boatwright's letter with that of Greever's. Boatwright was generally depressed by the desertion incident while Greever mentions it only as a postscript. Greever's letter is full of optimism because of the arrival of spring and the news of a supposed Southern victory in Mississippi. "I feel assured of the ultimate success of the South for a richeous [righteous] cause." Another officer in the brigade, from the 21st Virginia, reported on desertion in Jones's Brigade during the spring of 1864. Lieutenant Overton Stegar wrote that "several [of] our soldiers have deserted & gone over to the Yankees this week, how low & degraded those wretches must feel (if they have any) conscience must lash them for deserting their country at such a time," (Overton Stegar to unknown, 23 April 1864, Lewis Leigh Collection, USAMHI). Environmental factors, such as the weather, food (or lack of it), fatigue, boredom, and loneliness, could, of course, color the reports of soldiers during the war.

64 D. Alexander Brown, *The Galvanized Yankees* (Urbana: Univ. of Illinois Press, 1963), 67; Wesley C. Hebard, Compiled Service Records, 44th Virginia Infantry Regiment, RG 109, NA.

65 Muster roll of the consolidated Company I, 31 Dec. 1864, File of the 44th Virginia, RG 109, NA.

66 John D. Chapla, *42nd Virginia Infantry* (Lynchburg: H. E. Howard, 1983), 51–53. Alfriend fell ill during the summer campaign in 1864 and returned to his home in Richmond. He attempted to rejoin his unit during the fall of 1864 but once again returned to Richmond. He was arrested in Jan. 1865 and sent to the army under guard. Despite Alfriend's conviction, the officers of the brigade signed a petition asking President Davis to restore Alfriend's commission. No action was taken as the petition was written less than two weeks before the fall of Richmond (Edward M. Alfriend, Compiled Service Records, 44th Virginia Infantry Regiment, RG 109, NA).

67 George A. Bowles to Sallie, 1 Feb. 1865, Bowles Family Papers, Acc. 6450, UVA Lib. A study of two New York communities in the Civil war, for example, reveals that "a community's degree of unity and support had a direct influence on its soldiers' decision to desert. . . . the available evidence on enlistments and desertions indicates that Southold [New York] provided a stability lacking in Brookhaven, which its soldiers carried with them into military service. These Southold men had a strong sense of community support and approval, which not only added to their feelings of personal responsibility but also strengthened that obligation to meet the expectations of their home community" (Judith Lee Halleck, "The Role of Community in Civil War Desertions," *Civil War History* 29 [June 1983]: 134).

5

GREGG L. MICHEL

From Slavery to Freedom: Hickory Hill, 1850–80

IN 1850 A CENTRAL VIRGINIA PLANTATION WAS AS LIKELY TO grow wheat as tobacco, the traditional staple of the state. While a rich literature of memoir, fiction, and history describes life on Southern cotton plantations before, during, and after the Civil War, we know virtually nothing about how the owners and slaves on a plantation such as Virginia's Hickory Hill, near Richmond, coped with the pivotal event of the nineteenth century. The experience of Hickory Hill describes the paths many black and white Virginians followed through war and emancipation.[1]

As a large wheat plantation which remained in operation after the Civil War, Hickory Hill affords a unique perspective on critical issues in nineteenth-century Southern history. Life during slavery, the effects of the Civil War, the disintegration of forced labor, and the economic developments of the postwar years often took different shapes on the plantations of the Old Dominion than on the rice and cotton plantations of the Deep South. Hickory Hill, like much of Virginia, did not conform to our commonly held beliefs about what life was like in the nineteenth-century South. For a myriad of reasons, the bound and free inhabitants of Hickory Hill charted their own unique path through the century. Taking a close look at Hickory Hill offers a view of how the people on one plantation coped with the momentous events of the nineteenth century.

Hickory Hill is located in central Hanover County. Situated on the fall line between the Piedmont and Tidewater regions, the 512-square-mile county is "shaped like a bag of meal tied in the middle and swung diagonally to Richmond," five miles to the south. Home of the Wickham family since 1827, the sprawling, nearly 3,500-acre Hickory Hill plantation was one of the largest in the area by 1860. Transversed by both the Pamunkey River and the Virginia Central Railway, the land was divided into sixteen different tracts, ranging in size from one to 1,710 acres. Crops grew primarily on the two largest tracts, South Wales (1,710 acres) and

The Lane (972 acres), with the main grounds located on the tract known as Hickory Hill (284 acres).[2]

Hickory Hill was originally held by Robert Carter, owner of Shirley plantation in Charles City County, Virginia. In 1820 Carter gave 1,700 acres of this plantation to his daughter Anne Butler Carter Wickham and her husband, William Fanning Wickham (1793–1880). The Wickhams began constructing a house and laying extensive gardens immediately but did not move to Hickory Hill until 1827, when William Fanning Wickham retired from practicing law to devote the rest of his life to plantation management. Hickory Hill was directed by both William Fanning Wickham and his son throughout the mid-nineteenth century. Like his father, Williams Carter Wickham (1820–1888) was trained as a lawyer but abandoned the profession early to take up residence at Hickory Hill. A local militia officer before the Civil War, Williams Carter Wickham became a general in the cavalry of Northern Virginia. While both father and son played an active role in Virginia politics, only the younger Wickham made it his career, serving in both the state Senate and the Confederate Congress. In the years after the Civil War, Williams Carter Wickham also became involved in the railroad business, holding various executive level positions in the Chesapeake and Ohio Railroad. In 1891, three years after Williams Carter Wickham's death, his "comrades in the Confederate Army and employees of the Chesapeake and Ohio Railway Company" erected a statue of him in Richmond's Monroe Park. During the dedication ceremony, one of the speakers noted that Wickham's death had brought Virginia more "sorrow than any that had befallen her since the death of General Lee."[3]

By 1850 Hickory Hill had grown to 3,400 acres and was home to eight members of the Wickham family and their 191 slaves. During the fifties, Hickory Hill's slave population grew much faster than that of Hanover County—44 percent compared to 13 percent; by 1860, while the amount of land and number of Wickhams had remained constant, the slave population had increased dramatically to 275. In 1860 Hickory Hill was one of only two plantations in Hanover County, and nine in the entire state, on which more than 200 slaves lived and worked.[4]

Mixed farming dominated agricultural production at Hickory Hill. During the 1850s the slaves cultivated wheat, the plantation's primary crop, as well as oats, corn, and a wide array of fruits and vegetables. While a small amount of tobacco grew on the plantation, it was not—nor had it ever been—one of the primary crops on the plantation. One of six Hanover plantations larger than 1,000 acres, Hickory Hill produced an immense quantity of foodstuffs. In 1855, for instance, the plantation produced 5,700 bushels of wheat and over 1,000 bushels of corn. Because of the diverse nature of plantation operations, the failure, or partial failure, of the wheat crop was not the catastrophe it might seem. Instead, losses incurred on a poor wheat crop were often recouped with other crops or animal husbandry.[5]

Hickory Hill practiced the most up-to-date agricultural methods. Each year, the Wickhams planted several fields in clover to enhance the soil's fertility. Further, the Wickhams annually sowed large quantities of Peruvian guano, the latest and most expensive fertilizer at $45 to $65 a ton, in various crops both to improve the soil and to increase crop yields. Crops also were rotated annually on the plantation, with the three largest fields alternated among growing wheat and then corn and lying fallow. Additionally, the Wickhams purchased the most advanced farm tools and machinery for use at Hickory Hill. The slaves, for instance, used reapers during the harvest and threshers for the processing of wheat. Perhaps the greatest testimony to the plantation's technological advancement was the steam sawmill built on the plantation in 1849.[6]

Like other large plantations throughout the South, Hickory Hill was deeply involved in the market economy, mainly through its sale of wheat. Unlike other Virginia plantations, Hickory Hill did not sell any of its products to its immediate neighbors. Instead, each year the Wickhams sold anywhere from 80 to 90 percent of the wheat crop in Richmond— from where it was transported to distant markets—and retained the rest for the plantation's consumption. The same holds true for the surplus corn and oats produced at Hickory Hill. The Wickhams avoided the local markets because the high prices that the crops commanded in Richmond—wheat sold for between $1.50 and $2.50 per bushel throughout most of the decade—removed any incentive for selling or trading crops locally. Further, the plantation's railroad crossing and its proximity to Richmond allowed for quick, cheap, and easy delivery to the city. Thus, with its wheat, corn, oats, fruits, vegetables, and livestock, Hickory Hill not only achieved a high degree of self-sufficiency but isolated itself from the county's economy as well.[7]

The most important pillar of the Wickhams' financial security was the increasing value and number of slaves at Hickory Hill. In 1852 their 200 slaves were valued at $70,000—an average of $350 each. In 1860 the 275 slaves, averaging slightly more than $650 each, were worth $180,000. Therefore, low crop yields were not something the Wickhams had to worry about. If the Wickhams had to endure several consecutive years of crop failures, which they never did, they could always sell some of their slaves.[8]

Most of the changes in Hickory Hill's slave population occurred naturally, through births and deaths. There is no evidence that the Wickhams sold any slaves during the decade, and there is only one documented instance of a slave purchase—the July 1857 purchase of two women and five children. In the eleven years between 1850 and 1860, when the slave population increased from 191 to 275, an average of six more slave births than deaths occurred each year at Hickory Hill. The slave population, therefore, grew by natural increase to 251. It is likely, then, that the Wickhams purchased only 24 slaves during these years, including the seven at one time. Further, although going against the trend in Virginia, it is equally plausible that the Wickhams did not sell any slaves during the fifties. Virginia slaveowners determined that fewer slaves were needed for their mixed farming operations, as booming staple crop production on Deep South plantations drove the price of slaves upward. Although the number of slaves in the state continued to increase, Virginia became the leading supplier of slaves to the Deep South as the antebellum era came to a close. Hickory Hill, however, had long been oriented toward mixed farming and thus did not find itself with a sudden surplus of slaves in the last antebellum years.[9]

The field hands constituted the overwhelming majority of slaves at Hickory Hill. Approximately seven house servants lived at Hickory Hill, performing the traditional tasks of cooking, cleaning, caring for the children, and attending to the adults' various personal needs. The field hands lived a life vastly different from that of the house servants. Throughout the 1850s, these slaves followed the same yearly work routine. In late October or early November they planted wheat and about a month later harvested the year's corn crop. Field slaves spent most of the winter tending to the wheat crop and performing non-crop-related tasks, such as grubbing, repairing fences, filling the icehouse, or undertaking special projects such as building slave houses or clearing new land. As the weather improved in March, field slaves began preparing the land for the corn crop to be planted in mid-April. The pace of work picked up in the spring as the slaves then cared for two major crops. Forced to work hardest during the wheat harvest in June or July, field hands labored in often stifling heat from sunup to sundown. William Fanning Wickham hinted at the strain this caused the slaves when he remarked in his diary that "there have been a great many complaints among the people, but chiefly from the fatigue of the harvest." The field slaves then spent the next month preparing the crop for transportation to Richmond where it would be sold. By summer's end, the land was readied for a new planting of wheat, and by October the cycle started anew. Throughout the year, Hickory Hill's field slaves had few reprieves from work.[10]

The field hands formed their own community. There were a large number of married slave couples at Hickory Hill, and families tended to live together, though some undoubtedly shared their quarters with nonfamily members. In 1850 the 191 slaves constituted 49 separate families. Excluding the 12 slaves who were not part of any family, the average family size was 4.8. In 1860, excluding the nine nonattached slaves, there were 55 families of 266 people, an average of 4.8 again. That this number held constant over the decade indicates that stable family size characterized Hickory Hill's slave community. Typical was the Gibson family. The heads of the family, Peter Gibson and his wife Winney, lived on the plantation with several of their children. By 1859, however, two of their daughters, Mary and Beckey, had grown and no longer lived with their parents. Apparently Beckey recently had married Aaron, another slave on the plantation, for the two now lived alone together. They soon began a family, as Beckey gave birth to Mary in 1859 and Denis on Christmas Day 1861. Beckey Gibson, like her mother, would soon be surrounded by several children. As Peter and Winney Gibson's household became smaller, their children began to start families of their own.[11]

The Wickhams, like most large planters, employed an overseer at Hickory Hill throughout the 1850s. Planters tended to act as head manager of their farms—overseeing the entire operation, making important decisions, and solving the plantation's crucial problems—while preferring to hire an intermediary to perform the unpleasant tasks of driving and punishing the slaves. Since slaves worked in scattered areas throughout large plantations, planters could not take on the role of overseer while effectively carrying out their other responsibilities. Therefore, the Wickhams gave their overseer responsibility for assigning the slaves specific tasks, visiting the work squads throughout the plantation to ensure that the work was being done, and disciplining the slaves when necessary.[12]

Their detachment from the plantation's daily affairs increased many large slaveowners' emotional distance from their slaves. Masters of smaller farms might act as the alternately harsh and forgiving "father" of their "people" because they knew each of their slaves' character traits and special skills. This was a crucial component of paternalism, for a master needed to know his slaves individually to convince them that he was acting in their best interests. But William Fanning Wickham knew too little about his slaves to be an effective paternalist. He was not the overseer and had very little contact with his slaves. Except in the slave lists, his diary never mentions any slaves by name. Wickham considered the slaves as one large, uniform group, not as individuals. This impersonal relationship between Wickham and his slaves was not unlike that between employer and employees. Wickham valued the slaves primarily as laborers—as workers in his business—and, consequently, his interest in the slaves' identities and individual personality traits remained low. Interestingly, Wickham never referred to the slaves as "niggers," "negroes," or even "slaves," but rather as "the hands," "the house servants," or "the people." This, however, hardly qualifies him as a paternalist, for it was quite common for antebellum planters to fall into these bland euphemisms.[13]

Hickory Hill slaves exerted some control over their own time and labor; though the Wickhams possessed all the power on the plantation, it is clear that the slaves were not without influence. Shirking work, usually by feigning illness, was a favorite method by which Hickory Hill slaves sought to undermine their owners' authority. On numerous occasions William Fanning Wickham noted in his diary that sickness prevented many of the slaves from working. Often he seems to have suspected that the slaves were not actually ill: "A good many are laid up in the plantation with but little the matter."[14]

All in all, Hickory Hill displayed great stability on the eve of the Civil War. Wheat and corn still grew in great quantities, the slaves' workload remained unrelenting, the plantation continued to bring the Wickhams a profit, and the agricultural cycle loomed as the chief determinant of work patterns. A state senator by 1859, Williams Carter Wickham spent more time in Richmond than before, but that did not seem to affect the plantation's operations. William Fanning Wickham still kept his diary and continued to visit and receive relatives. While little had changed over the past decade, the plantation's stability was soon to be threatened by powerful external forces. Writing in his diary on the last day of 1860, William Fanning Wickham struck an ominous note: "The whole country is in a state of the greatest confusion from the secession of South Carolina and there seems a strong possibility of the dissolution of the Union and the entire breaking up of the government."[15]

Plantation life proceeded as it always had during the initial months of the war. The slaves worked the fields, the Wickhams purchased a new McCormick reaper, and William Fanning Wickham maintained high hopes for his corn and wheat crops. But the plantation soon felt the indirect impact of war. Williams Carter Wickham became a cavalryman in the Army of Northern Virginia and so could no longer aid his father in the directing of plantation operations. This was not the only problem the war created for Hickory Hill. In his diary entry for 31 August, William Fanning Wickham gloomily wrote that "there is no prospect of selling wheat. The price in Richmond is now from 90 cents to a dollar and were I inclined to take that price it would not be profitable to deliver the crop by the railroad which is fully occupied in transporting the troops and munitions of war." Not until 23 December 1861 could wheat be sent to Richmond, and then only one-third of the year's crop. While the price of wheat would rebound later in the war, the military's use of the railroad bedeviled Wickham throughout the conflict.[16]

In 1862 the war began to affect Hickory Hill and its inhabitants more directly. The Confederate government made its presence known early in the year. In March, William Fanning Wickham "was called on to furnish four mules for the use of the government for which they allowed me $500." Less than two weeks later the government came again, this time impressing fifteen young male slaves. Surprisingly, this did not initially upset Wickham, for plantation work was "so forward that we can spare them without much inconvenience." Though he tried to keep the plantation operating smoothly, it became harder to do so as the war and its effects came closer and closer. In April, soon after the slaves had planted the corn, soldiers from both sides began appearing in the neighborhood. Wickham expressed some concern, for they "are constantly coming here, asking for whatever they want. As yet they have done no injury here . . . but in the neighborhood I am told they have carried off some poultry." In mid-May, Williams Carter Wickham returned home to recuperate after suffering a severe wound from a saber thrust. It had become increasingly difficult to isolate the plantation from the war.[17]

The antebellum way of life was shattered forever at the end of May 1862. On 27 May the battle of Hanover Court House spilled over onto Hickory Hill when "an immense force of the Northern Cavalry," over 1,000 men strong, descended upon an outnumbered group of Southern soldiers who had been hiding on the plantation. The Southerners made a short stand before quickly retreating. The Union army "spent the night near the house" and "returned in large force on the plantation" for the next two days. Surprisingly, William Fanning Wickham had a high opinion of the Union forces that came to Hickory Hill, writing that "the officers all behave with the greatest politeness." Further, the plantation came through the fighting in good shape. The Union troops "took a little wheat for their horses . . . and trampled down some in riding over the field . . . and they broke down the fences in a great many places[;] but on the whole the damage was inconsiderable." Although this skirmish may have hardly affected the plantation's physical condition, it had a tremendous impact on Hickory Hill's slave population.[18]

Signs that the slaves were becoming anxious for their freedom became evident shortly after the battle of the twenty-seventh. "A party of the Hanover dragoons have just searched our [slave] quarters for muskets and found five. . . . They had been thrown away by the North Carolina troops after the battle." Soon after, on the nights of 9 and 10 June, fourteen slaves ran away. Two days later, another slave followed. Wickham believed they were "making, without doubt, for the Yankees who are about the Oaks along the Chickahomony." Throughout the South, slaves fled for the Union lines; if troops were near, or even rumored to be near, slaves often set out for freedom. The fact that numerous slaves ran away during the war dealt a debilitating blow to the proslavery argument that blacks were content in their bondage and satisfied with their lives. Hickory Hill's runaways showed William Fanning Wickham that they cared more for freedom than for his distant care and protection.[19]

Of the fifteen slaves who ran away from Hickory Hill, thirteen were men and two were women. Specifically, the group consisted of one couple, three male heads of household, one wife of a male head of household, five eldest sons, three noneldest sons, and one male slave whose family status is unclear. None of the runaways was very old, as they ranged in age from the teens to the mid-thirties. It is understandable that young, single, uncommitted males would run away. Restless on the plantation and in their bondage, males like Lewis Christian, the second of Tom and Jenny Christian's three children, left Hickory Hill in search of freedom and a better life. And Lucy Grayson, the lone slave who fled on 12 or 13 June, undoubtedly left to join her husband Edmund, one of the group of fourteen to leave a few days earlier. Less obvious, however, is why a male head of household such as Nelson Davis would flee, leaving his wife behind. While most slave marriages were consensual, based on mutual love and respect, this was not always the case. If slaves could not choose their own spouses, if the master forced a marriage upon them, or if they married simply for convenience, the bond between husband and wife was not likely to have been strong. Thus, the couple would have considered their marriage as something less than sacred, and the opportunity for freedom would have outweighed the commitment to one's spouse.[20]

The battle, the runaways, and the proximity of the Union army stirred feelings of hope and excitement among the slaves; they spent less time working in the fields and became harder to manage. On several occasions in 1862 a total breakdown of order on the plantation occurred, as the field slaves milled around the Big House instead of performing their tasks. "There are a great many hands in the house—and no discipline can be maintained among them," William Fanning Wickham complained in July 1862. One can infer that these slaves, unlike those who fled, did not want to leave their family and friends or Hickory Hill. This is not to say that they did not want freedom, but rather that they either had strong bonds with other slaves or knew of no other life beyond Hickory Hill.[21]

Hickory Hill slaves spent the first part of 1863 cleaning up fields, planting crops, mending fences, and performing other tasks to help the plantation recover from the events of the previous year. Despite their efforts, however, disaster struck in late June when Union troops again raided the plantation. This time the plantation suffered, and Wickham had few kind words for the Union army. As the troops left, Wickham bitterly recounted that they "carried away with them 18 of my Negroes—about all young men and boys—and five horses." Another raid occurred on 20 July, and this time the Union troops attacked the house as well, stealing wine and brandy from the cellar. Shortly after this raid twelve more slaves ran off, and, in Wickham's estimation, "the negroes who are left seem to work with no spirit." [22]

The loss of hands and the disruption of work by raids took time and labor away from the crops. The 1863 wheat crop appeared "indifferent" because "the coming of the yankees . . . prevented our securing it before it got wet." Further, the diminished labor force led the Wickhams to plant a much smaller wheat crop than usual. And to make matters worse, in December the Confederate government imposed taxes on the plantation's agricultural products at a rate of 10 percent in kind. [23]

Early the next year, as the plantation fought to continue operating, Union troops were rumored to be preparing to raid the plantation yet again. Fearing the loss of more slaves and animals, William Fanning Wickham tried to send his mules and horses to a friend's plantation in nearby Henrico County. But the Union army controlled the road to Henrico, and the slaves with the animals were forced to turn back to Hickory Hill. Although these slaves could have freed themselves by riding across Union lines, they chose to remain on the plantation with friends and family. That was the life they knew, and like the slaves who went to the Big House instead of fleeing after the raids of the earlier years, they preferred to wait for a secure freedom rather than force the issue. [24]

Fighting was never very far from Hickory Hill in the war's last two years. Some of the most bloody and destructive battles of the war took place nearby in May and June 1864. Though Wilderness, Spotsylvania, and Cold Harbor were the major battles of these months, several smaller ones took place in Hanover County, including the battle of the North Anna River. As the fighting drew closer, the plantation's residents "could hear the cannon and rattle of musketry all day long with scarcely a moments interuption." Little work was done on the plantation in May, and throughout the month Hickory Hill served as a Confederate safe house as well as a place where wounded soldiers were received and cared for. Throughout the conflict the plantation could never avoid the direct effects of being nearby the fighting. [25]

Hickory Hill struggled through the Civil War. During the war years crop production fell, the number of laborers decreased, Williams Carter Wickham was severely injured twice, and the plantation became run down. By the end of the war, everything on the plantation had changed. Blacks were no longer slaves. The Wickhams were significantly less wealthy and, like many other former slaveholders, hardened by their wartime experience. William Fanning Wickham in a letter to a northern cousin wrote that he had heard that robberies and murders had taken place near the plantation. But after four years of war the family was not worried, for "it would not be an easy matter to make us afraid of anything." With the end of the war, the Wickhams looked forward to a return of the stability and prosperity of earlier years. As Hickory Hill moved into the postwar era, however, its inhabitants would have to form a new set of relations and create a new way of life. Though the war had destroyed slavery, that institution was only vaguely replaced by the notion of free labor. It remained to be seen whether the Wickhams and their former slaves could find a workable definition of this term.[26]

In the summer of 1865, Hickory Hill's future looked bleak. Nearly two hundred Hickory Hill slaves had abandoned the plantation for freedom during the spring. The crops stood in poor condition, suffering primarily from lack of attention. Labor was clearly the main problem. William Fanning Wickham bitterly wrote of the freedmen that "we have no power to compel them to work, yet are obliged to furnish them with provisions. . . . While the uncertainty concerning the relation between the employer and the laborer continues, we can form no plans for the future and must go on pretty much as we now do." As a solution to the labor problem, he suggested that the government force the freedmen to contract for a "term of years" with the landowners. This was essentially the course the government followed.[27]

The Bureau of Refugees, Freedmen, and Abandoned Lands—the Freedmen's Bureau—was a temporary agency created in order to help the freedmen adjust to their newly won status. Many bureau agents, including their commissioner, General O. O. Howard, shared the common view that blacks were inherently lazy and shiftless and that unless forced to work they would be content simply to live off the bureau's support. Howard and other agents also believed in the transforming power of free labor—that the freed people must contract with planters soon so that both groups could adjust to the workings of a free labor economy and return the region to prosperity. Encouraging the freed people to contract with their former masters, then, became the bureau's central policy. As one historian concludes, the bureau, in the name of free labor, "ultimately delivered the black labor force back into the hands of the planters."[28]

The contract system governed labor relations at Hickory Hill during the immediate postwar years, but the dramatic decline in the labor force limited the plantation's productive capabilities. In 1863, after the last runaways had fled, over 200 slaves still remained on the plantation; but by the beginning of 1866 only 41 blacks worked at Hickory Hill, and the plantation's total freed population was not much more. Most of the freed people probably left at one of two junctures. In the spring of 1865, with the war officially over and the remaining slaves freed, most blacks probably chose to leave Hickory Hill as a way of exercising their newly found freedom. Another exodus likely occurred in late December 1865, when the Wickhams sought to contract labor for the coming year. The prospect of returning to work for the Wickhams surely must have disappointed the freed people, many of whom had expected to receive confiscated or abandoned land from the Freedmen's Bureau. While the Wickhams, like most whites, probably viewed the contract system as something radically new—an experiment in free labor—their former slaves, as a student of the Freedmen's Bureau points out, likely perceived it simply as "the resumption of things in the usual way."[29]

The stability of the antebellum years no longer characterized labor at Hickory Hill. Between 1866 and 1880 the number of laborers on the plantation changed constantly, as freedmen moved on and off the plantation with great frequency. Sometimes the same freedman left Hickory Hill only to return a year or two later, remain for a year, and then depart again. During these years, however, more laborers departed than settled at Hickory Hill: the forty-one laborers of 1866 had dwindled to twenty-six in 1880, with the bulk of this loss occurring within the first five years of emancipation. Whoever the freedmen were, they had definitely taken their freedom to heart.[30]

The contracts signed at Hickory Hill after the war stipulated that the freedmen work the entire year on the plantation in exchange for wages. Oliver Thornton and other adult men earned $7 a month, while Phil Hewlitt's son, George, and other young men earned from $3.50 to $5 a month. The laborers also received rations of meal and meat each month and could purchase additional food and supplies from the Wickhams as needed. The Wickhams also provided housing—the former slaves' quarters—for the laborers. The freedmen received two-thirds of their wages each quarter. Oliver Thornton, for instance, received $14, minus any expenditures, on 1 April, 1 July, and 1 October. The Wickhams deferred payment of the other third of the wages—$21—until the end of the year, at which time Thornton received this money along with his final quarter's wages. Withholding a portion of their laborers' wages allowed the Wickhams an interest-free extension of credit, while at the same time trapping the freedmen on the plantation until year's end. By binding their laborers to the plantation, the Wickhams ensured that the year's crops would receive the proper attention.[31]

The arrangements at Hickory Hill reflected the Wickhams' continued belief that slavery—or its closest substitute—was the system most suitable to plantation life. The work pattern had hardly changed, as laborers continued to labor in the fields and care for the animals. Further, an overseer still supervised the black laborers on a daily basis. The freedmen, as in slavery, continued to live in the slave quarters. And as in the antebellum years, the Wickhams supported some freedmen too old to work.[32]

Despite the similarities to the days of slavery, however, substantial changes had occurred in the laborers' lives after 1865. Most obviously, blacks now received wages for their labor, and receiving cash wages every four months signified that the freedman's labor was now worth something very tangible. Tom Christian, who had labored on Hickory Hill for many years as a slave, now received cash for his efforts. Further, he now had money to spend at his discretion or to save in hopes of renting or buying land. Additionally, the freedmen received extra pay for extra work. During harvest season, for instance, most laborers received $5 to $10 for "extra work in corn." It was clear to all that unless properly compensated, the freedmen might abandon the plantation at year's end. The Freedmen's Bureau agent in Hanover County, Assistant Superintendent Murphy, confirmed this possibility when he wrote that "no freedman will stay where he is not well treated." Hickory Hill's laborers also gained some control over their working lives. Women, for instance, withdrew from the work force. Of the forty-one laborers on the plantation in 1866, only nine were women, five of whom worked as house servants. Fewer black women worked because they could now choose to be with their children. Though Tom Tin still worked in the fields, his wife, Dalilah, did not. Instead, she now spent her days caring for their children, including six-year-old Barbara. Although their situation was not perfect, Hickory Hill's freedmen exerted as much control over their lives as the context permitted.[33]

Hickory Hill suffered through hard economic times during the initial postbellum years. With a dramatically reduced work force, the Wickhams planted significantly smaller crops than before the war, and yields and profits consequently declined. Between 1860 and 1870 laborers planted approximately 500 bushels of wheat each year, substantially less than in the antebellum era, when slaves consistently cultivated over 600 bushels a year. Yields dropped from the prewar level of 6,000 bushels to a low of 2,240 bushels in 1866. By 1870 the crop had recovered somewhat, yielding close to 4,000 bushels, but the Wickhams' strained financial situation prevented their hiring more laborers to cultivate the plantation on the antebellum scale. Further, the Wickhams lost much of their wealth and collateral for credit with emancipation. In 1860 their slaves were valued at $180,000; in 1866 free black labor cost the Wickhams over $3,000. And in 1870 Hickory Hill lost money for the first time since before the 1850s.[34]

Hickory Hill's economic situation continued to deteriorate over the 1870s. Both wheat and corn production continued their downward trend: wheat production averaged approximately 3,300 bushels a year, and the plantation did not market any corn in six of the decade's years, signaling a dramatic decline in production. Further, the selling price of these crops had also fallen. Corn brought in a paltry 57 cents per bushel during the decade, and wheat approximately $1.30 per bushel, a full 40 cents below wheat's prewar average. When compared to the county as a whole, Hickory Hill's decline appears even more marked: unlike their neighbors, the Wickhams did not compensate for declining wheat production by increasing corn production. And while the county's tobacco production exploded during the 1870s, greatly surpassing its antebellum output, Hickory Hill only experimented with the crop during the decade. Not surprisingly, Hickory Hill continued to lose money in the seventies, finishing in the red every year except 1872. Between 1867 and 1879 the plantation lost $11,556. Like other plantations throughout the South, Hickory Hill experienced gradual decline and relative poverty over these years.[35]

By the early 1870s most planters believed their search for an adequate substitute for slavery had failed, for the region remained "disordered, unstable, and poor." Though far from poor, the Wickhams had not regained their prewar prosperity. The freedmen, for their part, did not fare nearly as well as they had hoped in the years following emancipation. The ex-slaves deeply desired independence and land, and Hickory Hill's freedmen had neither. Throughout the South, then, both planters and laborers—employers and employees—became increasingly dissatisfied with the existing conditions. Sharecropping spread quickly across the region as a result.[36]

The development of sharecropping in Virginia's tobacco belt was typical of the process throughout the region. Immediately after the war, planters kept the freedmen on the plantations by signing them to wage contracts. The Freedmen's Bureau aided the planters in the task, for the bureau simply wanted to get blacks back to work. The experiment with wage contracts, however, lasted barely two years. By 1867 the shortage of agricultural workers and the freedmen's desire for land and independence, combined with the planters' lack of cash and their conviction that the wage system had failed, led to the spread of sharecropping throughout the region. Sharecropping reflected a compromise between planters who needed labor and freedmen who were seeking greater freedom and security than postharvest cash wages afforded them.[37]

Given its condition in the 1870s, and in light of what occurred on other plantations in similar situations, Hickory Hill was a prime candidate for the sharecropper's shack. But the system did not develop at Hickory Hill. Instead, wage labor became even more entrenched as the plantation moved toward the complete rationalization of labor relations. A capitalistic wage-labor system developed at Hickory Hill during the 1870s, complementing the plantation's well-entrenched market focus. This labor system became increasingly based on the anonymous bond of wages, and not, as in sharecropping and paternalistic slavery, on personal relations.[38]

Wages remained constant at Hickory Hill over the 1870s, as adult men continued to earn $7 a month, and younger men and women approximately $2.50 to $5.00. But in 1877 the Wickhams ended the practice of retaining a portion of the laborers' wages until the end of the year. They did not take this course of action because the work force had stabilized. The number of laborers remained between twenty-five to thirty, but individual laborers continuously joined or abandoned the plantation. To combat this high rate of turnover, the Wickhams began paying the freedmen their full wages each quarter. Lacking close personal relations with their slaves, the Wickhams had an easier time adjusting to a free labor system than many of their more paternalistic contemporaries. Transactions between the Wickhams and their workers now became cut-and-dried: the freedmen received their full wages each quarter, and the Wickhams cleared their books, dissolving the yearlong tie with their workers that the retention of wages had ensured.[39]

In addition to year-round wage earners, Hickory Hill began taking on seasonal day labor in 1873. During the wheat harvest, when the need for extra help was most acute, over forty day workers labored on the plantation. The appearance of these workers at Hickory Hill signified the further rationalization of labor relations. The Wickhams had no commitment to these workers beyond the season in which the plantation required their labor. Since they did not live at Hickory Hill, day laborers remained anonymous to the Wickhams. In fact, the Wickhams often only knew these laborers by their first names. The presence of day laborers, combined with the overtime the regular workers performed, significantly altered the breakdown of the plantation's labor costs. Between 1866 and 1875 the number of regular laborers at Hickory Hill fell by nearly half. Total labor costs, however, remained virtually unchanged, indicating that day laborers had become an increasingly significant part of life at Hickory Hill.[40]

The Wickhams were able to use day laborers instead of sharecroppers because, unlike most planters, they maintained a ready source of cash throughout the postbellum era: in 1860, in addition to 275 slaves valued at $180,000, the Wickhams owned $32,000 worth of stocks and bonds. Though they lost an enormous sum of property when the slaves were freed, they still owned their stocks and bonds, which, unlike land, they could easily convert to cash. Further, throughout the 1870s Williams Carter Wickham probably brought in a steady income from his high position in the Chesapeake and Ohio Railroad. With cash available, then, the Wickhams need not become involved in the cumbersome credit relations of sharecropping. A simpler system of wage labor could be established at Hickory Hill.[41]

Though planters benefited from sharecropping to the extent that production resumed, it was the refusal of blacks to labor in gangs as they had during slavery that led to the development of the system. The shortage of labor gave the freed people the power to force the creation of a new system of labor. Freedmen often desired sharecropping agreements since it gave them some semblance of what they had long wanted—land and independence. But an abundance of labor in the area surrounding Hickory Hill denied freedmen the threat of withholding their labor as a means of forcing the Wickhams to change the plantation's labor system. Most of this excess labor came from Richmond, only five miles away. Between 1860 and 1880 Richmond's black population nearly doubled. Rural blacks arrived in search of work and greater freedom, but the city's economy could not absorb the influx. Therefore, a significant number of unemployed freedmen lived in Richmond, a group from which the Wickhams could attract workers when needed. In fact, it is quite likely that most of the day laborers at Hickory Hill came from Richmond, for Hanover County did not have a surplus of black labor. With a large source of underemployed blacks nearby, Hickory Hill's freedmen could not gain much leverage by withholding their labor.[42]

The needs of the plantation, however, required that the Wickhams maintain a minimum number of year-round laborers. Although some of the resident laborers left Hickory Hill in search of better opportunities, many stayed on. These laborers, such as Daniel Hewlett, remained on the plantation year after year, no doubt because they feared their situation would probably worsen if they left Hickory Hill. If Hewlett had gone elsewhere, he probably would have been forced to settle for postharvest payments—either annual cash wages or shares of the crop. At Hickory Hill, on the other hand, Hewlett at least received quarterly cash payments. The salient point, which certainly did not escape Hewlett and the other year-round laborers, was that wage payments at any interval shorter than a year were preferable to sharecropping and other arrangements in which they were paid only once a year (and not necessarily in cash). Thus, the resident laborers' economic situation, while not ideal, was better than that of most Southern black farm laborers.

Regardless of the type of labor arrangement established in the years after the Civil War, plantations rarely regained their former prosperity. On those where sharecropping developed, the planters no longer owned all of the crop yields, now having to give a portion to the croppers. Although it remained intact and did not witness the development of sharecropping, Hickory Hill, like other plantations, suffered economically throughout the postwar era. Crop yields declined, profits fell, and the number of laborers on the plantation decreased. Labor relations had changed as well. The Civil War destroyed slavery, and by 1880 a full wage system of labor, characterized by anonymous and impersonal relations, had assumed its place. The emergence of this system was the most important development at Hickory Hill after the war. Not only does that development distinguish postbellum from antebellum Hickory Hill, but it was the key factor separating Hickory Hill from other Southern plantations after 1865.

During the 1880s, Hickory Hill continued to run a deficit. Beginning in the 1890s, however, the plantation's economic condition improved— largely as a result of further diversification. In 1893, for instance, the plantation sold corn, wheat, oats, hay, a wide variety of vegetables (cabbage, potatoes, cucumbers, spinach), cows, and hogs. The Wickhams also began a dairy business (from which they sold butter) as well as a poultry farm. Because they had diversified, the Wickhams' financial well-being depended even less on any one crop. Now the Wickhams could become more flexible in their operation of the plantation, adjusting crop production according to the prevailing market conditions. In 1893, because wheat prices were so low, the plantation's laborers planted the smallest crop in twenty years. In 1900 wheat prices had sufficiently recovered so that it was again profitable to cultivate a large wheat crop. By shifting the plantation's crop mix, the Wickhams succeeded in bettering their economic standing despite the agricultural depression of the 1890s. And the first year of the new century brought the Wickhams their first profit in nearly thirty years.[43]

The rationalization of labor relations continued throughout the latter years of the nineteenth century as the Wickhams increasingly turned to day labor. As in earlier years, the Wickhams took on a large number of day laborers in the wheat-harvesting months of June and July. These laborers earned pay by the day and received rations and housing while they worked at Hickory Hill. Further, as the nineteenth century faded, the number of regular resident laborers on the plantation declined, their places taken by day laborers. By 1913 day laborers worked throughout the year and on all aspects of plantation operations. Residential farm labor was still present at Hickory Hill but diminished in importance with each passing year. Day labor became the dominant form of labor at Hickory Hill before the end of the twentieth century's second decade.[44]

Hickory Hill, like the rest of the rural South, felt the effects of the Great Depression. But because it was not tied to a single cash crop, especially cotton, the plantation fared better than many others elsewhere in the South. In order to boost wheat prices in these hard economic times, acreage limits were placed on the crop's production. The Wickhams could withstand a decrease in wheat production by simply altering the crop mix and focusing on the production of a different crop. A reduction in wheat cultivation, however, did affect the plantation's labor needs. With less work to do in these strained economic times, the laborers worked one day less a week in 1934 than previously—five days instead of six—and earned $1.35 per day rather than the $1.50 paid in 1929. Still, this was a better situation than most cotton sharecroppers faced. With no work for these croppers, owing to the strict limitations placed on cotton production, planters chose to evict their tenants rather than continue to support them. Though times became hard, Hickory Hill's laborers were not driven away.[45]

Hickory Hill, because it produced wheat and because the Wickhams possessed cash, had always faced different challenges from the rest of the agricultural South. The Wickhams turned to wage labor immediately after the Civil War and diversified their operation well before acreage reduction laws encouraged them to do so. Similarly, the Wickhams adopted the latest technological improvements as soon as they became available and practical to own, and before World War II ended much of the plantation's operation was mechanized. By 1942, for instance, the Wickhams owned a bailer, a combine, a tractor, and a truck for deliver-ies to Richmond. As a result of this process, the plantation's labor force was sharply reduced. In 1942 only six laborers worked at Hickory Hill, all as full-time wage laborers; mechanization enabled them to harvest the wheat themselves without the addition of other day laborers.[46] Thus, as they had for the previous one hundred years, the Wickhams kept their plantation intact in the face of new challenges, forcing the black laborers to bear the costs of their evolving strategies.

NOTES

I would like to thank the staff of the Virginia Historical Society for their assistance in the researching of this chapter. Also, thanks is owed to Gulfstream of Virginia for its generous funding of the research of this chapter.

1   The shift from tobacco to grain production in Virginia was largely complete by 1800. Owing to a variety of factors, such as soil exhaustion in tobacco lands and the settlement of the central and northern Piedmont areas where the soil and climate were well suited to grain production, wheat plantations became more widespread and economically important in the state as the nineteenth century progressed. On the development of wheat production in Virginia, see Lewis Cecil Gray, *History of Agriculture in the Southern United States to 1860* (Washington, D.C.: Carnegie Institution, 1933), 161–67, 606–9; David C. Klingaman, *Colonial Virginia's Coastwise and Grain Trade* (New York: Arno, 1975); Gerald W. Mullin, *Flight and Rebellion: Slave Resistance in Eighteenth-Century Virginia* (New York: Oxford Univ. Press, 1972), 125–28; Lynda J. Morgan, "Emancipation in the Virginia Tobacco Belt, 1850–1870" (Ph.D. diss., Univ. of Virginia, 1986), 7, 19; John T. Schlotterbeck, "The 'Social Economy' of an Upper South Community: Orange and Greene Counties, Virginia, 1815–1860," in Orville Vernon Burton and Robert C. McMath, Jr., eds. *Class, Conflict, and Consensus: Antebellum Southern Community Studies* (Westport, Conn.: Greenwood, 1982), 9–10.

2   Rosewell Page, *Hanover County: Its History and Legends* (privately published by the author, 1926), 1. The information on the division of the plantation's land is based on an 1878 survey of Hickory Hill, located in Wickham Family Papers (WFP), box 7, folder 1, Virginia Historical Society.

3   William Fanning Wickham (WFW) was the son of John Wickham, a prominent Virginia lawyer and owner of the town house that now forms part of the Valentine Museum in Richmond (Hanover County Historical Society, *Portraits in the Historic Hanover County Courthouse* [Hanover County, Va., 1985], 8; Calder Loth, ed., *The Virginia Landmark Register*, 3d ed. [Charlottesville: Univ. Press of Virginia, 1986]). Williams Carter Wickham (WCW) saw action in several important Civil War battles, including Second Manassas and Gettysburg, and was twice severely injured—once when he received a severe saber wound and again when a shell fragment lodged in his neck (Jed Hotchkiss, *Confederate Military History*, vol. 3, *Virginia*, ed. Clement A. Evans [Atlanta: Confederate Publishing Company, 1899], 686). WCW served in the state senate 1859–60, the Confederate Congress 1863–64, and again in the state senate 1883–88. He also was chairman of

the Board of Supervisors of Hanover County 1871–88. The Virginia Central Railway was renamed the Chesapeake and Ohio Railway in 1868; WCW was vice president of the C&O 1869–75, receiver 1875–78, and second vice president 1878–88. On the statue of WCW, see the statue's base and Walter Fredric Brooks, *History of the Fanning Family*, 2 vols. (Worcester, Mass.: privately printed by the author, 1905), 663.

4 Joseph F. and Isabel B. Inman, *Hanover County Virginia, 1850 United States Census* (Richmond,: privately printed by the authors, 1974); WFW Diaries, 4 and 5, WFP. Hanover County's slave population increased from 8,393 in 1850 to 9,483 in 1860 (U.S. Bureau of the Census, *The Seventh Census of the United States, 1850*, vol. 1, *Population* [Washington, D.C.: Robert Armstrong, public printer, 1853], 256; U.S. Bureau of the Census, *The Eighth Census of the United States, 1860* [Washington, D.C.: GPO, 1864], vol. 1, *Population* 516, 598–99; ibid., vol. 3, *Agriculture*, 243, 247).

5 U.S. Bureau of the Census, *Eighth Census*, vol. 3, *Agriculture*, 221, 228.

6 Since they possessed the necessary capital, land, and labor, large planters such as the Wickhams led the way in adopting the latest agricultural reforms and innovations (see John T. Schlotterbeck, "Plantation and Farm: Social and Economic Changes in Orange and Greene Counties, Virginia, 1716 to 1860" [Ph.D. diss., Johns Hopkins Univ., 1980], 270; Gray, *History of Agriculture*, 794). For an overview of the agricultural improvements and reforms introduced in the South during the nineteenth century, see ibid., 797–810. For a discussion of the changes at the county level, see Schlotterbeck, "Plantation and Farm," 255–81; WFW Diaries, 4: 1 Jan. 1850, 7: 16 Nov. 1860.

7 WFW Diaries, 7: 31 Aug. 1859. Of the 1859 wheat crop, for instance, 700 of the 5,800 bushels produced were retained at Hickory Hill; John T. Schlotterbeck found that the large plantations of Orange and Greene counties "supplied foodstuffs for the local nonfarm population" (Schlotterbeck, "The 'Social Economy' of an Upper South Community," 10; WFW Diaries, 7: 31 Aug. 1859). The per bushel price of wheat dropped below $1.50 only once in the decade—in 1859, when it sold for $1.40 per bushel; Schlotterbeck found that transporting the crops to market by rail cost half as much as transporting by wagon ("Plantation and Farm," 310).

8 "Value of Estate," box 7, folder 1, WFP. Between 1852 and 1860 the number of slaves increased 38 percent, the value of each slave 86 percent, and the value of the entire slave population 157 percent. On slave prices and the profitability of slavery, see Robert W. Fogel and Stanley Engerman, *Time on the Cross: The Economics of American Negro Slavery* (Boston: Little, Brown, 1974), 4–5, 59–78, 86–94, 103–6; Roger Ransom and Richard Sutch, "Capitalists without Capital: The Burden of Slavery and the Impact of Emancipation," *Agricultural History* 62 (Fall 1988): 133–60; Kenneth Stampp, *The Peculiar Institution: Slavery in the Antebellum South* (New York: Random House, 1956), 414. As Stampp has written, "the high valuation of Negro labor during the 1850's was the best and most direct evidence of the continued profitability of slavery."

9 Slave lists, 1850–60, including lists of births and deaths, located in WFW Diaries, 4–7. In the diary entry for 20 July 1857, WFW noted that he had recently purchased two slave women and five slave children. The sex of the children and names of the slaves are not known. For a discussion of the state's shift to mixed farming, see note 1. Virginia's slave population was growing as the antebellum era came to an end. In the era's last decade,

the slave population increased 4 percent, giving the state 490,865 bonds-men, more than in any other state (U.S. Bureau of the Census, *Eighth Census*, vol. 1, *Population*, 516, 598–99). One point must be remembered about slavery in Virginia on the eve of the war: white Virginians' ideological commitment to slavery remained strong and, perhaps, became stronger as the institution came under increased attacks from abolitionists.

10 Although never mentioned in the Wickham diaries, there was a "mammy" on the plantation. To this day her quarters, a small three-room shack adjacent to the Big House, still exist (WFW Diaries, 4–7, esp. 4: 12 July 1850; U.S. Bureau of the Census, *Eighth Census*, vol. 3, *Agriculture*, 221, 228).

11 Slave lists, 1850–60, WFW Diaries, 4–7. Family units are demarcated on Hickory Hill's slaves lists by lines drawn between the slaves' names. Nearly all of the units are headed by a male and female, followed by several other slaves. Some, no doubt, were children, but others may have been either part of the extended family or nonrelated slaves who simply lived with the family. Although the average family size remained constant, the slave population was not static during the 1850s. Rather, as exemplified by the Gibson family, individual slaves moved around within the slave community, as couples separated, children moved out of the family's quarters, and singles married. That the average family size did not change over the decade, however, signifies that a pattern had emerged in slave family life.

12 It would not have been unusual for Williams Carter Wickham to serve as Hickory Hill's overseer in the early 1850s; overseers were often "the sons or close kin of the planters, who were learning to be planters in their own right" (Eugene D. Genovese, *Roll, Jordan, Roll: The World the Slaves Made* [New York: Pantheon, 1974], 12–21). On slave management and overseers, see William Kauffman Scarborough, *The Overseer: Plantation Management in the Old South* (Baton Rouge: Louisiana State Univ. Press, 1966), esp. 5–7, 54–56, 67–101; Gray, *History of Agriculture*, 545–46; Stampp, *The Peculiar Institution*, 38; Schlotterbeck, "Plantation and Farm," 190; Mullin, *Flight and Rebellion*, 20–23; Ulrich Bonnell Phillips, *American Negro Slavery* (New York: D. Appleton, 1929), 240–41, 280.

13 On paternalism, see Genovese, *Roll, Jordan, Roll*, 3–7, 187–91; Phillips, *American Negro Slavery*, 327–28; Mullin, *Flight and Rebellion*, 6–33; James Oakes, *The Ruling Race: A History of American Slaveholders* (New York: Knopf, 1982), 192–224. While Mullin and Oakes agreed on the characteristics of a paternalistic planter, they differed on the question of how the planter's role as paternalist affected his role as farm manager. Mullin saw the two roles as being inherently contradictory. Oakes, on the other hand, believed that paternalism did not affect the planter's role as manager. Instead, he argued that paternalism prevented the dehumanization of the slaves. If William Fanning Wickham had behaved paternalistically, his diaries would have attested to the fact. Slaveowners throughout the South recorded their thoughts and feelings about their slaves in their diaries. The absence of the slaves from WFW's diaries makes it clear that his thoughts and concerns lay elsewhere on the plantation.

14 WFW Diaries, 7: 14 Sept. 1859. For a discussion of shirking and other forms of slave resistance, see Stampp, *The Peculiar Institution*, 101–9; Oakes, *The Ruling Race*, 179–80; Mullin, *Flight and Rebellion*, 55; Phillips, *American Negro Slavery*, 327.

15 WFW Diaries, 7: 31 Dec. 1860.

16   Though there is no mention of an overseer in WFW's diaries during the war years, it is likely one remained at Hickory Hill owing to the Confederate Conscription Act of 1862. This law contained a provision exempting from military service overseers and owners of plantations with twenty or more slaves. Since WCW joined the war effort immediately, and because WFW was beyond the fighting age, this exemption could have been applied to Hickory Hill's overseer (Scarborough, *The Overseer*, 139–40; WFW Diaries, 7: 25 May, 22 June, 6 July, 31 Aug., 26 Sept., 23 Dec. 1861). Approximately 2,200 of the 6,500 bushels of wheat produced in 1861 reached Richmond before the end of 1861.

17   WFW Diaries, 8: 13, 25, March, 14 April, 13 May 1862. For a general treatment of the war's effect on plantations throughout the South, see James Roark, *Masters without Slaves: Southern Planters in the Civil War and Reconstruction* (New York: Norton, 1977), 44–55.

18   WFW Diaries, 8: 31 May 1862.

19   Ibid., 11, 14, June 1862. A single slave also departed Hickory Hill two weeks before the exodus of 9 and 10 June. There was no apparent connection between this slave's fleeing and the group's subsequent departure. For discussions on slave runaways during the war, see Bell Irvin Wiley, *Southern Negroes, 1861–65* (New Haven: Yale Univ. Press, 1938), 3–4, 8, 19, 23; Leon F. Litwack, *Been in the Storm So Long: The Aftermath of Slavery* (New York: Random House, 1979), 132–35; Morgan, "Emancipation in the Virginia Tobacco Belt, 1850–1870," 123–60.

20   WFW included the names of the runaways on the 1862 slave list. I then located these slaves on earlier slave lists (as far back as the 1830s) in order to determine their age, marital status, and family size. It should be noted that it is possible that some of the male non-heads of household runaways may have been members of the extended family or boarders rather than sons. The family situation of one of the runaways, Talbot, is not clear: Talbot and a second slave, Harry, are listed as comprising one family, but the exact relationship between Harry and Talbot is not known. Slave marriages are discussed in Deborah Gray White, *Ar'n't I a Woman?: Female Slaves in the Plantation South* (New York: Norton, 1985), 105–11, 149–55; Litwack, *Been in the Storm So Long*, 234, 238–40; Genovese, *Roll, Jordan, Roll*, 450–75, 482–501; Herbert G. Gutman, *The Black Family in Slavery and Freedom, 1850–1925* (New York: Pantheon 1976).

21   WFW Diaries, 8: 11, 29, July 1862. A wide range of the slaves' response to freedom, including ambivalence, is discussed in Litwack, *Been in the Storm So Long*, 169–93, 222–29.

22   WFW Diaries, 8: 18 Feb. 1863. The raid occurred while Robert E. Lee's son Rooney Lee recuperated at Hickory Hill from wounds he had recently received. The Union forces took Lee prisoner while his brother Robert E. Lee, Jr., who had been caring for him, escaped capture by hiding in the plantation's boxwood garden. The Lees had been at Hickory Hill because their father was the first cousin of Anne Carter Wickham, William Fanning Wickham's wife (ibid., 29 June, 20 July 1863). Undoubtedly, the raids and runaways affected the remaining slaves' thoughts and attitudes. WFW only noticed and recorded in his diaries those obvious manifestations of slave feelings, such as lackluster work. There were probably, however, many other more subtle ways in which slaves expressed their changing attitude (e.g., casual conversation, social activities). Because of their fear of slave revolts

during the war, planters in general were very sensitive to any shifts in slave behavior, but they were not usually aware of changes in slave attitudes. See Roark, *Masters without Slaves*, 71–76, 78.

23 WFW Diaries, 8: 26 Aug., 10 Nov. 1863; tax list, Dec. 1863, box 7, folder 1, WFP. Because no data exist on crop production at Hickory Hill during the Civil War, the exact amount of wheat planted in 1863 is unknown.

24 WFW Diaries, 8: 1 March 1864.

25 Ibid., 14 May 1864. Information on activity at Hickory Hill during the battle of Cold Harbor is missing; Hickory Hill was in the line of battle, but WFW's diary ends before the end of May when the most intense fighting took place. It is possible that once the fighting neared Hickory Hill he stopped making entries.

26 According to WFW's diaries, 46 slaves fled Hickory Hill during the war, all between June 1862 and August 1863. Seventeen percent of the prewar slave population of 275 had fled by war's end, reducing the number of blacks on the plantation to 229. Between 1861 and 1864 (no figures are available for 1865), Hickory Hill averaged roughly five more slave births than deaths per year. By 1865, then, the black population had naturally increased by approximately 22 people. This increase partially offset the number of slaves who ran away during the war, so that by the spring of 1865, the black population stood at approximately 251 (ibid., 7–8). Williams Carter Wickham was injured a second time in 1864 when a piece of a shell lodged in his neck (Hotchkiss, *Confederate Military History*, 686; WFW to Charles Carter, 25 April 1865, box 6, folder 1, WFP).

27 WFW to Charles Carter, 9 July 1865, WFP. Immediately upon the war's completion, WFW began the process of obtaining a presidential pardon for his support of the rebellion. First, on 17 April 1865, only eight days after Lee's surrender, he took the loyalty oath, in which he pledged to support the Union; next, on 30 June 1865, he sent a petition to President Johnson asking to be pardoned. He received the pardon on 3 Nov. 1865 (box 9, folder 5, WFP).

28 Morgan, "Emancipation in Virginia's Tobacco Belt, 1850–1870," 162. On free labor ideology and the Freedmen's Bureau, see Eric Foner, *Reconstruction: America's Unfinished Revolution, 1863–1877* (New York: Harper and Row, 1988), 68–70, 153–70; The best study of the Freedmen's Bureau is William McFeely's *Yankee Stepfather: General O. O. Howard and the Freedmen* (New Haven: Yale Univ. Press, 1968); see also Roark, *Masters without Slaves*, 138–41. The Bureau's role in the tobacco belt of Virginia is discussed in Morgan, "Emancipation in Virginia's Tobacco Belt, 1850–1870," 161–62, 173–76. Debate within the federal government on the freedmen's place in a free labor system is discussed Gerald David Jaynes, *Branches without Roots: Genesis of the Black Working Class in the American South, 1862–1882* (New York: Oxford Univ. Press, 1986), 3–15.

29 List of laborers contained in WCW's Farm Accounts, WFP; McFeely, *Yankee Stepfather*, 152. In addition to the laborers, nearly all of whom were men, several nonworking women resided on the plantation. These women were likely the wives of the male laborers. The total freedmen population at Hickory Hill was approximately fifty to fifty-five. Southern freedmen's response to freedom is also discussed in Litwack, *Been in the Storm So Long*, 169–93, 296–301. On the Freedmen's Bureau's land policy, see Foner, *Reconstruction*, 69–70, 158–63.

30 The forty-one laborers of 1866 had shrunk to twenty-five laborers in 1870. In the ensuing ten years, there were never less than twenty-two or more than thirty laborers at Hickory Hill, with twenty-six present in 1880. On labor turnover rates throughout the South, see Gavin Wright, *Old South, New South: Revolutions in the Southern Economy since the Civil War* (New York: Basic, 1986), 65–78. The reason only a few of the postwar laborers can be identified as former Hickory Hill slaves has much to do with slaves' response to freedom. While few slaves had surnames, all of the plantation's freedmen had two names. There was no apparent pattern or special significance attached to most of the laborers' surnames. Ordinary names such as Carter, Lewis, and Scott were quite common. Some, though, had names that might have referred to their occupation on the plantation, such as Jack Tin or Edward Woody. And one laborer adopted a name which proclaimed his new status in life: Aaron Freeman. That none of the freedmen took the Wickhams' name suggests the desire of those who had once lived on the plantation as slaves to establish an identity apart from their former owners. See Litwack, *Been in the Storm So Long*, 248–51, for a discussion of freedmen naming patterns.

31 Accounts of individual laborers, as well as accounts for labor as a whole, are contained in WCW, Farm Accounts, WFP. Between 1865 and 1870 what few female laborers there were earned approximately $2.50; during these years, male laborers' annual net profit was approximately $65. Since his annual wage was $84, approximately $20 a year was spent on food and supplies. The $7 per month male laborers received supports Litwack's finding that Virginia freedmen earned no more than $5 to $10 per month, much less than Lower South freedmen (Litwack, *Been in the Storm So Long*, 411–12). For a helpful discussion of the causes and consequences of the planters' retention of wages, see Foner, *Reconstruction*, 171–72; Jaynes, *Branches without Roots*, 26–53; Wright, *Old South, New South*, 87–89.

32 Roark, *Masters without Slaves*, 141. Maynard Dyson held the position of overseer on Hickory Hill in the years after the Civil War. It is not known if he was the overseer of the antebellum years. On overseers after the Civil War, see Scarborough, *The Overseer*, 157, and J. William Harris, "Plantations and Power: Emancipation on the David Barrow Plantation," in Orville Vernon Burton and Robert C. McMath, Jr., eds., *Toward a New South: Studies in Post-Civil War Southern Communities* (Westport, Conn.: Greenwood, 1982), 246–64. During these years the Wickhams supplied rations for nine elderly freedmen (WCW Farm Accounts, 1866–70).

33 Slave lists, 1859–61, WFW Diaries; WCW Farm Accounts, 1866; Bureau of Refugees, Freedmen, and Abandoned Lands, "Monthly Reports of Operations and Conditions in Subdistricts," 30 April 1866, in Records of the Assistant Commissioner for Virginia, 1865–69, RG 105, microfilm reels 44–49, National Archives. The ratio of female-to-male laborers before the war was certainly much higher. But the slave lists—the only source of evidence on women at Hickory Hill—give only the total number of women on the plantation before the war, and not the number of working women. Thus, the exact number of working slave women cannot be deduced. On the different ways in which emancipation affected the former slaves, see Morgan, "Emancipation in Virginia's Tobacco Belt, 1850–1870," 141–204, 249–50; Alrutheus Ambush Taylor, *The Negro in the Reconstruction of Virginia* (Lancaster, Pa.: Men of Mark, 1926); Roger L. Ransom and Richard Sutch, *One Kind of Freedom: The Economic Consequences of Emancipa-*

tion (New York: Cambridge Univ. Press, 1977), 44–46; Harris, "Plantations and Power," 246–64.

34   WCW Farm Accounts, 1866–70; "Monthly Reports of Operations and Conditions in the Subdistricts," 28 June 1867. In 1870 Hickory Hill's receipts totaled $5,533 and expenditures totaled $6,091, for a net loss of $558.

35   WFW Diaries, 12: 31 Dec. 1872; WCW Farm Accounts, 1870–79; Roark, *Masters without Slaves*, 172–73, 176. The year 1880 is excluded from the final balance calculations because the accuracy of its figures are in doubt.

36   Roark, *Masters without Slaves*, 141.

37   Morgan, "Emancipation in Virginia's Tobacco Belt, 1850–1870," 9, 161–62, 240–49.

38   The concept of the rationalization of labor relations implies that the employer-employee relationship is impersonal, based solely on the business at hand.

39   Data on laborers and labor costs in WCW Farm Accounts, 1866–80.

40   In 1866, before the addition of day laborers and when overtime payments were still relatively small, the Wickhams spent $3,053 on labor: the regular wages of forty-one laborers, $2,244 (74 percent); extra labor (overtime), $509 (17 percent); and overseer, $300 (9 percent). In 1877, although the number of regular laborers had fallen by nearly half to twenty-two, total labor costs had hardly declined ($2,995). However, regular wages now represented only 55 percent of this total ($1,656) while extra labor—in the form of both day labor and overtime pay—represented 35 percent ($1,039) (ibid., 1866, 1873–80).

41   While the Wickhams retained stocks and bonds after the war, their value most likely fell owing to the virtual collapse of the Southern economy. Buckingham County's Robert Hubard, formerly a large slaveholder, had a similar experience after the war. Initially, the selling of his stocks and bonds kept his family out of debt. But by his death in 1871, the stocks and bonds could no longer support the family, and most of his children fell into debt. The only one to avoid debt was Robert Hubard II who, like WCW, brought in outside income to supplement his farm earnings (John Burdick, "From Virtue to Fitness: The Accommodation of a Planter Family to Postbellum Virginia," *Virginia Magazine of History and Biography* 93 (1985): 14–35). Though WCW undoubtedly earned a high salary from the C&O Railroad, his exact compensation is unknown.

42   Ransom and Sutch, *One Kind of Freedom*, 67. Richmond's black population increased from 14,275 in 1860 to 27,832 in 1880 (U.S. Bureau of the Census, *Eighth Census*, vol. 1, *Population*, 280; U.S. Bureau of the Census, *Tenth Census of the United States, 1880*, vol. 1, *Population* (Washington, D.C.: GPO, 1883), 425). On the influx of blacks to Southern cities, see Jaynes, *Branches without Roots*, 64, 143, and C. Vann Woodward, *Origins of the New South, 1877–1913* (Baton Rouge: Louisiana State Univ. Press, 1951), 207–9. On a plantation's proximity to surplus labor, Gavin Wright has written that "where transient labor was abundant, as in the vicinity of towns, it was 'esteemed a great advantage to farmers and they always have a full supply of day labor to draw on without any charges for its keep'" (Wright, *Old South, New South*, 94–96, quoting from *Report of the Industrial Commission on Agriculture and Agricultural Labor*, 10 [Washington,

D.C.: GPO, 1901], p. 819). Hanover County's Freedmen's Bureau agent attested to the fact that the county did not have a surplus of black labor when he wrote, "most [freedmen] have secured places for the year and all will be able to find employment with the opening of spring" ("Monthly Reports of Operations and Conditions in Subdistricts," 28 March 1867). Their proximity to a major city with a large black population was the chief source of the difference between the Wickhams' and Hubards' experience with free black labor. The Hubards "failed to pay freedmen wages high enough to secure a reliable and productive labor force." While the Wickhams did not pay especially high wages either, their proximity to a large supply of black labor enabled them to replace immediately any worker who quit because he felt the wages were too low (Burdick, "From Virtue to Fitness," 14–35).

43 WCW Farm Accounts, 1885–87; Henry Taylor Wickham (HTW) Farm Accounts, 1893, 1900, WFP. HTW was WCW's eldest child; he began managing the plantation in 1892. The Wickhams established a poultry farm on the periphery of the plantation in 1888, and they leased the land to C. C. Evans in exchange for his running the farm. In the first decade of the twentieth century, Hickory Hill's final yearly balance fluctuated from year to year. Though in the end the Wickhams lost money during the decade, they were doing considerably better than in earlier years.

44 That day laborers replaced regular laborers can be verified by the fact that although there were eight fewer regular laborers in 1900 than in 1893, labor costs did not fall even $200 (HTW Farm Accounts, 1893, 1900). Labor costs for 1913 were: day labor—$1,030; regular labor—$1,015 (ibid., 1913). The Wickhams could afford to reduce their resident labor force because wheat and other crops typical of mixed farming operations require less year-round attention than the major southern crop, cotton (Jack Temple Kirby, *Rural Worlds Lost: The American South, 1920–1960* [Baton Rouge: Louisiana State Univ. Press, 1987]). Hickory Hill's labor relations after 1880 were similar to those on rice and sugar plantations. Like wheat production, rice cultivation is capital, not labor, intensive. Thus, wages were a natural, if somewhat ephemeral, development in this industry. Louisiana sugar planters could turn to wages because, like the Wickhams, they had the cash necessary to pay wages (Pete Daniel, *Breaking the Land: The Transformation of Cotton, Tobacco, and Rice Cultures since 1880* [Urbana: Univ. of Illinois Press, 1985], 39–53; Kirby, *Rural Worlds Lost*, 37–38). Daniel and Kirby also have interesting, if brief, discussions on "neo-plantations"—large, centralized commercial farms. A case could be made that Hickory Hill fits this description (Daniel, *Breaking the Land*, 241–42; Kirby, *Rural Worlds Lost*, 52–53).

45 HTW Farm Accounts, 1929, 1934. On the effect that agricultural production limits had on farm labor, see Wright, *Old South, New South*, 227–35; Gilbert C. Fite, *Cotton Fields No More: Southern Agriculture, 1865–1980* (Lexington: Univ. Press of Kentucky, 1984), 131–43; Lee J. Alston, "The Wright Interpretation of Southern U.S. Economic Development: A Review Essay of *Old South, New South* by Gavin Wright," *Agricultural History* 61 (Fall 1987): 52–67 (esp. 61–65).

46 HTW Farm Accounts, 1939, 1942.

6

LAWRENCE L. HARTZELL

The Exploration of Freedom in Black Petersburg, Virginia, 1865–1902

IN THE ANTEBELLUM ERA PETERSBURG WAS A BUSTLING transportation and manufacturing hub of the Southern economy; it was the seventh largest city in the South in 1860, and its railroads, factories, and mills made it one of the most important cities of its day. The Civil War brought great destruction to Petersburg and set in motion forces that would render the city an economic backwater by 1900. This reversal in the postbellum era was unusual in the urban South; most cities grew significantly in size and economic output throughout the late nineteenth century.

At the same time, Petersburg's black community, building from a foundation laid down by the largest urban free black population in antebellum Virginia, experienced brief periods of significant political influence and tremendous growth in its institutional life.[1] These experiences, coming as they did within the context of economic decline, led to great tension as blacks strove to define what freedom meant. This chapter explores that tension and describes the various methods blacks pursued in their desperate struggle to achieve full participation in American life.

In 1867, to meet Radical Reconstruction's demands for readmission to the Union, Virginia registered both black and white voters to elect delegates to a constitutional convention. Radical Republicans dominated the convention, and 25 blacks stood among the 105 delegates. This body, which produced the Underwood Constitution, provided for black suffrage, a public school system, and the disfranchisement of all those whites who had aided the Confederacy. The newly formed Conservative party vehemently opposed the constitution, fearing it would lead to "Negro rule."

The results of the balloting in 1869 pointed in two different directions. Virginia voters overwhelmingly approved the new constitution and rejected the disfranchising provision; they also chose conservative Republican Gilbert C. Walker as governor, who opposed the constitution. At the same time, voters gave Conservatives a large majority in the General Assembly and five of the state's nine congressmen.[2] Even though twenty-seven blacks won seats in the General Assembly—three as Conservatives—by 1870 Virginia was "redeemed"; that is, white Virginians generally opposed to black rights controlled state government.

The city of Petersburg, however, was not redeemed with Virginia in 1870. Even though Conservatives had a majority of city council seats, most elected city officials, including the mayor, were Radicals. Petersburg had 2,583 registered black voters and only 1,390 registered white voters.[3] This black majority formed the backbone of the city's Radical coalition and elected two black Radicals to the House of Delegates in 1869, Peter G. Morgan and George Fayerman. Both had been free before the war. Morgan, a shoemaker, had earned enough money hiring himself out to purchase his freedom and that of other family members. Born in Nottoway County, he came to Petersburg during the war and freed his family. He later claimed he had learned to read by strapping a speller to his plow. After his term in the House, Morgan served on the city's school board and city council. Fayerman, on the other hand, was born free in Louisiana, the son of a Haitian refugee. He came to Petersburg immediately after the war, opened a grocery store, and "at once assumed a position of leadership." Both he and Morgan owned property in the city.[4]

The success of Morgan and Fayerman demonstrates the strength of the city's large antebellum free black class. Riding the wave of Petersburg's economic success, approximately one-fourth of the free black families owned taxable property in 1860.[5] Although most free blacks were near the bottom of the economic ladder, working as laborers, many were skilled craftsmen and entrepreneurs. Earnings from these occupations helped free blacks to begin building a separate community by constructing churches, creating a benevolent society, and procuring a basic education. These institutions filled a crucial role in an impoverished community, and their leaders—men like Morgan and Fayerman—were at the forefront of black Petersburg in the early postwar period.

The early 1870s saw Radical strength in Petersburg grow. In 1871 blacks Joseph Evans and John Matthews represented the city in the House of Delegates. Evans, born a slave, bought his freedom in 1859 for $900 and came to Petersburg right after the Civil War. In 1873 he served in the state Senate and was a prominent politician until the 1880s. In many ways Matthews represented the wealthiest stratum of antebellum black society. Born free, his family owned slaves and hired them out; the slaves were part of a bequest, presumably to Matthews's grandmother, from a white man, who also left the family some valuable real estate. As a result of their affluence, Matthews and other members of his family received a good education, his sister being among the first group of blacks to teach in Petersburg's public schools.[6]

After the 1873 municipal elections, every councilman and executive official of the city was, like Morgan, Fayerman, Evans, and Matthews, a Radical; nine blacks served on the city council. Radical-controlled city government provided jobs, education, and services that did much to help blacks. Petersburg, in fact, was said to have the best public school system in the state. Created in 1868, the city's school board set up four elementary schools for black children. Six blacks sat on the board from 1872 to 1890, helping to ensure some continuity of city support. White teachers and principals oversaw the teaching of about one thousand black students for ten months each year, one of the nation's longest school years. Male teachers' salaries were the highest in the state. Blacks served on the police force beginning in 1869. The city's Board of Health gave out free vaccinations and set up a hospital for treatment during the smallpox epidemic of 1873.[7]

Petersburg's black citizens outvoted their white counterparts in every election between 1870 and 1874, thanks to their majority among registered voters. War Clubs, set up by the Republican party, and the Loyal League, a social organization which almost all black political aspirants joined, combined to bring out black voters in large numbers. The dominance of the Republican party at every level of voting indicates that black aspirations were at least receiving a hearing. In Petersburg, that also meant that blacks were representing their community in state and local government.[8]

Unfortunately, the economic devastation of Petersburg during the war made governance especially difficult in the years following the Confederate surrender. City services, such as gas streetlights and the street drainage system, remained in terrible condition for many years. Many tobacco factories and cotton mills were sold to anyone with cash enough to pay, and some had to close. By 1870 the number of cotton mills in Petersburg stood at four, down from eight in 1860. Capital was scarce; many business operations stayed afloat only by taking on huge debt. Hundreds of homes had to be rebuilt or repaired. The city created the Petersburg Agricultural, Horticultural and Immigration Society of Southside Virginia to encourage white immigration to the city and to promote economic cooperation between city businesses and local agricultural interests. Northern capital aided some of the area's railroads, but bitter fights among their owners restricted many needed improvements. In short, the economic condition of the city restricted its government's ability to provide much beyond basic services.

Thus, by the early 1870s Petersburg's blacks were subjected to countervailing forces that would plague them throughout the rest of the century. They were part of a triumphant political team as voters and representatives, and together they did much to demonstrate their ability to define their interests and work responsibly to attain them. Simultaneously, however, they were exerting political power over an economically crumbling city. Given that circumstance, political power so exercised did not have the ability it might otherwise have had to make blacks powerful political players.

The panic of 1873 only exacerbated the city's difficulties. Petersburg banks had cash-flow problems when their frightened depositors withdrew large sums in September. Businesses were forced to reduce wages, some by as much as 20 percent. The Atlantic, Mississippi and Ohio Railroad, headquartered in Petersburg, could not meet the payments on its bonded debts and fell into receivership.[9]

The 1870 manuscript census for Petersburg demonstrates the poverty of the city's blacks and the importance of even low-level political posts. Although policemen, public school teachers, and the city gauger were black, two-thirds of the male household heads were laborers of one sort or another, the vast majority working as day laborers or tobacco workers. Twenty percent were engaged in skilled crafts. But fewer than 5 percent could be characterized as professionals or businessmen, including ministers, grocers, bakers, and livery stable keepers.[10]

Other characteristics of black Petersburg also denote poverty. Women headed over a fourth of black Petersburg's households in 1870. Most listed their occupation as "housekeeper." Other occupations included laundress, seamstress, and maid. Very few of these women could be said to be anything but poor, and they made up a large percentage of black households. They combined with the male heads who were laborers to account for about three-fourths of all black households—a huge number of families who lived on very little income. Despite the efforts of the Freedmen's Bureau and the city schools, 75 percent of male heads were illiterate, as were almost 90 percent of female heads. Children under the age of sixteen were no better off; over 80 percent of them could neither read nor write.

This snapshot from 1870 reveals a community mired in the lowest levels of economic activity and plagued by a high illiteracy rate. Those who attained higher levels of education and occupation had more often than not been free before the war. Some, like Peter Morgan, were native to the region; others, such as George Fayerman, were immigrants to Petersburg.

Black Petersburgers long suffered the aftershocks of economic distress. One casualty of the depression of 1873 was the city's Radical Republican government. Despite high taxes, the city government borrowed heavily to finance everything from its school system to the dredging of the Appomattox River. Forced to offer high rates of interest on its bonds, the city soon found itself with an enormous debt load. As the problem worsened throughout the 1870s, the Conservative opposition used the debt as an election issue and was returned to city hall in full force. After the 1874 municipal election, Conservatives held the mayorship and a two-to-one margin on city council. Though blacks continued to hold some seats on council, they were effectively nullified as a force. Redemption came to Petersburg, then, four years after it arrived in Virginia.[11]

While political strength waxed and waned in the 1870s and the city struggled to keep its economic head above turbulent water, black institutional life flourished. Social organizations of all types sprang into being during the late 1870s and 1880s, while there had been only a single such organization during the antebellum period. Over three hundred blacks in the city supported thirteen Masonic lodges. Blacks also organized chapters of the Odd Fellows, the Knights of Templar, and the Independent Order of St. Luke's, one of the most visible black self-help organizations in America. Other social societies included the Sisters of David and the Beaumonde, Ugly, and Callioux clubs. Because blacks lacked access to the city's public library, they began the Chorraneesee Literary Society and the James G. Blaine Lyceum and Library Association, among others. Many clubs used the Masonic Hall or the Ramsdell Building for meetings or events such as debates, lectures, spelling bees, and glee club practice. Several baseball teams traveled around Virginia and to neighboring states, sometimes accompanied by fans.[12]

Petersburg's blacks also formed militia companies, a new addition to black culture in the 1870s. These groups—the Petersburg Guards, the Flipper Guards, and the Petersburg Blues—became the source of much black self-respect, as the companies were well trained and highly visible, often participating in parades and performing at special ceremonies and before baseball games. But the companies fell beyond the means of most blacks. Despite state financing for weapons, ammunition, and accessories, members had to supply their own uniforms; most black men could not afford the necessary coats, trousers, boots, belts, and plumes worn by the militiamen.[13]

The black church in Petersburg underwent a great growth and trans-formation after 1870. Gillfield Baptist Church enlarged its seating capacity to sixteen hundred, making it one of the largest black churches in America, and four churches built new structures. The churches sponsored reading and writing classes, seminars, foreign missions, YMCAs, recitation clubs, and sister congregations throughout the South. Churches probably had greater relative significance in the black community than in the white. Not only did black church membership exceed the white by over 30 percent, but black ministers commanded a relatively higher status within society than did white ministers. In a world without captains of industry, professors, and high-level politicians, black pastors represented the most visible position of leadership in the black world.[14]

By all statistical measures, then, black Petersburg was an economically and educationally impoverished community in the 1870s. Although those statistics mask the richness of black Petersburg society, the depth and breadth of its religious and social life, it was blacks who had been free in the antebellum period, not the recently emancipated ex-slaves, who were the foundation of this culture. Political, religious, economic, and social leadership sprang primarily from the prewar free black class; it was through their money, status, and visibility that black Petersburg became a dynamic society. As the community matured and more blacks prospered, however, established leaders were challenged by younger, more success-ful blacks. As the two groups struggled over the process of defining the community's larger interests, conflicts occurred.

The 1880s brought to Petersburg a new set of circumstances that boded well for its black citizens. At the beginning of the decade, political change was at hand, as a third party, courting the black vote, challenged Democratic control. Two blacks—Alfred W. Harris and Armistead Green—represented Petersburg in the General Assembly. Harris, born into a free black family in Fairfax County in 1854, received a formal education at Howard University, graduating in 1881, then studied law under the tute-lage of a local black lawyer. He set up his legal practice in Petersburg in 1882 and lived outside town on a farm he owned. Harris was considered the most eloquent black legislator of the era. Armistead Green was a Petersburg native, having been born a slave in 1841. By the 1870s he had become one of the most successful black grocers in Petersburg—so prosperous, in fact, that he owned three parcels of land in town.[15]

Green and Harris represented the new generation of black Virginia politicians. Some, like Harris, were younger than those politicians who preceded them; others, like Green, were ex-slaves. Whatever their ori-gins, these men broke new ground by supporting the Readjuster party.

The Readjusters rode the issue of Virginia's large antebellum debt into prominence.[16] Largely replacing the Republicans as the main challengers to the Democratic party, the Readjusters, led by Confederate hero General William Mahone, were a patchwork coalition of Republicans, blacks, dissident Democrats, and small farmers from the Shenandoah Valley and Southwest Virginia. They first showed electoral strength in 1879, electing 24 of the 40 state senators and 56 of the 100 delegates, thus giving the new party control of the General Assembly.[17] In 1881 the Readjusters elected Petersburg's William Cameron governor.

The Readjusters' success meant that no longer was the Republican party the only one blacks could trust to fight for their interests; indeed, the GOP did not even nominate candidates for statewide office in 1877. Instead, the new party sought the black vote and pledged to stand up for black interests, even though it refused to nominate blacks for high office. When presented with choices, limited though they were, blacks took the risk and spurned their old allies in favor of new ones. The risk was real: since blacks were a vital part of a political revolution which aided black causes, making up two-thirds of the Readjuster voters in 1881, they could expect a serious backlash should that revolution falter. And they understood the magnitude of their action: "This is a war for true freedom," proclaimed the most prominent black-owned Petersburg newspaper.[18]

The payoff, however, was also real. All black Virginians were rewarded for their support of the winning team—the Readjuster legislature abolished the poll tax and the whipping post, allowed blacks to serve on juries, and required equal pay for black teachers. But nowhere were the gains greater than in Petersburg.[19] The city played a vital role in the Readjuster ascension, with both Mahone and Governor Cameron calling Petersburg home. Its black citizens made up a large percentage of the city's consistently large vote for Readjuster candidates. And the Readjusters repaid the city for its support. The Readjuster legislature in 1882 bestowed upon Petersburg the state's first college for blacks, the Virginia Normal and Collegiate Institute (now known as Virginia State University; see fig 6.1). VNCI opened for classes in 1883 on a site just outside the city. Petersburg also received the state's first black insane asylum; before its advent, mentally handicapped blacks were held in local jails. And Governor Cameron even appointed a Petersburg black as his personal secretary.

A further sign of political development came from the city's leading black newspaper. The Petersburg *Lancet*, established in 1882 and edited by nineteen-year-old George F. Bragg, Jr., had as its motto, "Sworn to no Party; of no Sect am I; I can be silent, but will not be." In truth,

Fig 6.1. The first Normal graduating class of the Virginia Normal and Collegiate Institute, 1886. (Courtesy of the Special Collections/University Archives, Virginia State University Library, Ettrick)

the *Lancet* was a Readjuster organ, but Bragg exhibited a political sensitivity which belied that label. Speaking of blacks, he said, "We desire to state that we do not endorse the rascality and meanness in the Readjuster party no more than we endorse the hide-bound meanness and proscriptive policy of the Bourbons [Conservatives]. . . . The Readjuster party, just like the Republican party, has shown a disposition to ignore the negro in the distribution of its patronage; yet we can say in all truthfulness that that party has approximated nearer the principles of right than even the Republican party." More than anything, blacks sought a way to get the most out of the political system, and if that meant supporting a new party, so be it. Bragg summarized black feelings on the matter: "They are not such fools as to vote against their own interests, and put men in office who give no evidence of their honest intentions." [20]

And yet to judge by the actions of many Petersburg blacks, there was disagreement over what those interests were. While most blacks voted for the Readjuster ticket, others behaved quite differently. In the early 1870s Petersburg boasted a Colored Conservative Club, led by W. F. C.

Gregory, a white Conservative leader, and former Union army general Walter Newberry; few black politicians emerged from this organization. The Republican faction that did not join the Readjuster movement, known as "Straightout" Republicans, was represented in Petersburg by, among others, Peter Morgan and William Stevens. Stevens was born free in Petersburg and "carpetbagged" from Petersburg to Suffolk, which he served in the state Senate. His family was wealthy, and he practiced law in both his native and adopted cities. It is impossible to know the biographies of all blacks who were Straightouts, but if Morgan and Stevens are at all indicative, it would seem that many free blacks remained loyal to the Republican party out of a sense of duty and self-interest. In any case, it is clear that Petersburg's blacks had no one idea of what was in their best interests, nor were they agreed on how best to realize their common goals of equality and full participation.[21]

Readjusterism was destined to be a short-lived phenomenon, suffering defeat largely because of its racial policies, however meager their return seemed to many blacks. The 1883 statewide election was its Waterloo. Capitalizing on the racial fears of white Virginians, Conservatives claimed that Readjusterism was really about mixed marriages and integrated schools. This viciousness was most prominent in Danville, where blacks had made spectacular gains in municipal officeholding. The result was the Danville Riot, a racial conflagration in which four blacks were killed by a white mob. Occurring just days before the election, the riot secured the Conservatives' revival; they won large majorities in both houses of state government, and in 1885 they would elect the next governor.[22]

With the demise of Readjusterism, blacks found their rights steadily eroded. The Anderson-McCormick Act of 1884 and the Walton Act of 1894 effectively made black voting almost impossible. After the 1891 elections, there were no blacks in the General Assembly for the first time since 1870. The Republican party returned to its earlier ailing state; it put forward no statewide candidates in 1893. With no one to defend their rights in either party, as Beth Schweiger argues in her chapter in this volume, many black voters simply stayed at home; those who did try to vote often sold their ballots to the Democrats or were intimidated at the polls.

Despite this dispiriting history of black politics in Virginia as a whole, the story was somewhat different for Petersburg's blacks. Before the crucial statewide election of 1883, the *Lancet* understood the role that blacks played within the Readjuster party: "We are regarded as a mere cipher, a pygmy among elephants." Yet it remained loyal to the party: "It is the only one in which we feel that we have the right to humiliate ourselves and receive whatever is doled out to us as a reward." After the election, editor Bragg was livid when he reported seeing blacks with Conservative ballots in their hands: "Colored men like white men have a right to vote the Democratic ticket if they think that the success of that party will best conserve their interest. . . . But the low dirty infamous, scurlous renegade colored man who in consideration of bad whiskey or money, bart[er]ed away his franchise, is too despicable a character to think of." He commented on this practice a week later: "Before the war a Negro would sell for twelve hundred dollars, but in these days of enlightenment and understanding they will sell themselves for one Dollar. O! ingratitude, the worst of all crimes!"[23]

Even after Readjuster defeat, the *Lancet* was still ready to fight the good fight—against the Conservatives. If the anti-Conservative forces were to win, "we must roll up our sleeves and work." In early 1884 the abandonment of blacks by the Republican and Readjuster parties was not the foregone conclusion it appears today. Bragg told his readers, "The political status of the Negro is the same as that of other citizens. . . . It behooves us to fight for the rights that are due us as citizens." All blacks wanted was to be "given an equal chance with other citizens in the race of life, [to disprove] the assertion that he is unworthy to be a part and parcel of this great polyglot people."[24]

In September 1884 the state Republican party held its convention to nominate a candidate for Congress in Petersburg's district. One faction supported a white, James Brady; a smaller faction wanted Joseph Evans, a black. Mahone, the state party chairman, ruled in favor of the Brady faction. Evans's supporters promptly left the convention site and held their own convention, nominating Evans to run as an independent. For many of Petersburg's blacks, this snubbing by Mahone was the last straw, the final act of white betrayal. Mahone used his power as state party chairman to defeat Evans and the Democratic candidate; Brady barely won, and Evans finished a distant third. Bragg knew the reasons for Evans's defeat: "Our men fought nobly and gallantly to the last for the People's cause, but Brady's money, the party Machinery and worst of all the treachery and perfidy of our own race, was too powerful over us." Bragg and his readers saw that money talked: "It is no use for any colored man to make an attempt to go [to] Congress unless he has plenty of money to buy up the leaders, because as long as there are two white men in the party in this district one of them will want to go to Congress and his money will elect them."[25]

This loss convinced the *Lancet* that blacks were expending too much energy in politics for too little return. In politics blacks were no more free from white control than they were under slavery. Perhaps it was time to look elsewhere for freedom. Bragg wrote in the *Lancet*, "In our mistaken zeal for our commonweal we have esteemed too highly an undying and never ending deathlike grasp upon politics. . . . Let us first learn to be true to ourselves, and in no better and more substantial manner can we do it than by cooperation in business." Blacks should spend their hard-earned money at black businesses; men should combine their capital to create new ones. Bragg also believed that political corruption was brought on mostly by ignorance and illiteracy. Thus, blacks should do everything possible to protect "our free schools, that lie dearest to the bosom of the poor man." The *Lancet* warned that "illiteracy must be exterminated or the republic cannot remain safe." Finally, religion remained the backbone of black life. In 1886 Bragg changed the focus of his paper to religion, and he gave it a new motto: "For what is a man profited, if he shall gain the whole world, and lose his soul."[26] A month later, he changed the paper's title to the *Afro-American Churchman*.

The lack of an organized party interested in representing their interests discouraged potential black voters. Blacks in the area were too poor to mount an independent organization capable of taking on the powerful Democratic machine. It would require a black man with deep pockets and broad connections to succeed, and there were few of them available. The tremendous growth of black institutions in the 1880s demanded much attention and money, and success in this area was more immediate and tangible in the lives of Petersburg's black citizens. Given the frustrating experience of politics and the satisfaction to be found in churches, businesses, schools, and social clubs, many blacks understandably turned away from politics and concentrated their energies elsewhere. Their citizenship could be expressed through success here as well, and often more fully, as in the political arena.

The longing for a political voice, for complete citizenship, was never extinguished, though. Many blacks bided their time, waiting for the opportunity to throw their energies into politics once again. They fiercely wanted to elect a black man to Congress, feeling their large share of the voters of their district earned them such representation. In 1888 they got their wish. Ironically, that man, John Mercer Langston, was not one of them, having been born in Louisa County, Virginia, but raised free in Ohio. Extremely intelligent, arrogant, and well-connected to national political figures, Langston was a graduate of Oberlin College in Ohio and the first black in Ohio to be admitted to the bar. He came to Petersburg in 1885 to be president of Virginia Normal and Collegiate Institute, having already served as dean of Howard University Law School and minister to Haiti.[27]

Langston used the presidency of VNCI as a stepping-stone to political office. The presidency put him in the midst of state and national politics, although not always to his advantage. Mahone was still state Republican chairman and used his dislike of Langston to deny him the Republican nomination for congressman of the Fourth District. But Langston's campaign for Congress differed vastly from Evans's effort, though both ran as independents, for it drew attention from politicians around the country. The national Republican party was anxious to see how a black politician from a heavily black district would fare without the support of a longtime state GOP leader like Mahone.

With practically no party backing, Langston relied on charisma, speaking ability, overwhelming black and significant white support, and an excellent districtwide organization to run a strong race.[28] It was precisely these qualities that earlier black candidates in the Fourth lacked. Despite these benefits, on election day Langston lost to the Democratic candidate, Petersburg businessman E. C. Venable; the regular (white) Republican candidate finished third. In the election the Democrats resorted to fraud, vote buying, and intimidation to prevent the popular Langston from winning. Mahone probably conspired with the Democrats to prevent Langston's election after he realized his own candidate would not win. The final count showed Langston losing by 654 votes out of 29,000 cast.[29]

Langston was incredulous that the State Electoral Board would declare Venable the winner in a district where blacks outnumbered whites by more than two thousand. Certain he had been cheated out of victory, Langston asked the U.S. House of Representatives to investigate the election and to rule on its validity. After a delay of almost two years, the House declared Langston the winner and swore him in as Virginia's first black congressman. Because of the lengthy delay, though, Langston served only a few months in the lame-duck session of the Fifty-first Congress.[30]

The election of Langston to Congress shows what blacks could do with an overwhelming voting majority, a popular candidate, and the will to overcome white Republican intransigence. They did not completely abandon political activity; they became more circumspect in its viability. In 1888 Langston faced the right set of circumstances. Petersburg blacks had previously seen Mahone's manipulation of party machinery and Democratic fraud, but this time they did not let that deter them. Having voted for Langston in sufficient numbers, they still had to rely on the only Republican-controlled Congress between 1882 and

1894 to consider Langston's contest case. That it took so long in the end suggests exactly how hesitant national Republicans were to challenge Mahone's control over the state party's machinery. On the other hand, the fact that Congress nevertheless awarded Langston the election indicates how necessary massive electoral fraud was to deny him victory in a heavily black district. In short, Langston's election symbolizes the effective use of black political power in a hostile environment.

In turn, Langston's unsuccessful reelection effort in 1890 symbolizes how quickly political sands shifted under blacks' feet and how uncertain many blacks felt about political activity. Again Langston ran as an independent; the Republican party chose not to nominate a candidate rather than endorse him. But other factors assisting Langston in 1888 were absent in 1890. The candidate himself was broke, having spent a large part of his fortune on the 1888 campaign and subsequent legal contest. Because he was now a congressman, ironically, Langston could devote much less time to organizing his reelection campaign. Intemperate remarks made during a speech addressed to a huge throng the day after taking his place in the House hurt him badly: "If it is courage that is wanted we will give it by hogsheads, even until the blood shall run in streams; if necessary, till by the commingling of white men's blood and black men's blood our country shall be the grandest and our Government the greatest and most lasting the world has ever seen or ever will see." White Democrats used his words, and the fact of his election, to raise the issue of "Negro rule" much more successfully than in the past. This tack had special relevance in 1890 as Southerners roundly opposed the Force Bill, which called for federal supervision of Southern congressional elections to ensure black suffrage. The Fourth District election became a referendum on whether whites or blacks would control Virginia politics.[31]

Many Petersburg blacks seemed less interested in Langston's second effort. Attendance at his appearances throughout the district "were considerably smaller and less enthusiastic" than in 1888. Voters cast almost 6,000 fewer ballots in 1890, suggesting that many blacks stayed at home. Although the reasons for this lower turnout are elusive, some blacks undoubtedly felt that the luster of their dream of having a black congressman was gone. Langston had incumbency, but many blacks "couldn't understand that their representative had had no time to reap the benefits he had promised."[32] The excitement of his initial campaign also could not be duplicated.

On Election Day 1890 Democrat J. F. Epes defeated Langston by 3,300 votes. Low turnout hurt, but Democratic fraud and intimidation were again major factors in the outcome. Langston and his workers monitored behavior at the polling places as they had in 1888 and recorded acts of fraud, but this time Langston chose not to contest the election before Congress. The margin of defeat was great, Democrats now controlled Congress, and the candidate had neither the time, money, nor energy to expend on a costly legal campaign. Langston returned to Washington to finish out his congressional term a beaten man.[33]

After 1888 the political paths of blacks in Petersburg and Virginia merged once again. With the demise of the Republican party in the 1890s —it offered no candidates for statewide office in 1893—black Virginians backed, in opposition to the Democrats, the Populist party. In contrast to those in other Southern states, Virginia Populists eschewed black voters, for the party was "led by gentlemen—by disgruntled, liberal-minded Democrats of social and economic standing—but men whose liberalism did not include political equality for the Negro." Corruption pervaded postwar Virginia politics, for "probably at no time in the history of the state have election frauds been so openly practiced as during the years between 1870 and 1902."[34] The purchasing of votes was the main avenue for fraud, and it was primarily the black vote that was bought. In the Fourth District, not only was Langston cheated, but in 1900 one Democratic politician could write "that for eight or ten dollars he could hire twenty-five to fifty Negroes to hiss a Republican opponent off the speaker's platform at the courthouse in Nottoway county."[35] Many blacks were, as Bragg accused, more interested in getting what they could for their vote, be it money, whiskey, or food, than in participating honestly in elections where their interests were not being represented.

In her chapter in this volume, Beth Schweiger writes of the efforts of white Democrats to create a new constitution in 1900 and 1901. The impact of the new constitution, which disfranchised most blacks and many whites, should be apparent. In the effort to obtain fair elections, Virginia's white politicians "sacrificed politically the injured party—the very ones who were being bought, used, defrauded, and cheated out of their constitutional rights," rather than pass legislation against those doing the cheating. And at any rate, elections after the constitution went into effect could hardly be called honest; voter registration depended almost exclusively on the local registrar, in most parts of Virginia a Democrat, who could apply the literacy test with unequal standards depending on the registrant. The cumulative effect of the 1901 electoral changes was to cast black Virginians into the political wilderness.[36]

Over the course of the late nineteenth century, then, politics gradually became a disheartening experience for Petersburg's black citizens.

Losing white political support, blacks realized the necessity of running independent candidates such as Evans and Langston if they were to have any chance at electoral success. Such success was so unlikely, however, that many blacks simply gave up on their prospects of electing representative officials and sold their vote to the highest bidder. By 1890 many in black Petersburg had come to the conclusion that politics was corrupting them and that they should withdraw until they could exercise the franchise responsibly. In 1902 such exercise, responsible or not, became a pipe dream as disfranchisement capped a tumultuous thirty years of black political involvement.

In the 1880s, when black Petersburg looked away from politics, what it saw was not comforting. The city could not keep pace with the economic growth of the nearby cities of Norfolk, Danville, Lynchburg, Durham, and Winston-Salem, all of which experienced economic booms after the Civil War. The example of Richmond, more or less successfully overcoming the economic woes of war and depression, made the failure of Petersburg that much more apparent. From its position as an important manufacturing city in 1860, Petersburg gradually sank into obscurity as a commercial backwater.

A major cause of Petersburg's decline was the downfall of its transportation systems. River activity on the Appomattox, aided by the construction of a canal to bypass the falls just west of the city, had been an important part of Petersburg's economic growth in the antebellum era. But the river began to lose its importance with the appearance of the Southside Railroad in the 1850s. By the 1880s river trade, hampered by an inability to keep the lower Appomattox navigable—it was constantly filling up with silt—had been surpassed by rail commerce. But Petersburg's railroads also suffered in the postwar era. High freight rates, competition from lines in Norfolk and Baltimore, and takeovers from outside interests combined to lessen the city's importance as a passenger and freight center. The loss of the Atlantic, Mississippi and Ohio Railroad, run with a dictatorial hand by William Mahone, in 1876 hurt the city badly; the railroad was crucial to the city's growth as a manufacturing hub. The city government suffered with the demise of the line; it owned $300,000 of AM&O stock.[37] By the end of the century, decisions affecting all railroads running through Petersburg were made by corporations not having the city's best interests in mind, a drastic change from the early 1870s.

Economically, tobacco manufacturing had always been Petersburg's main source of income. In 1860 Petersburg was the second largest producer of manufactured tobacco in the state, trailing only Richmond, with tobacco making up about 60 percent of Dinwiddie County's manufacturing output. In 1890 processed tobacco comprised only about 43 percent of the city's $7 million manufacturing output. By 1900, with the total value of manufactured products having fallen below $7 million, that proportion dropped to 35 percent.[38]

The Civil War siege of the city and the Union's naval blockade of Southern ports crumpled tobacco production—the number of workers in Petersburg's tobacco industry dropped 31 percent in the decade after 1860—cutting the legs out from under the city's economy. Another major contributor to the decline of tobacco in Petersburg was the failure of foreign tobacco consumption to match that in the United States— half of all the tobacco made in Petersburg was sold outside the United States.[39] To make matters worse, the city's tobacco manufacturers persisted in making a product increasingly unpopular with consumers. While Petersburg tobacconists continued to make chewing tobacco, their Southern competitors switched to cigarette production.[40] As a result, the Petersburg-Richmond area steadily lost ground to Danville, Winston-Salem, and Durham as the region's tobacco manufacturing centers. The total value of tobacco manufactured in Petersburg declined about 20 percent in the last ten years of the century alone.[41]

The combined effect of these reversals was devastating. In 1860 Petersburg had been second among Virginia's cities in manufacturing output; by 1900 it was fifth. Norfolk, Newport News, and Danville had all moved ahead of Petersburg. The decade of the nineties was particularly harsh for the city's industries. Over the course of the decade, Petersburg's industrial output actually fell 10 percent, its total wages slumped 8 percent, and its number of establishments dropped 17 percent. Petersburg's collapse occurred as the value of output in Virginia increased by half, its total wages paid rose over 40 percent, and its number of establishments grew 40 percent. The city was not simply failing to grow; it was dying.[42]

Population stagnation accompanied economic decline. During the 1880s Petersburg's population increased only 5 percent, while the average for urban areas in the United States was 56 percent. And during the 1890s the number of residents actually fell slightly.[43] Black residents of Petersburg, being the poorest, were most affected by the city's misfortunes. Most blacks worked hard and long each day for extremely low wages, among the lowest in the nation according to one source.[44] The most striking figure about postwar black Petersburg is this: between 1872 and 1889 the number of black males in Petersburg over the age of twenty-one fell by 23 percent. Only the presence of female, young, and elderly blacks kept the total black population in 1889 above that of 1872.

One episode shows why young black men left Petersburg and where they went. In 1875 forty tobacco workers left Petersburg for the Bull Durham tobacco plant in North Carolina to act as strikebreakers. Tobacco workers there called a strike to protest their $1.50 daily wages, which were about 50 percent higher than those in Petersburg.[45] Young black males from Petersburg also migrated to other places in search of work. Many undoubtedly left for Southwest Virginia's booming coalfields or nearby urban tobacco centers, where their work experience in Petersburg might prove to be of some advantage. Others headed north along with thousands of other black Virginians, hoping to find work in Northern cities. Many worked on the railroad, which took them places where there was greater opportunity.

Tobacco workers in Petersburg did, however, take a stand in response to their worsening situation. In 1883 black workers formed a union and called a strike to protest harsh work conditions. Although nine hundred blacks participated, the strike was broken when factory owners brought in white strikebreakers to do work usually performed by blacks. Less confrontationally, Petersburg blacks created the Colored Agricultural and Industrial Association in 1886. Chartered by the General Assembly, this union set up agricultural and industrial fairs where black and white manufacturers exhibited their wares. William Mahone and Governor Lee attended the second fair in 1887.[46]

Another sign of Petersburg blacks' difficult economic times was a great rise in the number of female household heads who were pushed into the labor force. In 1870 most were housekeepers, maids, or laundresses. In 1900 that was still true, but over one-fifth of female household heads also worked in tobacco factories or as laborers, where few toiled in 1870. Also, 40 percent of the wives of male heads in 1900 were employed in some fashion.[47] These figures suggest that black workers in late nineteenth-century Petersburg were suffering greater hardship than in the 1870s, and that households were experiencing greater strains. Blacks in Petersburg did make some positive strides in employment between 1870 and 1900. Even as the city's economy withered, it experienced a transformation similar to that felt in other urban areas by the end of the century, and those changes appear in data on black occupations. Most notably, the percentage of male heads who were businessmen or professionals increased almost threefold by 1900. Professor, druggist, restaurateur, insurance agent, confectioner, beer bottler, florist—all were new jobs for blacks. Occupational data also show a decline in those jobs that required black political strength. In 1870 blacks were policemen, the city gauger, and a post office janitor; in 1900 only the professor (at VNCI) could be said to have a job which required some political connections.[48]

The alteration of black Petersburg's occupational structure was not revolutionary. Even in 1900, the vast majority of household heads still performed menial, servile tasks. The economic decline of the city over the thirty years since 1870 exacerbated the situation; most male and female laborers earned the same wages in 1900 as in 1870. Moreover, the great majority of black businessmen and professionals had an almost exclusively black clientele, which, despite the gains made by certain members, remained decidedly poor.[49] Most household heads worked as hard and long for the same pay as had their parents, and the number of working female heads grew enormously in that period.

Figures on home ownership reflect the positive occupational strides of some black Petersburgers. Luther P. Jackson found that about 25 percent of the free black household heads owned real estate in 1860, while data from the 1900 census indicate that the figure for black Petersburg was 28 percent. Considering the postwar addition of thousands of poor ex-slave families to the free black community and the difficult economic environment of postwar Petersburg, the slight increase indicates some progress. Another study of the city's real estate tax books shows that black home ownership increased threefold between 1870 and 1889, while white home ownership did not go up significantly. At the latter date, Petersburg's blacks owned a greater percentage of their city's real estate than did blacks living in Danville or Richmond.[50]

The most significant advancement made within the black community in the last third of the nineteenth century came in literacy. Due to the proliferation of schools for black children in the 1870s and 1880s, the literacy rate skyrocketed. By 1900 illiteracy had fallen greatly among both household heads and children, though seven of ten female heads and half of the children still could not read or write. For male household heads, the illiteracy rate dropped from 76 percent to 47 percent. In the field of education, then, blacks made important strides, taking full advantage of the new educational opportunities available to them. Despite the setbacks delivered to the black community, blacks maintained their thirst for education, acquiring skills that could never be taken away.

By 1900 black society in Petersburg had undergone great changes. The institutional structure erected in the city presented a variety and activity which belied its inhabitants' poverty. Some black men moved into occupations that gave them greater chances for more income and leisure time. Overall, blacks in the city became better educated. More blacks owned property than at any time in the past. Unfortunately, Petersburg's black women were compelled to find wage-paying work, adding to their already arduous roles as mothers, wives, and sometimes as household heads. Young black men were increasingly scarce in the city as many had gone elsewhere looking for more remunerative work. Since the city's faltering economy was a force over which its black residents had no control, they were left to manage as best they could.

Politically, blacks had already seen the best of times and were embarking upon the worst at the turn of the century. In the early 1870s blacks took part in the city's Radical governing coalition. The decade of the 1880s had been the most promising one for Petersburg's blacks, as Readjusterism gave them a key role in state government and rewarded their support with jobs, a college, and better public schools. The eighties also saw the election of John Mercer Langston to Congress. By 1888 blacks had been elected to every position except statewide office, and they distinguished themselves wherever they served. By 1902 black Virginians saw the political world crumble around them, as the state's white Democrats disfranchised them.

Blacks in Petersburg understood from the beginning, however, that there was more to being an American than just going to the polls to express political opinions. There was nonelectoral life—schools, churches, work, family, and social organizations. These social areas were just as important to blacks as politics, for they would allow blacks the freedom from white control they had sought since 1619. Though begun mostly in the postbellum period, these areas of community life took on more importance after the turn of the century, when political involvement ceased.

In sum, black Petersburgers were the captives of forces beyond their control. Their city was dying, and they were trapped. Those who could get out, did. Most, however, stayed and struggled to control what they could. When political activity appeared beneficial, many blacks eagerly participated, and the rewards were great. When it did not, they retreated and looked for other ways to express their hopes and ideals. In the *Lancet*, George Bragg exhorted, "There is no use of talking about failures, we must do something. . . . Let us be up and doing."[51] And blacks responded, building an institutional structure which was an eloquent statement of their desire to become full Americans. But despite their efforts, there was little they could do as the failures mounted around them, unmoved by their dreams and their struggle.

NOTES

I would like to thank the following people for the encouragement, time, and effort they gave toward making this chapter better than it otherwise would have been: Polly Hartzell, Edward L. Ayers, John C. Willis, Janette Greenwood, Beth Barton Schweiger, and Lucious Edwards, Jr., Archivist at the Johnston Memorial Library at Virginia State University.

1 Luther P. Jackson, *Free Negro Labor and Property Holding in Virginia, 1830–1860* (New York: Appleton-Century, 1942), 91.

2 Allen W. Moger, *Virginia: Bourbonism to Byrd, 1870–1925* (Charlottesville: Univ. Press of Virginia, 1968), 12.

3 William D. Henderson, *The Unredeemed City: Reconstruction in Petersburg, Virginia, 1865–1874* (Lanham, Md.: Univ. Press of America, 1977), 175.

4 Luther P. Jackson, *Negro Officeholders in Virginia, 1865–1895* (Norfolk: Guide Quality Press, 1945), 28, 16.

5 Luther P. Jackson, "Free Negroes of Petersburg, Virginia," *Journal of Negro History* 12 (July 1927): 388.

6 Jackson, *Officeholders*, 26–28.

7 See Henderson, *Unredeemed City*, chap. 9 and pp. 183–88. John Claiborne listed school enrollment in 1900: 1,563 whites, 1,694 blacks. The city employed 29 white and 24 black teachers in 1900 (Claiborne, *Seventy-Five Years in Old Virginia* [New York: Neale, 1904], 97).

8 Henderson, *Unredeemed City*, 226.

9 The information in the previous two paragraphs comes from ibid., chap. 6.

10 To acquire data on Petersburg's blacks, I chose the United States manuscript censuses of 1870 and 1900, on microfilm, as the basis for information. A one-third selective sample was taken for both censuses, from which the statistics making up the core of this study were drawn. The census of 1870 has serious limitations in terms of household composition and wealth; the 1900 census rectifies the first and ignores the second. For any local study, the manuscript census is an invaluable source of information but must be supplemented by other primary materials to achieve depth. For the complete tables compiled from the censuses, see Lawrence L. Hartzell, "Black Life in Petersburg, Virginia, 1870–1902" (M.A. thesis, Univ. of Virginia, 1985), Appendix.

11 Henderson, *Unredeemed City*, 260–62.

12 Ibid., 98–100; William D. Henderson, *Gilded Age City: Politics, Life, and Labor in Petersburg, Virginia, 1874–1889* (Lanham, Md.: Univ. Press of America, 1980), 321–25.

13 Henderson, *Gilded Age City*, 326–29.

14 Ibid., 313. The churches with new buildings were Shiloh Baptist, Union Street Methodist, St. Stephen's Episcopal (ministered to by Rev. Giles B. Cooke, a white), and Oak St. A.M.E. Zion (James G. Scott and Edward A. Wyatt, *Petersburg's Story: A History* [Petersburg: Titmus Optical Co., 1960], 286–87; J. H. Chataigne, comp., *Chataigne's Petersburg Directory, 1882–83* [Petersburg: T. S. Beckwith, 1882], 20).

15 Jackson, *Officeholders*, 20, 18.

16 The Readjusters favored "readjusting," or scaling down, the debt. Conservatives wanted to repay it in full more or less along the lines of the Funding Act of 1871; they became known during this era as "Funders." See Beth Barton Schweiger's chapter 9 below; Charles C. Pearson, *The Readjuster Movement in Virginia* (New Haven: Yale Univ. Press, 1917); James Tice Moore, *Two Paths to the New South: The Virginia Debt Controversy, 1870–1883* (Lexington: Univ. of Kentucky Press, 1974).

17 Richard L. Morton, *The Negro in Virginia Politics, 1865–1902* (1918; rept. Spartanburg, S.C.: Reprint Co., 1973), 107; Virginius Dabney, *Virginia: The New Dominion* (Garden City, N.Y.: Doubleday, 1971), 384. Thirteen black Readjusters were elected in 1879.

18 James Tice Moore, "Black Militancy in Readjuster Virginia, 1879–1883," *Journal of Southern History* 41 (May 1975): 181; Petersburg *Lancet*, 28 Oct. 1882.

19 Charles E. Wynes, *Race Relations in Virginia, 1870–1902* (Charlottesville: Univ. of Virginia Press, 1961), 22–25; Moore, *Two Paths*, 103.

20 Petersburg *Lancet*, 9 Sept., 28 Oct. 1882.

21 Henderson, *Unredeemed City*, 98–99; Jackson, *Officeholders*, 40. The Straightouts continued to elect some officials throughout the era of Readjusterism, but most Republicans signed on with the Readjusters. For more on the infighting among Republicans in response to Readjusterism, see Moore, *Two Paths*, chap. 6.

22 Wynes, *Race Relations*, 29–32; Moore, "Black Militancy," 184–85.

23 Petersburg *Lancet*, 18 Aug., 10, 17 Nov. 1883.

24 Ibid., 26 Jan., 29 March 1884, 20 Jan. 1883.

25 Henderson, *Gilded Age City*, 177–86; Petersburg *Lancet*, 20, 27 Sept., 8, 18 Nov. 1884.

26 Petersburg *Lancet*, 23, 16 May 1885, 15 Nov., 22 March 1884, 2 Jan. 1886.

27 See William F. Cheek, "Forgotten Prophet: The Life of John Mercer Langston" (Ph.D. diss., Univ. of Virginia, 1961).

28 For example, Langston had over five hundred precinct-level workers getting out the vote and observing activity at the polling places on election day (ibid., 294).

29 Ibid., chap. 10. For more information on Langston's race for Congress, see William F. Cheek, "A Negro Runs for Congress: John Mercer Langston and the Virginia Campaign of 1888," *Journal of Negro History* 52 (Jan. 1967): 14–35, and John Mercer Langston, *From the Virginia Plantation to the National Capitol* (Hartford: American Publishing Co., 1894; rept., New York: Arno, 1969), chaps. 28 and 29.

30 Cheek, "Forgotten Prophet," 295.

31 Richmond *Dispatch*, 26 Sept. 1890, quoted in Cheek, "Forgotten Prophet," 336. See also ibid., chap. 12.

32 Cheek, "Forgotten Prophet," 344–45, 348, 346.

33 Ibid., 347, 348–50.

34 Wynes, *Race Relations*, 48; Albert O. Porter, *County Government in Virginia: A Legislative History, 1607–1904*, no. 506, Columbia University Studies in History, Economics, and Public Law (New York: Columbia Univ. Press, 1947), 304, quoted in ibid., p. 55.

35 Wynes, *Race Relations*, 54.

36 Ibid., 56.

37 Henderson, *Gilded Age City*, 372.

38 U.S. Bureau of the Census, *The Eighth Census of the United States, 1860*, vol. 2, *Manufactures* (Washington, D.C.: GPO, 1865), 604–34; U.S. Bureau of the Census, *The Eleventh Census of the United States, 1890*, vol. 12, pt. 2, *States and Territories* (Washington, D.C.: GPO, 1895), 437; U.S. Bureau of the Census, *The Twelfth Census of the United States, 1900*, vol. 8, *Manufactures* (Washington, D.C.: GPO, 1902), 916–18.

39 Henderson, *Gilded Age City*, 436, 444. Petersburg's tobacco manufacturers produced about a third of all American tobacco exports in 1885 (ibid., 439).

40 Growing tobacco is a sensitive, unpredictable practice. The area around Petersburg was capable of producing only dark-leaf tobacco, used primarily for chewing tobacco. As the market for chewing tobacco declined in the late nineteenth century in favor of cigarettes, bright and burley tobaccos became the favorite varieties. Bright tobacco, however, could not be profitably grown in the soil and climate around Petersburg; the Virginia and North Carolina Piedmont became the center of bright tobacco production. With this shift in tobacco taste came technological developments in the industry; James B. Duke's mammoth firm in Durham led the way.

41 U.S. Bureau of the Census, *Eleventh Census*, vol. 12, *Report on Manufacturing Industries*, 437; U.S. Bureau of the Census, *Twelfth Census*, vol. 8, *Manufactures*, 918–19. See Nannie May Tilley, *The Bright-Tobacco Industry, 1860–1929* (Chapel Hill: Univ. of North Carolina Press, 1948), 150–52, for the shift in tobacco production from dark leaf to bright leaf and burley tobaccos.

42 U.S. Bureau of the Census, *Twelfth Census*, vol. 8, *Manufactures*, 908.

43 Henderson, *Gilded Age City*, 473; Scott and Wyatt, *Petersburg's Story*, 351.

44 Henderson, *Gilded Age City*, 473–74. Henderson cites an 1886 study which showed that the typical Petersburg factory worker earned only about two-thirds of the income necessary to feed a family of four.

45 Tilley, *Bright-Tobacco*, 518.

46 Henderson, *Gilded Age City*, 321–22.

47 These data come from my manuscript census sample, as do all following data about 1870 and 1900 black Petersburg. Information on marriage is extremely difficult to determine from the 1870 census, so no effort was made to speculate on the topic for that year.

48 Robert Engs's study of Hampton, Virginia, during the same period demonstrates a very similar pattern. His analysis of an 1896 city directory found that 13 percent of Hampton's workers were professionals and businessmen, 36 percent were skilled and service workers, and 50 percent were laborers. Combining the 1900 data for Petersburg's males and females, one discovers these comparable figures: 10.1 percent professionals/businessmen, 32.9 percent skilled and service workers, and 47.7 percent laborers. Herbert Gutman's analysis of a largely black ward in Richmond in 1900 cited slightly different statistics. In looking at the occupations of adult black males, Gutman discovered that 77 percent were classified as unskilled and service workers, 16 percent as skilled workers, and 7 percent as white collar workers and entrepreneurs. These two studies suggest that similar trends

were taking place in Hampton and Petersburg, while Richmond was traveling down a different path. It could be that Hampton, like Petersburg, could not keep pace with its economic competitor, namely Norfolk. Gutman's figures for Richmond imply that the city's manufacturing sector was continuing to grow, as evidenced by a high percentage of laborers and unskilled workers, though such growth clearly was a mixed blessing for blacks, who comprised a large portion of the lower skill groups (Robert Engs, *Freedom's First Generation: Black Hampton, Virginia, 1861–1890* [Philadelphia: Univ. of Pennsylvania, 1979], 168–69; Herbert G. Gutman, *The Black Family in Slavery and Freedom, 1750–1925* [New York: Pantheon, 1976], table A-22, p. 497).

49 Henderson, *Gilded Age City*, 6–9, 440; Howard Rabinowitz, *Race Relations in the Urban South, 1865–1890* (Urbana: Univ. of Illinois Press, 1978), 90, 83–92. See also Engs, *Freedom's First Generation*, 199–200.

50 Jackson, "Free Negroes," 388; Henderson, *Gilded Age City*, 473. My one-third sample of the 1900 manuscript census showed 166 household heads out of 602 households (27.6 percent) owning their homes. Thus, of a total number of roughly 1,800 households, about 500 blacks owned homes (Hartzell, "Black Life in Petersburg," Appendix, table 9).

51 Petersburg *Lancet*, 19 Sept. 1885.

7

ELIZABETH ATWOOD

"Saratoga of the South": Tourism in Luray, Virginia, 1878–1905

IN 1865 THE CONFEDERATE ARMIES LAID DOWN THEIR weapons and returned home to rebuild the South. Lacking the capital and resources to complete the task themselves, Southerners turned to their former adversaries for assistance, embracing the industrialization many had once scorned. Some communities offered their cotton, their coal, their iron, and their labor in exchange for prosperity; those lacking these resources bargained with what they had. But the deals Southerners struck did not always bring the affluence they expected.

This is the story of one Southern town that looked to the North to pull it from economic stagnation. Isolated, rural, and agricultural, Luray, Virginia, did not have cotton, or coal, or even very many laborers. The resources it offered to the Northern investors were natural beauty and great caverns; the industry the town sought to attract was tourism. Although the town of Luray had existed for many years, in some ways its history really began in 1878 with the discovery of the Luray Caverns. The next twenty-five years are the subject of this chapter.

Tourism played an important but largely unexplored role in Virginia and the New South. The conditions of the South in the nineteenth century made the region the destination of thousands of visitors each year. Railroads aided their travel; hotels were built for their comfort; and Southerners, with their regional pride and courtesy, eagerly acted as hosts and guides. Despite its neglect by historians, tourism was as much a part of the New South ideology as textile mills, steel plants, or coal mines. Fittingly, the travel industry shared both the optimism and the limitations of the New South.

In March 1881 Mann Almond saw the New South come to the town where he had lived all his life. His father had been one of the earliest settlers in the part of the Shenandoah Valley that was to become Page County and had bought one of the first town lots in Luray, the county seat. Mann Almond had been a storekeeper in the town and had helped raise money to uniform the county's sons to fight in the Confederate army. Two decades later, he had outlived most of his friends and, at the age of eighty-five, had become the town's oldest citizen. For this accomplishment, he was given the honor of driving the last spike in the railroad his town had awaited eagerly for more than a decade. With the spike driven, he might have stopped to reflect on the changes he had witnessed in his lifetime and wonder what the future might bring to his hometown.

Set between the Blue Ridge and Massanutten mountains, Luray was isolated from much of the political and social turmoil that engulfed the South in the nineteenth century. Founded in 1812 as a central location for a county seat, the town grew slowly throughout the century. In 1820 its population was only 173 persons, and by the eve of the Civil War, the number had grown to only about 600. Without an efficient transportation network, staple-crop agriculture, and, for the most part, slavery, Luray was a world of yeoman farmers. Before 1881 the only transportation to Luray was by horse or flatboat. The nearest railroad was in Woodstock, nearly forty miles across the mountain—a long haul for farmers taking their wheat and corn harvests to market. Despite its isolation, during the Civil War Page County was one of the areas in the Valley hardest hit by the destruction of the invading armies. In 1863 a local newspaper reported that Sheridan's army destroyed 300 barns in the county.[1]

After the war, it became clear that a railroad held the key to prosperity in the new order of things. A railroad was chartered in 1867 to run through Luray to the ironworks and minerals at one end of the county, but its construction was repeatedly delayed. Editorials in the town's weekly newspaper, the *Page Courier*, voiced the county's disillusionment. "Throughout our whole section of the country there is one universal cry of hard times," the editor, Andrew Broaddus, wrote in early 1871. A disastrous flood the previous fall had destroyed the corn and wheat crops, creating an especially dismal financial situation for the farmers that winter. A few months later, Broaddus pleaded, "We want confidence. We must get it or die." Three years later, however, the rails remained far from town. Hopes of the Pennsylvania Railroad taking over construction were dashed with the company's financial losses during the panic of 1873. Broaddus kept up his campaign for a railroad, but his editorials became more desperate. "We want a road—must have one— and will have one. To die as our people must like rats caught in a trap is intolerable."[2]

Not until 1878, when Northern capitalists began pouring money into the railroad, was real progress made. But in June the work was stopped for the summer—forty miles from Luray. The trestles and bridges required in that area promised to make those few miles the most expensive section of track. Plans for Luray's prosperity were frustrated again, but that summer the town had something else to talk about. A stranger had arrived and was combing the hillsides looking for caves.

The stranger was Benton Pixley Stebbins. He was born in New York State in 1825 and seems to have been one of those itinerants who never find their place in life. He had sought his fortune as a carpenter, a teacher, and a newspaper publisher. Although he came to Luray to set up a photography business, his dream was to find a fantastic cavern which would rival Kentucky's famous Mammoth Cave, a tourist attraction since before the Civil War. The Shenandoah Valley seemed the perfect place to begin explorations. Already Weyer's and Fountain caves had been discovered on the other side of the mountain, and the hills around Luray were dotted with small caves.

Stebbins enlisted the help of some local men and began his search. William Campbell, a twenty-six-year-old farmer, took him to Ruffner's Cave, which had been discovered a number of years earlier. This was not the grand cavern Stebbins dreamed of, but it encouraged him to keep trying. For several weeks he explored the hills around Luray and became the butt of the town's jokes. The townsmen laughed at the strange Yankee and his foolish accomplices, calling them "phantom chasers." But on 13 August 1878, after taking a closer look at a trash pile in a rocky field near Ruffner's Cave, Stebbins found his dream. Cool air coming from a hole in the ground alerted the "phantom chasers" to a cave. William Campbell's uncle, Andrew Campbell, lit a candle and squeezed through the opening. In the dim light, he saw glistening stalactites in a room which appeared to be about forty feet wide. A huge column stood before him. Holding his candle higher, he saw passageways leading out into the darkness. This was what they had searched for—a tremendous cavern. What wonders lay beyond his faint candlelight, Campbell could only guess. He had discovered the Luray Caverns.

The cave lay beneath a twenty-eight-acre parcel of land belonging to Samuel Buracker, a town storekeeper who had been hit hard by the war and owed $15,000 to bankers and friends around town. To settle his debts, he planned to sell the land at an auction in September. With only a month to wait before they could purchase the property, Stebbins and the others kept their discovery a secret.

On 10 September the amateur spelunkers bought the land for $17 an acre—nearly twice its value as farmland. Nine days later, the local newspaper reported rumors about the caverns. "Some of the citizens of the town and near vicinity are greatly excited at the reported discovery of a cave in what is known as 'Cave Hill,' one mile from town, rivaling in extent the wonders of Weyer's Cave. . . . We understand some owners of the land contigious to the cave are asking fabulous prices."[3]

A week later, the rumors were verified and the paper reported the wonders beneath the field that had been too rocky to farm:

> A Wonderful Cave!
> Subterranean Vaults of Mammoth Dimensions!
> Only One Mile From Luray
> Altogether it is considered second to no natural curiosity in the state and once fully explored and thoroughly developed may prove the equal of any upon the continent.[4]

But almost immediately a damper was put on the excitement when Samuel Buracker's son-in-law, William T. Biedler, sued Stebbins and William Campbell for fraud, contending that the sale of the cave land had not been advertised properly and that the purchasers had not revealed the true value of the property. The case would be tied up in court for two years. Meanwhile, Stebbins, Andrew Campbell, and William Campbell began reaping the benefits of their discovery.

They held the first grand public illumination of the caverns 6 November 1878 and charged fifty cents per person. Two hundred people from as far away as Arlington, Virginia, viewed the underworld chambers. The New York *Herald* carried an article describing the excitement of the day: "From early morn until two or three o'clock wagons, carriages, and horseback riders poured into town on the way to the opening of the great caverns. . . . though only partially lighted they presented an imposing subterranean spectacle. A thousand candles illuminated the antechamber making it nearly as bright as day. Hundreds of lights were placed in the left-hand chambers, and the illuminations extended along through the great corridor."[5] In order to capture the imaginations of the visitors, Stebbins gave descriptive names to the caverns' glistening formations: Fish Market, Organ, Totem Pole, Spectre, Cathedral, and Ballroom. The first illumination was a great success. The owners collected $91 and revealed plans to build a hotel.

The next illumination came two days after Christmas and featured a dance in the Ballroom. Andrew and William Campbell rigged wires across the larger rooms and arranged pulleys for the attachment of candelabra. Fifteen chandeliers, holding twenty-five to thirty candles each, were hoisted onto cables. A plank floor was laid in the Ballroom for the dance, and handrails and stairs were completed. Admission was one dollar per person, and 600 came, their wagons clogging the town's streets from early morning until the illumination at eleven o'clock. Inside the cavern, ladies struggled to keep their best dresses from touching the damp floor, and gentlemen peered behind the stone columns hoping to discover for themselves some new secret within the cave.[6]

Luray's future as a tourist mecca was launched. Soon, the town began sprucing up for visitors. In 1879 telephone wires were strung across the town, and the Luray council passed a set of ordinances to keep the town clean and safe. The new laws prohibited swimming in the Hawksbill Creek, loose pigs on the street, fast driving through the town, and cows roaming at large after eight o'clock at night. Another ordinance required residents on Main Street to sweep to the middle of the road in front of their premises on the first and third Saturday of every month or face a twenty-five-cent fine.

In the spring of 1879 illuminations at the caverns became weekly events, and the town's two hotels were filled to capacity. With the railroad still not completed, the stage-line business boomed. About 700 visitors poured into the town each week—a number greater than Luray's entire population. "Big crowd, big hole, big money," the *Page Courier* said succinctly. Meanwhile, the caverns' reputation was spreading. Some of their stalactites, mounted in plaster of paris, were exhibited in the window of Tiffany's in New York. In the summer of 1880 a group from the Smithsonian Institution visited the cave.[7]

Anticipating the profits that the caverns could bring, the railroad executives pushed to complete their project. Shenandoah Valley Railroad president William Milnes visited the town and publicly predicted that with the completion of the railroad, Luray's population would increase to 40,000. With such lucrative prospects, the railroad executives sought a larger stake in the budding tourism industry. In the winter of 1880 Milnes offered Stebbins $40,000 for the caverns, pending the outcome of the court decision on the ownership. Believing Stebbins's title to the property would be upheld, the railroad officials revealed plans to construct a grand hotel near the station and chartered a syndicate, the Luray Cave and Hotel Company, with a capital stock of $100,000. The officers of the corporation were Philadelphia railroad entrepreneurs F. J. Kimball and W. C. MacDonald.[8]

The railroad was finally completed in March 1881. It extended from the Norfolk and Western connection in Hagerstown, Maryland, through Luray and on to the Cumberland and Ohio railroad in Waynesboro, Virginia. Two months later, the first rail excursion to the caverns came, bringing more than 200 people. Excursions were weekly occurrences the rest of the summer.[9]

Luray soon found its way into the travel guidebooks of the day. The reference book of the Norfolk and Western Railroad praised Luray as "a beautiful town and of considerable commercial importance. . . . The wonderful Luray Caverns have made this place familiar to the traveling public." The Cumberland and Ohio Railroad offered excursion packages to Antietam battlefield; Shepherdstown, West Virginia; the Luray Caverns; Weyer's Cave; and White Sulphur Springs. Its glowing description of the caverns read: "No straining or expansion of a terminology derived from the upperworld will enable it to describe adequately the wonderful phenomenon presented in the realm of stalacta." [10]

It was the terminology of the upperworld's Virginia Supreme Court of Appeals, however, that handed down a startling decision on the ownership of the caverns after two and a half years of litigation. The court ruled in favor of William Biedler, setting aside the circuit court's ruling of September 1879 that had sided with Stebbins and Campbell. Campbell had replied to Biedler's charges of fraud by arguing that if the cave was of great value, "it has been made so by the efforts, explorations, researches and expenditures of money by the present owners." Circuit court judge Mark Bird obviously agreed and dismissed the charges. But Biedler appealed, and on 21 April 1881 the high court ruled in his favor. The court ordered that the caverns be put up for sale again and granted Biedler permission to post the first bid on the land. He offered $10,000. Stebbins and Campbell were unable to come up with a larger amount, and the land was sold to Biedler. He promptly sold the caverns to the railroad for $39,450.[11]

The railroad kept its promise to build a grand hotel. The gigantic structure in an Old English Tudor style was built in 1881, looking down on the town from a hill near the depot (fig. 7.1). That fall, the newspaper was pressed to decide which was more portentous, the death of President Garfield or the first lighting of the caverns by electricity. Thirteen electric lamps operated by a dynamo at the railroad station marked the first use of electric lamps in any cavern. A few months later, the town contracted with the caverns to extend electricity into the corporate limits. The following year, the town installed its first pump for its first public well. The newspaper noted that one of the many improvements in the town in the summer of 1882 was the construction of pigpens on Main Street. In August the paper reported another big step. "The citizens of Luray have raised by subscription funds for the purpose of uniforming

Fig 7.1. The Luray Inn. (Courtesy of the Manuscripts Division, Special Collections, University of Virginia Library)

Mr. C. E. Young, chief of police. The uniform is to be navy blue with Virginia buttons. This is a move ahead of any neighboring villages and proves Luray to be a progressive town." [12]

What was transpiring in Luray was not very different from what happened in other small towns across the South. Railroads provided relatively cheap transportation for Northerners and urban Southerners, industrialization increased disposable income, and urbanization produced a group of people with plenty of leisure time. Northern newspapers encouraged their subscribers to visit the Southern resorts. The New York *Daily Tribune* wrote that a vacation in the South would prove pleasant and could help Southerners overcome their prejudices against Yankees and give them fresh ideas. The newspaper also made suggestions on the appropriate traveling attire and printed a clothing list in 1888 which totaled $1,500. [13]

Virginia recognized the importance of the travel industry and tried to encourage tourism. The Virginia Code of 1887, which outlawed rail traffic on Sundays, exempted trains carrying mail or passengers and their baggage. The state laws also reflected the growing popularity of hotels. In 1860 the only mention of resorts or hotels in the state code was a requirement that the owners keep a license and pay taxes. In 1887 the code provided for the protection of innkeepers from boarders who did not pay for their rooms. The new law permitted the innkeepers to confiscate the customers' baggage and provided a $50 fine and a three-month jail term for offenders. In 1904 the Virginia Code sought to protect the guests as well as the owners by mandating fire escapes on public buildings higher than three stories and requiring hotel operators to post warnings and directions on the use of gas fixtures.[14]

Under the railroad's ownership, the Luray Caverns became increasingly prosperous. More than 3,000 visitors came into the town each month from all over the world. The newspaper reported that in one month in 1882 visitors arrived from twenty-five states, South America, England, Germany, and Australia. In the first five years of its operation, the cave was viewed by more than 30,000 people.[15] Half that number came in 1883 alone. The Smithsonian Institution published a pamphlet praising the town's "handsomely equipped trains on the Shenandoah Valley Railroad, courteous, well-informed employees, beautiful scenery and historic associations; luxurious hotel accommodations close to the railroad station; and everywhere commodious facilities with reasonable charges."[16] With so many tourists, Luray found its facilities strained. In 1884 the town council adopted a resolution asking the General Assembly to permit a town debt of $5,000 for laying sidewalks and improving streets.[17]

Contemporary Virginians praised the caverns for the benefits they brought to both the town and the Valley. "The discovery and opening of the caverns at Luray and the Grottoes of the Shenandoah had a marked effect upon the development of the Shenandoah Valley and may be assigned as one of the causes of its growth," Thomas Bruce wrote in 1891. Bruce believed that the caverns "played an important part in the whole section of the country by drawing visitors . . . and giving an impetus never before known in Luray."[18]

Business came to Luray as well as tourists. Soon after old Mann Almond drove in the last rail spike, the new Deford tannery, the largest in the country and employing 100 workers, was completed. A Richmond newspaper reported the town's growth:

> Luray, shut off hitherto from the world is bursting into life like the trees in the valley of the orchards of the South river, an immense impulse has been given by the railroad and on every side the busy note of preparation is heard. New stores near the railroad and near hotels, old stores revamped, a new hotel in a grand scale, a tannery that is to cost $100,000 before a vat is used, hammer and saw, pick, shovel and spade, wagons and teams, the blasting of rocks, crowds of negroes—life, motion, activity all around. The mere sight of it stirs the pulse.
>
> The cave . . . has been bought by the railroad folk and is to be made the

Mecca of hosts of Northern wonder worshipers. For them the new hotel is being pushed on with hottest haste, for them this vale of Tempe is to unbosom its maiden charms and become as famous as the brush of artists and the pen of poets and prose critics can make it.[19]

The *Page Courier* noted the demand for houses, a steam planing-mill was built, and a second newspaper rolled off the presses. A glass-paneled hearse was a new pride of the town in September 1881. At the same time, the *Courier* boasted of its new power press. A new restaurant opened at the beginning of the year, and an editorial in the newspaper called for an expansion of the town's corporate limits. In 1884 Andrew Broaddus estimated that ten times as many goods were being sold in Luray as five years before. By 1890 the town had a cigar factory, a new flour mill, and a furniture factory, but Broaddus still demanded more industry. "Luray wants more factories. Factories bring workmen and workmen build houses," he wrote.[20]

Hotels naturally were among the most prosperous businesses in Luray. In 1871 only one hotel was advertised in the *Page Courier*, although another existed by the time the caverns were discovered. The grandest hotel was the Luray Inn, built by the railroad in 1881 at a cost of more than $25,000. An elegant dining room and beautiful gardens and pools were designed to give its guests the most luxurious accommodations. Three years later, the Laurance Hotel opened with a capacity for 100 guests. The Arlington Hotel achieved a milestone in Luray's history in 1885 when it received a liquor license after more than a decade of prohibition in the town.[21]

The newspaper boasted of what the town had accomplished in just a few years:

> A walk through the various streets of our town will convince the most casual observer that Luray is a live, progressive town. Her splendid churches, handsome private residences, wonderful caverns and beautiful natural scenery cannot be surpassed by any town of similar size in the state. In fact, we have found almost everything that belongs to a first-class town and the few other public improvements that are needed will be accomplished within the next few years by our enterprising and public-spirited citizens. It is surprising to see how many changes the lapse of a few years brings around, and if a former resident of Luray absent a decade or two were to return to our midst, he would be utterly unable to recognize it as the same town of "ye olden times."[22]

Although the town appeared to be booming, life was not prosperous for everyone. The county board of supervisors decided to add four or five rooms to the county poorhouse. The newspaper reported people leaving town to look for better lives in the West. In February 1884 alone the paper noted that thirty families had caught "Kansas fever" and were going to move.[23]

The early 1890s brought Luray and the rest of the Shenandoah Valley expectations of boom times. The *Page Courier*, in the role of promoter press, sought to sell the town's attractions as the best place for Northern money. "Luray has one very superior advantage over all other towns with a boom," the editor wrote. "It is the best-known town in the United States. It is visited every year by capitalists from the north and east and frequently from the great money centers of the old world. It takes no effort to get people here. It has the best hotel in the South for their entertainment when they are here. So all that remains is for our people to show off the town and county with all their great natural wealth."[24]

The boom fever became stronger during the year. "Luray is preparing vigorously for her boom. Look out for it!" the newspaper cried. A few weeks later, the boom did come under the auspices of the Valley Land and Improvement Company. Like other boom companies in the Valley, it was a Northern-based land-speculating firm with most of its investors from Pennsylvania and Maryland. With an authorized capital of $2 million, the company bought 8,000 acres of mineral land in Page County and 2,500 acres of land around Luray. Among those properties were the Luray Caverns and the Luray Inn. But the company's "great land sale" that year sold only 285 lots for $150,000, with the largest number of buyers from Baltimore, New York, Philadelphia, and Richmond. Although the sale was disappointing, in 1890 Luray's future still looked bright. The newspaper reported that negotiations were in progress for a shoe factory, steel plant, furniture factory, and pulp mill. A historian at the time praised Luray as both a resort and an emerging industrial center. "Taking the place as a whole," he said, "with its many advantages and resources—both in an agricultural and mineral sense—its wonderful caverns, its scenery and admirable climate, its educational facilities and Christian principles, its beautiful surrounding country, we feel safe in saying that its future as the 'Saratoga of the South' and a manufacturing town can scarcely be controverted, although by some enemies it may be denied."[25]

Only one year later, Luray's faith in the New South prosperity was dashed. The properties bought by the Valley Land and Improvement Company were never developed. The company went broke, sold most of its holdings—including the caverns—and its trustees resigned. Attempting to explain the catastrophe, the editor of the *Page Courier* wrote: "The

Valley Land & Improvement Company bought too much land to develop. . . . We are positively assured by those in a position to know
that the company will make an honest effort to build up and develop
the reduced area it retains. . . . We hope to see Luray start again upon an
era of prosperity and growth."[26]

The company was unable to develop the few remaining lands it held
and sold what it could back to the original owners. Luray's experience
was repeated all across the Shenandoah Valley between 1889 and 1893.
Lots were laid out in tiny or nonexistent towns. Electric lights were
strung along empty streets, elaborate maps drawn, big plans made to
arouse the interests of the investors. Towns were given grander sound-
ing names: Big Lick was renamed Roanoke, Williamson became Clifton
Forge. Investors had to improve the land as quickly and cheaply as
possible. Top priority was given to massive hotels. "The emphasis was
always on bigness," historian Stuart Seely Sprague has written. If the land
sales succeeded, the news was broadcast over the area to promote other
projects. As in Luray, most of these riches were never realized, and a
national depression in 1893 laid to rest any remaining hopes. Sprague
has contended that even without the depression, most of these ventures
would have failed. "They were too numerous and too close together, and
in many cases land improvement company promises proved empty."[27]

Marking the end of the great era was the fire that destroyed the Luray
Inn in 1891. "The country for miles around was lighted up with the lurid
glare brighter than day," the newspaper reported. Although the *Page
Courier* for years had urged the town to upgrade its fire-fighting system, the advice was ignored. Only a little furniture was salvaged, and
the grand hotel on the hill was reduced to ashes.[28]

With the depression that followed, Luray's only bank failed, and tourism declined to only about 3,000 people a year. Broaddus was forced
again to turn to his press to comfort the town in the midst of hard times.
In an editorial entitled "Let Luray Flourish" he strove to retain his pride
and offer encouragement, but his words rang with disillusionment and
humiliation. "We are not in the unfortunate position that many towns
are in of having to beg for outside help," he wrote, but, he added, "we
extend a hearty welcome to anyone who will, to come and dwell in this
garden spot of the prettiest valley in Virginia and to share with our prosperous destiny."[29]

After the Valley Land and Improvement Company sold the caverns,
a new corporation was chartered in 1894. Again, most of the investors
were Northern businessmen. J. K. Bartlett, a lawyer from Philadelphia,
was named trustee, with other board members coming from Delaware

and Maryland. But for the remainder of the decade, the tourism industry dwindled to only a fraction of what it had been in the 1880s. In 1905 the caverns were sold again to yet another Northerner, Theodore C. North-cott of New York, a former Union soldier, friend of Abraham Lincoln, and air-conditioning engineer. Under the Northcott era, which lasted nearly forty years, the caverns regained their popularity, and tourism became increasingly important to the town's economy.[30]

Prosperity returned by the turn of the century. Visitors to the caverns declined, but the number of businesses increased 93 percent, the amount of capital invested 261 percent, the number of wage earners 79 percent and the value of products 179 percent. The county ranked fifteenth in the state in terms of the value of goods produced.

As with other places in the South, Luray's work force reflected increasing industrialization and urbanization, but this growth did not mirror the substantial increase in service industries one might expect in a prosperous tourist town. Few workers listed in the census manuscript for the Luray magisterial district were identified as workers at the caverns, hotels, or restaurants. In 1870 farmers and farm laborers represented the bulk of the town's 540 workers. Only one person was listed as a hotel-keeper. In 1880 the work force was still dominated by agriculture, and only six persons listed their employment with the hotels. In 1900 hotel work provided income for twelve people, and two persons listed their employment with the caverns—the superintendent and a guide.[31]

It thus seems the caverns and tourism had little if any effect on the economic conditions of the county. Did anyone benefit from the development of the caverns as a tourist attraction? Modern tourism studies have shown that those who own the land at the tourist site and those with the capital to develop the area reap the greatest benefits. A look into the county tax records, deeds of sale, and Luray Caverns account books between 1892 and 1902 verifies this pattern in Luray. One measure of the benefits the caverns brought their owners appears simply in the prices the caverns were sold for over the years. Stebbins and Campbell bought the original twenty-eight acres in 1878 at the public auction for $476. After the sale was overturned by the courts, Biedler bought the property for $10,000 and sold it to the railroad in 1881 for $39,450. Other lands adjacent to the original tract brought $6,616 at various sales throughout the decade. In 1890 the caverns and Luray Inn were sold to the Valley Land and Improvement Company for $180,000. After the land bust and depression, the cave was sold in 1893 for $49,100. The caverns were sold the last time, in 1905, for $60,000.[32]

Another measure of the prosperity the caverns brought their owners is the profits from sales and admission charges. Account books from 1892 to 1902 show that the owners were able to bank 75 percent of their receipts of $43,521. The number of tourists visiting the caverns at this time was about 3,000 a year, compared to 3,000 a month a decade earlier. As a result, the Luray Caverns Company did not realize the full amount of its investment until it sold the caverns in 1905. The ledger suggests the caverns' profitability during the earlier peak years; while costs of upkeep, labor, and taxes would have been virtually the same, the receipts would have been twelve times greater. The property tax structure of the late nineteenth century did not give the community a very large share in the prosperity of the caverns. For most of the period, the tax on real estate was 30 cents for the government and 10 cents for the public schools per $100 value of property. From 1882 to 1904 the caverns paid approximately $2,000 in property taxes.[33]

Although tourism injects money directly into the local economy, modern studies have shown it also creates an increasingly unequal distribution of wealth. Tourism contributes to fluctuations in employment because of the seasonal nature of the industry, overcrowding during peak seasons, a low rate of return on capital investments, and a strain on public facilities. Although tourism may create entertainment facilities that the entire community can enjoy, in less developed areas tourism may be a source of frustration and resentment. Small areas near tourist attractions receive good roads and utilities while the rest of the community is neglected.[34]

The tourist industry in modern times aids complementary businesses such as gas stations, hotels, restaurants, and entertainment facilities. In the nineteenth-century South, most of the people in a community did not profit from the money the tourists brought to their area. A tour of the Luray Caverns, for example, usually benefited only the caverns' owners and the railroad—one and the same in the prosperous 1880s. These entrepreneurs also owned the major hotel and a restaurant and provided liveries to the caverns.

While Luray's disheartening experience was repeated throughout the South, in the West the concept of a national park became popular in the late nineteenth century. The idea was first suggested by Cornelius Hedges, who explored the Yellowstone region in 1870 and believed that such a natural treasure should be set aside for all to enjoy. He discouraged one man on the expedition who believed that they should buy the lands and become wealthy either by speculating or charging admission to the area.

In the East, though, natural wonders remained in private hands until the twentieth century when the National Park Service was founded and began buying tourist attractions such as Mammoth Cave in Kentucky and the Everglades in Florida.[35] The Luray Caverns and most tourist attractions in the South continued to operate under private ownership.

The Luray Caverns never brought the widespread prosperity for which the town residents longed. Like many other towns, Luray learned that following the New South creed brought dependency, outside control over investments, and underlying poverty and unproductiveness. These were problems Mann Almond probably never expected when he laid down his hammer.

More than a century after the first rail excursions rolled through the South, tourism remains a vital part of the region's economy. In 1987 the eleven Southern states received $63 billion from the travel industry, with Virginia's $6.9 billion second only to Florida in total tourist dollars spent in the state. Tourism created 157,882 jobs in Virginia, generated $365 million in state and local taxes, and accounted for 19 percent of Virginia's retail business.

Tourism is more vital to Page County today than it was a century ago when other industry in Luray competed with the hotels, restaurants, and caverns for laborers. In 1932 the Shenandoah National Park opened near Luray, creating another attraction for tourists to the area. In 1987 tourists spent $23 million in the county, and the travel industry generated 524 jobs. Local tax receipts from tourism that year were $233,000.[36]

Today gas stations, restaurants, and hotels enjoy the benefits of the tourists who come from all over the world to view the caverns. The number of jobs created and the amount of money spent by tourists in the county have increased significantly in recent years. Yet the town's economy lags behind the rest of the state. Unemployment in Page County in 1988 was 6.6 percent, compared with 3.9 percent for all of Virginia. Even in June 1989, during the height of the travel season, Page's employment rate ranked number 122 out of 136 counties and cities in the state. Many of the old factories have closed, and workers must commute to areas outside the county for jobs. A full century after its great days as a resort for Northern tourists, Luray still feels the effects of the colonial economy.

NOTES

I would like to thank John D. Waybright, editor of the *Page News and Courier*, for his assistance.

1   Harry M. Strickler, *A Short History of Page County, Virginia* (Richmond: Dietz, 1952), 96–97, 172–77; *Page Courier*, 24 March 1881.

2 *Page Courier*, 20 Jan., 24 Sept. 1871, 16 April 1874.

3 Russell H. Gurnee, *Discovery of the Luray Caverns, Virginia* (Closter, N.J.: R. H. Gurnee, 1978), 80, 1, 17–23; *Page Courier*, 19 Sept. 1878.

4 *Page Courier*, 3 Oct. 1878.

5 Gurnee, *Discovery*, 42, 52, 82.

6 Ibid., 77.

7 Ibid., 82; *Page Courier*, n.d., 1878.

8 Page County Corporation Charter Book, 2: 5–7, Page County Circuit Courthouse, Luray.

9 *Page Courier*, 12 May 1881.

10 *Reference Book of the Norfolk and Western Railroad Company* (New York: Giles, 1880), 78; E. W. Clark and Co., *Description of the Shenandoah Valley Railroad and Its Connections, Resources, and Proposed Extensions with Particulars concerning the Security of the Company* (Philadelphia: Allen, Lane & Scott, 1881), 11.

11 W. T. Biedler v. William Campbell, Chancery Cause box 19, Page County Circuit Court, Luray; Gurnee, *Discovery*, 99. The Virginia Supreme Court of Appeals could find no record of the case, and the circuit court files contain no explanation for the reversal.

12 *Page Courier*, 27 Sept., 21 July 1881, 6 April, 3, 24 Aug. 1882.

13 Horace Sutton, *Travelers: The American Tourist from Stagecoach to Space Shuttle* (New York: William Morrow, 1980), 56, 59, 61–64; Brian Archers, *The Impact of Domestic Tourism* (Cardiff: Univ. of Wales Press, 1973), 6; Valene L. Smith, ed., *Hosts and Guests: The Anthropology of Tourism* (Philadelphia: Univ. of Pennsylvania Press, 1977), 37–38; Donald C. Lundberg, *The Tourist Business*, 4th ed. (Boston: CBI, 1980), 9.

14 *Virginia Code of 1887*, chap. 185, title 52, sec. 3801, p. 901; *Virginia Code of 1860*, chap. 38, title 12, sec. 1, p. 224; *Virginia Code of 1887* (Supplement), chap. 181, title 52, sec. 3722b and chap. 110, title 30, sec. 2489, p. 110; *Virginia Code of 1904*, chap. 45, title 16, sec. 1067a, p. 512.

15 *Page Courier*, 28 Sept. 1882, 10 Aug. 1888.

16 *The Caverns of Luray* (Washington, D.C.: Smithsonian Institution, 1882).

17 *Page Courier*, 28 Feb. 1884.

18 Thomas Bruce, *South-west Virginia and the Valley* (Richmond: J. L. Hill, 1891), 223.

19 *Richmond State*, 20 June 1881, reprinted in *Page News and Courier*, 22 Nov. 1927.

20 *Page Courier*, 17 Feb., 15 Sept. 1881, 24 Jan. 1884, 6 March 1889.

21 Ibid., 5 May 1881, 13 March 1884, 30 July 1885.

22 Ibid., 18 Sept. 1884.

23 Ibid., 28 Feb. 1884.

24 Ibid., 1 May 1890.

25 Ibid., 17, 24 April, 26 June 1890, 30 June 1930; Bruce, *Virginia*, 223.

26 *Page Courier*, 10 Sept. 1891.

27 Sprague, "Investing in Appalachia: The Virginia Valley Boom of 1889–1893," *Virginia Cavalcade* 24 (1975): 135–36, 141–42.

28 *Page Courier*, 12 Nov. 1891.

29 Ibid., 21 April 1892.

30 Page County Corporation Charter Book, 2: 17–20; *Page News and Courier*, 8 July 1941.

31 Population schedules, Page County, Va., 1870, 1880, 1900, National Archives.

32 Page County Deed Book, Y:233–34, 235, X:163, 184–85, W:390, N:31, 243, 15:260, 17:131–41, 53:97–101, Page County Circuit Courthouse, Luray.

33 Luray Caverns Account Ledgers, 1891–1902, Zerkel Family Papers, Acc. 6364, Manuscripts Division, Special Collections Department, Univ. of Virginia Library; Page County Circuit Court tax records, 1882–1904, Page County Circuit Courthouse, Luray.

34 Lundberg, *The Tourist Business*, 156.

35 Jenks Cameron, *The National Park Service: Its History, Activities, and Organization*, Service Monographs of the United States Government, no. 11 (New York: D. Appleton, 1892), 3; Alfred Runte, *National Parks and the American Experience* (Lincoln: Univ. of Nebraska Press, 1979), 12, 67, 116.

36 U.S. Travel Data Center, *Travel in Virginia, 1987: An Economic Report*, prepared by the Virginia Division of Tourism (Washington, D.C., 1987).

8

ROBERT WEISE

Big Stone Gap and
the New South,
1880–1900

"Beyond a shadow of a doubt, Big Stone Gap will be
one of the mightiest manufacturing cities and railroad centers on the
continent," predicted the Big Stone Gap *Herald* shortly before 1890, and
with some accuracy.[1] The vast, untouched coal resources of Wise County,
located in Virginia's mountainous southwest corner, attracted industri-
alists from several Northern and Southern states. Centered around the
new town of Big Stone Gap, chosen as the capital of the industrialists' "Mountain Empire," Wise County's economic base underwent a
tumultuous change. A lightly commercialized, cash-poor farm economy
in 1880, Wise County was dominated by logging, coal-mining, and coke-
manufacturing interests before the turn of the century.

The economic boom did not always proceed peacefully, and with the
bustle and commotion came frequent bouts of street violence. The Big
Stone Gap *Post* lamented that "the rowdy element that is found in every
section, and especially in places that have long been remote from the
civilizing influences of railroads and their accompaniments would come
to town, fire up on moonshine, and then hold high carnival with pistol
practice with one another, Comanche yells, and drunken orgies." The developers attributed discord to local "toughs" or "desperados" from "the
most lawless section of Kentucky," only forty miles away from Big Stone
Gap, whose barbarism would soon be wiped out by the tide of Progress.[2]

Most historians of Appalachian industrialization, however, contend
that this kind of boisterous, unruly behavior stemmed from the mountain natives' hostility toward the newcomers and rejection of the new
order they represented. In this view, the "colonialism" model, industrialization brought the local farmers only profound social dislocation,
a loss of a coherent, healthy culture. These scholars represent preindustrial Appalachian society as set apart from the mainstream of American
capitalism and peripheral to the industrial developments taking place

elsewhere. Economic and social life, they believe, was founded on community self-sufficiency, and the strong bonds of land and familialism created a cultural consciousness fundamentally different from and antagonistic to that created by industrial capitalism.

When the coal industry established itself in the Kentucky, Virginia, and West Virginia mountains, proponents of this colonialism model continue, outside capitalists imposed their will and culture upon a reluctant mountain populace, gaining control over the land and its people by force and by guile. At its most extreme, the colonialist thesis portrays a stark dichotomy between natives and newcomers and locates the sources of conflict and defiance in the struggles of a traditional culture exploited for profit by outside industrial capitalists. Some mountain natives tried their hands in the coal game themselves, but these local entrepreneurs have been labeled a "local elite" unconnected culturally with their neighbors or as "colonizers of their own people" who sold out to the new industrial ruling class.[3] The strength of the colonialism model is its insistence that economic development in the mountains often served the interests of Northern or foreign industry rather than the local population. Elizabeth Atwood's chapter on the Luray Caverns in this volume gives an example of outside capitalists who reaped benefits from tourism to the detriment of real needs in the surrounding area.

The treatment of the local elite's role in coal development, however, underscores deficiencies in the colonialism model that make it unable to explain fully the complexities of Appalachian industrialization. Drawing so definite a line between insiders and outsiders requires simplifying Appalachian society to artificially homogenous terms and ignoring anyone whose background, motives, or actions did not conform to the caricature. The colonialism model accepts too easily the stereotype of the isolated mountaineer, set wholly apart from the rest of American society, who knew little and cared less about what went on away from his local community. Appalachian natives may have considered themselves mountaineers before all else, but they (men more than women) had always had dealings with the world outside the hollow in which they lived. Merchants and wealthier farmers, especially, traveled and traded with people far beyond the borders of their counties.[4] In Wise County, in the decades after the Civil War, local farmers, merchants, and lawyers increased their contacts with outside speculators, industrial corporations, and railroads. These contacts created tensions and conflicts not only of the sort described by the colonialism model—between natives and outsiders—but also among natives themselves, all legitimately Appalachian, who conceived their financial self-interests or regional allegiances differently. In Wise County, local farmers, lawyers, and merchants interacted with outside speculators, industrial corporations, and railroads on many levels, from outright hostility to positive association. At the same time that local "toughs" protested the growing power of the new order by disturbing the peace in Big Stone Gap, other Wise County natives, in no betrayal of cultural loyalty, threw their lot in with industrial development.[5]

Hidden within the Cumberland Mountains along the Kentucky border, Wise County in 1880 still depended almost entirely on agriculture for its sustenance. Farmers headed 72 percent of Wise County's 1,098 households, and farm laborers another 9 percent. Those listed by census enumerations as housekeepers, generally unmarried or widowed women, accounted for another 8 percent of household heads, leaving only 10 percent to encompass all other occupations, including doctors, lawyers, blacksmiths, carpenters, teachers, coopers, millers, and county officials. Only a handful of merchants operated out of Wise County in the preindustrial years. Between 1856 and 1880 perhaps only four or five businesses operated in Gladeville, the county seat and only town in Wise before the incorporation of Big Stone Gap in the late 1880s.[6] The most successful of these was owned by Creed F. Flanary, one of four Gladeville men listed as a merchant in the 1880 census and the wealthiest man in Wise County.[7]

Because of the difficult terrain and lack of railroad transportation, the region's farms were generally small, diversified, and not fully linked to the market networks that operated outside the mountain region. Nonetheless, agriculture in Wise County, as throughout the central Appalachians, provided at least a modest living for most farm families. Over 80 percent of Wise's landowners lived within the county, and unlike the cotton South, 85 percent of the farmers owned the land they cultivated. The 1,145 farms in Wise County averaged 213 acres in size, and only 106 farms contained over 500 acres. Most of the farm acreage consisted of unimproved land. On the average farm, farmers planted their corn and vegetables on only 35 acres, generally along the creek bottoms, while the sheep, cattle, and swine that were their mainstay ranged on the steep, forested hillsides. While less than two-thirds of the farmers owned even one horse, 88 percent herded cattle, usually about three per farmer, and 77 percent owned hogs, usually eight or nine. A lesser number, about 61 percent, raised sheep, averaging eight or nine head per flock.[8]

Underneath the farms and hillsides lay millions of tons of high-quality coal, a substance in increasing demand by American steel and iron factories. Beginning around 1880, individual speculators and agents of coal and land corporations began purchasing mineral and timber rights in large sections of Wise County. The most important of these corporations was the Virginia Coal and Iron Company, which conceived, built, and promoted Big Stone Gap around its coke furnaces. Developers from both Connellsville, Pennsylvania, and southwest Virginia combined to form the Virginia Company, including former Confederate general John Daniel Imboden, of Bristol, and former attorney general for the commonwealth Rufus A. Ayers, from Scott County, on the Wise County border.[9]

The Virginia Company, as the colonialism model would predict, pursued any means available to establish its mining operations, often ignoring the concerns and worries of the local farmers whose land it coveted. In securing title to large sections of Wise County soil, the Virginia Company took advantage of obscure patents granted long before to Revolutionary War veterans, which generally went unsettled by their owners. Never adequately surveyed, these patents frequently overlapped, and within their nebulous boundaries squatters had staked their claims. After purchasing the property, the Virginia Company's lawyers ordered a new survey of the tracts, stretching the boundaries to include as much area as possible. Squatters within the company's holdings were then evicted.[10] As a result of these tactics, the Virginia Company found itself mired for several years in a series of complicated lawsuits in which the company, according to its early historian, "met a resentful spirit on the part of the natives because the appearance of a native in court fighting a corporation aroused feeling against the corporation."[11]

Most of the squatter claims, though, did not go to court. Instead, the Virginia Company often compromised by dropping its claims on the surface of the property in exchange for a conveyance of the mineral rights. Farmers, hoping to retain land for cultivation, either did not recognize the full implications of this strategy, believed it would not inconvenience them, or saw no other option. Although the farmer still held full control over the surface of the property for agricultural purposes, the terms of the deeds made this control worthless. For either fifty cents an acre or nothing more than a simple exchange of mineral for surface rights, the farmers conveyed to the Virginia Company

> all of the Coal, Iron, Stone, and other minerals of whatever name, nature, or description, and all of the timber trees of every kind whatever . . . together with as much of the surface . . . as may be necessary for the purpose of opening mines, raising, storing, and transporting said coal, iron, stone . . . and of felling, preparing, manufacturing, storing, removing and transporting all such timber trees . . . with a full free and perfect right of

entry upon . . . said land . . . as to the said Hyndman [company agent] may seem fit and proper . . . and the said Hyndman is to have the further right for any and all purposes to resort to have and use water from any running stream, spring or pond upon said land without let or hinderance.[12]

In short, the Virginia Company was free to do anything to the land necessary in extracting its minerals, and the farmer had no recourse to protect his crops from damages caused by mining. After all the claims based on the Revolutionary War patents had been settled in the courts, the Virginia Coal and Iron Company gained control of about 70,000 acres of property in minerals and in fee, losing only 4,564 acres to prior claimants.[13]

The Virginia Company was not alone in its speculation. Local residents also attempted to buy up rights in expectation of future profits, but these speculators dealt directly with the farmers rather than through the courts, generally paying between 50 cents and $1.50 per acre of coal. The team of Creed F. Flanary, Gladeville merchant, and Patrick Hagan, Irish immigrant and lawyer from Scott County, for example, purchased upwards of 162 tracts of mineral lands throughout the 1880s. The wording of these deeds may seem more benevolent than the Virginia Coal and Iron deeds; grantors to Flanary and Hagan retained rights to "coal for domestic purposes, and the surface of yard, garden, orchard or barn lot is not to be disturbed provided the same does not exceed five acres." But the contracts still provided the grantee with "right of ingress and egress upon said lands for the purpose of mining . . . said coal, oil, gas, and minerals and . . . of utilizing the same to the fullest and most ample extent," guaranteeing that ultimate control over those properties passed from the hands of farmers to those of industrial developers.[14] Both native and outside speculators, then, negotiated land use contracts that, when fully executed, left many Wise County farmers without farms.

While mining corporations busily secured mineral lands for exploitation, three railroads—the Louisville and Nashville (L&N), Norfolk and Western (N&W), and South Atlantic and Ohio (SA&O)—extended lines into Wise County, planning to converge at Big Stone Gap. Under Virginia's railroad laws, county courts could condemn land lying in the railroad's route by eminent domain if it considered the right-of-way to be in the public interest. The three railroad companies initially attemted to come to terms with the owners of land in their paths but quickly urged condemnation proceedings when an agreement could not be reached. Since the mountainous terrain restricted proposed routes to the river valleys, the tracks usually ran through the best farmland in the county. Tracks absorbed tillable land, isolated water sources from farm-houses and grazing areas, and created a new danger to livestock. Several farmers brought suit (often successfully) against the railroads when, due to the "negligent and careless manner" in which the trains were operated, horses, cows, and steers—and, in at least one case, a human being—met an early death on the tracks.[15]

Though written by the railroad companies, the terms of the right-of-way deeds reflected the farmer's concerns over the viability of his farm. Compensation given for a right-of-way varied considerably from farm to farm and railroad to railroad. SA&O and L&N deeds paid up to fifty dollars an acre and included assorted promises to leave water sources un-disturbed, build cattle fences and crossings, and allow cultivation around the track when it was not in use. N&W deeds generally provided no direct compensation for rights-of-way at all but instead stated, in typi-cally wordy fashion, that "should it become necessary in the location and building of said proposed Railroad to take any yard, garden, orchard, or building, or any part thereof, that the said company shall pay to said [name] the actual damage sustained by said [name] by the taking of said yard, garden, orchard, or building." Apparently, that deal caused more trouble than it prevented for the railroad, which in 1888 began exchang-ing a monetary compensation at the outset for a release of liability from property damages.[16]

Right-of-way controversies with the railroads underscored the fluidity and ambiguity that characterized relations among speculators, industri-alists, and farmers. When landowners and railroads could not agree on compensation for the right-of-way, the railroads asked the county court to condemn the property through eminent domain. Condemnation suits arose not only with native farmers but also with newly arrived develop-ers who had bought property in the county and with mineral and land corporations. Lines of conflict and allegiance shifted continuously and were not defined solely by a person's "insider" or "outsider" status.

To ascertain just compensation in a suit, the county court established a commission of "five disinterested freeholders." In the fifty-four con-demnation proceedings heard by the court between 1888 and 1893, forty-two men served as commissioners. At least two-thirds of these men came from the ranks of the more successful local farmers, but the rest had ar-rived in the county only when the boom began around 1890.[17] A few recent arrivals, such as W. E. Harris and J. R. Goodloe, also became involved in condemnation suits of their own. While local farmers often came out quite well in the hearings—the widow Sarah Blondell picked up $205 for little more than five acres of land—the newcomers did not:

Harris received the chastening sum of 46 cents for a half-acre strip of land, and Goodloe received $2 for his two acres. Harris and Goodloe each served as commissioner for the other's condemnation hearing.[18]

Whatever hostility farmers may have held for the railroads and their agents has not survived in any written records. The L&N apparently had some difficulty acquiring rights of way in the Kentucky mountains where, the railroad's historian tells us, "arbitrary edicts against the march of progress [were] enforced by the owners who sat on their rail fences all day long, rifles in hand," and it most likely encountered similar obstacles in Wise County.[19] And yet, tracks ran through the property of traditionalists and progressives alike. Wealthy planters, county executives, and local development promoters sometimes objected to the railroad rumbling through their own cornfields, but they could hardly have objected to the industrial order it represented.[20]

The railroads even encountered difficulties in their dealings with their ostensible industrial allies, the coal and land companies. Normally, the necessity of rail transportation induced the mining corporations to give rights of way without compensation. On occasion, however, corporations and railroads could not come to mutually beneficial terms. The L&N had the most trouble and in 1891 paid $18,000 in compensation to the Southwest Virginia Mineral Land Company for eleven acres of land. The land company objected to even that settlement, arguing that the L&N and the Big Stone Gap Improvement Company had exerted undue and illegal pressure to force the conveyance.[21] The biggest controversy came between the L&N and the Virginia Coal and Iron Company, not regarding compensation but over hauling rates on Callahan Creek. The squabble ran from 1892 to 1918, when the Interstate Commerce Commission decided against the railroad, causing "very bad feelings between the Louisville & Nashville and the Virginia and Stonega Companies."[22]

Big Stone Gap had its own problems with both the L&N and the N&W that might have spelled the end of the town. Both railroads had received rights-of-way through Big Stone Gap, which needed to connect its ironworks and its citizens to the outside world. As the tracks came closer, however, it became increasingly clear that neither line had any intention of running through the town. Instead, they veered to the northwest into the Callahan Creek coalfields, threatening to leave Big Stone Gap isolated. The town quickly raised more capital, secured rights-of-way, and built on its own the Big Stone Gap and Powell Valley Railroad to connect the SA&O, which did run through Big Stone Gap, with the L&N.[23] The industrial elements displayed neither a unified voice nor a concerted organization of interests. Although railroads, coal companies, and speculators all pushed for the exploitation of Wise County's mineral resources, they did not act as a single unit. Instead, each group pursued its own financial gain, cooperating with the others when advantageous but rejecting initiatives that hindered its position in the developing economy.

With the appearance of railroads and the opening of coalfields came a flood of speculators and investors hoping to make their fortune in the rapidly expanding boom economy. Into Big Stone Gap poured, in the words of novelist and Gap investor John Fox, Jr., "shrewd investors, reckless speculators, land-sharks . . . real estate agents, curbstone brokers, saloon-keepers, gamblers, card sharks, railroad hands—all the flotsam and jetsam of the terrible boom." An "unidentified old-timer" described the Gap "boomers" as "just like speculators on the New York Stock Exchange, except that they dealt in town lots." "The best way to handle boom lots," he went on, "was to base the value on future expectations and hypnotize the purchaser by fair or unfair means. No land boomer, or man courting a lady, is expected to tell the truth!" The boomers in the Gap "slept eight in a room [at the] Grand Central Hotel," which "was a humming real estate exchange, and, day and night, the occupants of any room could hear, through the thin partitions, lots booming to the right, left, behind, and in front of them." The price of town lots rose considerably as the boom went on; speculators could expect to pay up to $550 per lot in 1888, but by 1890 prices of over $2,000 were not uncommon.[24]

The boom played no favorites and excluded no one; anyone willing to take the risks could join in. Well over one hundred men and women came from places as disparate as Madison, Wisconsin, and Essex, England, and many places in between. The Tidewater and Piedmont sections of Virginia and the bluegrass region of Kentucky supplied a sizable minority of investors, many of whom came not as "reckless speculators" but to set up their homes. Kentucky's mountain counties also had representatives at Big Stone Gap. G. A. Eversole of Harlan County and J. H. Frazier of Letcher crossed over Black or Pine Mountain and got a taste of the coal industrialization that would not hit their own area for another fifteen years.[25]

The original planners and initiators of Big Stone Gap, however, wanted their town to be a home for businessmen and workers, and not just a meeting place for boomers. Rufus Ayers, a board member of the Virginia Coal and Iron Company and president of the Big Stone Gap Improvement Company, and Colonel C. E. Sears, editor of the *Post*, rejected the boom idea and aimed their advertising at men with "a spirit of town building and not of speculation." Ayers, Sears, and the flatlander Kentuckians and Virginians who settled permanently in Big Stone Gap dedicated their efforts to raising the town "to queenly supremacy in the midst of the greatest wealth-producing section on earth." Mere speculators, the *Post* argued, pursued only their own selfish gain and not the good of the town.

> They have come, bought lots, running the price up, in many instances, beyond the reach of those who wished to purchase property and improve it, and they have gone away again to wait for some one to pay 200 or 300 percent . . . and leaving their lots as naked as Nature made them. They have not added one soul to the population; they have not contributed one dime to the productive industry of the place; they have not pushed it along one inch in the race we are making with competing towns. The man who builds a $25 shed is of more value than many of them.

Rather than fill the town with "real estate agents, lawyers, and speculators," the *Post* called for "men of muscle, with families whom they must work for and support" to make their homes in the mountains. Left in the hands of speculators, Big Stone Gap would "remain as we are, a petty town squat in a hollow." [26]

While the development of coal resources in eastern Kentucky and West Virginia was geared toward the interests of Northern corporations, Wise County developers attempted to remain independent of Northern control. The *Post* and the improvement company saw in Wise County an opportunity for Southern states to build an industrial economy and challenge the Midwest and Northeast in industrial production. The Virginia Coal and Iron Company built coke furnaces and steel plants near their mines, shipping only surplus raw materials to plants in Birmingham and the Midwest. Most of the firms operating in Wise County had their headquarters in Big Stone Gap, and company officials living there dedicated their efforts to making their environs more suitable to the tastes of upper-class Victorian gentlemen. In addition to the coke furnaces, steel plant, tannery, and brickyard, Big Stone Gap boasted an extensive municipal lighting system and waterworks, a 300-room hotel, a streetcar system, and a 3,000-acre game park on High Knob.[27]

As the improvement company struggled to establish the industrial centrality of Big Stone Gap, the *Post* lambasted other Southern newspapers for standing in the way of industrial progress throughout the South. "One looks in vain," the newspaper reported, "for news about the great developing and manufacturing movement which has in ten years restored to the South all she lost by the war, and upon the continuance of which depends not only the prosperity of her people but her influence in national politics and affairs." The *Post* left no doubt about the position Big Stone Gap would occupy in the New South: "here is the seat and mid-region of the future wealth and power of the South. Here are the elements that are to render her the richest half of an already rich nation. Here is her empire and the throne of her glory."[28] The *Post* dreamed of restoring national prominence to the Southern states and saw industry at Big Stone Gap as the foundation of new Southern greatness. Big Stone Gap's promoters envisioned, planned, and built the town not to be an outpost of Northern colonialism but to be the heart of a Southern, indigenous, and locally run economy.

Realization of the Big Stone Gap dream required, paradoxically, large quantities of Northern capital. In depending so heavily on investors who would not come to Wise County to live, Big Stone Gap ran the risk of falling under Northern control. The *Post* worried that Southerners might not profit much from development while "the best gleaning has fallen to our Northern friends." Still, the paper predicted, "it will probably be different hereafter. At almost every point of any importance you will find Southerners taking the lead in developing the smaller industries, and these will grow in number and magnitude. Many that have had to rely on Northern capital heretofore are now able to stand alone; and thus, gradually, our own people will have a better chance to utilize the marvellous resources of this marvellous country."[29]

Significantly, the *Post* considered all Southerners—not just mountaineers—"our own people," including newcomers to Big Stone Gap from Kentucky and Tidewater Virginia. Mountaineers, for their part, held loyalties to places beyond their mountain homes—to their state and to the South—they could, if they chose, consider themselves part of the audience the *Post* tried to reach. At least twenty Wise County residents contributed to development by venturing in Big Stone Gap town lots. Among them were J. J. Kelly and Thomas Rutherford, who had both lost property to the Virginia Coal and Iron Company during its land-grabbing maneuvers in the early 1880s.[30] Whatever conflicts Kelly and Rutherford may have had with the Virginia Company did not prevent them, ten years later, from pursuing their own profit from industrial development.

All along the N&W line, more towns popped up that experienced smaller booms of their own. While outside capital drove the development of two of these towns, two others were far more open to investment from local sources. In St. Paul, between 1885 and 1889, six Wise County residents purchased fifteen of the first twenty town lots sold, initially for $250 and eventually for upwards of $1,200.[31] In 1888 R. P. Dickenson, one of the county's wealthiest farmers, joined with the N&W in platting out the town of Coeburn on the N&W line that ran through his property. More than half of Coeburn's twenty-seven lot buyers came from outside Wise County, but at least seven, and possibly up to eleven, were insiders who had been living in the county since before development began.[32]

Outsiders, on the other hand, dominated the real estate market in Tacoma and Norton, both located on the N&W line, much more than they did in Coeburn or St. Paul. Tacoma, advertised as the "Gem of the Mountains," attracted no fewer than eighty-seven investors from beyond Wise County, compared with only eight local investors. Norton also depended for its development on investments from outside the county, but almost all of these investors moved into Norton and claimed it as their residence. Of the thirty-eight purchasers of Norton town lots, only six claimed residency outside the county. Only three of the remaining thirty-two, however, had lived in the county in 1885, six years before the lots went up for sale.[33] Development promoters in Norton, like those in Big Stone Gap, solicited people who would set down roots in the town, rather than speculators who hoped simply for quick profits.

All together, at least thirty-six Wise County men from thirty-one different families invested in the manufacturing and railroad boomtowns, a figure which should make untenable any assumption of uniformly antagonistic relations between locals and development.[34] Of course, these men represented the financially well-to-do portion of the local population. Their median taxable wealth assessment for 1885 of $175 was more than double the county's median of $83. A few of these investors, particularly Creed Flanary and Elbert Fulton, were among the very richest men in the county. At least six were lawyers and judges, and one, J. B. F. Mills, later became a state senator. But not all the investors earned their living as merchants or lawyers. Judging from their entries in the tax books under the livestock and value of farming implements categories, thirteen investors can be safely labeled farmers, a group which historians have previously assumed rejected market orientation.[35] Needless to say, thirteen farmers and a total of thirty-six men hardly constitute a popular mandate for industrialization. Still, the presence of a local minority which cast its lot with development suggests that some of the Wise County population wanted to take advantage of the new economic opportunities.

But the street brawling that disrupted Big Stone Gap in its early years was the expression of another significant part of the mountain population, people who explicitly sought to undermine the kind of order and stability required by industry. John Fox, Jr., described a typical afternoon scene in Big Stone Gap as an "exhilaration of moonshine, much

yelling and shooting and bantering, an occasional fist-fight, and, sometimes, . . . an exchange of shots." Worse problems arose when "Kentucky feudsmen would chase each other over Black Mountain and into
the Gap. . . . Sometimes they would quite take the town, and the store-
keepers would close up and go to the woods to wait for the festivities to
come to a natural end."[36]

Amidst the turbulent atmosphere, workers at the brickyard went on
strike and proceeded to "[shoot] out the lights and [puncture] the chro-
mos in the boarding house. Then they got sticks, clubs, knives, and pis-
tols, and marched up through town, intimidating and threatening."[37]
Several of the more respectable townsfolk, mostly young lawyers, tired
of the incessant tumult, finally banded together and confronted the brickworkers, who backed down at the show of force.

Pleased with their success, these lawyers remained together and
dubbed themselves the Big Stone Gap Home Guard, a civilian police
force dedicated to preserving law and order. Over the next few years, the
home guard protected "the streets, day and night . . . without swerving
a hair's-breadth from the plain line of the law," established a "civilized
atmosphere" in the Gap, and "successfully controlled the mighty element
that naturally drifts into mountain towns." Fox, who eventually joined
the guard himself, later portrayed its members as "lawyers, bankers, real
estate brokers . . . speculators, and several men of leisure . . . all were
active in business and . . . represented the best people of the blue-grass
of [Kentucky] and the tidewater country of [Virginia]." The *Post* predicted that the guard "shall one day put down feuds, street fights, assas-
sinations, and in general kill this mountain spirit of murder."[38]

Fox and the *Post* considered the "mountain spirit" entirely contradictory to the values necessary in a progressive, capitalist society. The home
guard, according to the colonialist model, served to enforce the new
values at the expense of the old and aided "the process whereby the new-
comer gained control and subdued the native population." "Under the
guise of law and order," one historian writes, "the newcomers defeated
the family-clan system and replaced it with a network controlled by economic interests."[39] But lines cannot be sharply drawn between capitalist newcomers and traditional natives. Forty-one Big Stone Gap citizens
had enlisted in the guard by 1890, and at least seven of them were native
to Wise County. Three of those seven served as lieutenants, the guard's
highest rank below the captain. The guard gradually extended out of
Big Stone Gap into the rest of the county and eventually boasted eighty-
six members. Of these, at least twenty-one came from local families, including Carico, Gilly, Gilliam, Kilbourn, Kilgore, Kelly, Miller, Robinett,

Wright, and Wells families, all names commonly found among the local investors in town lots.[40]

Wise County natives joined the guard for the same reasons the newcomers did, to prevent the "rowdy element" of the mountains from hindering the economic progress of the county. The native guardsmen identified themselves more closely with the new industrial society than the old and, in a role the colonialism model confines to outsiders, helped impose on all Wise Countians virtues conducive to development. Native businessmen and lawyers held much the same attitudes as the newcomers toward the backwoods mountaineer, seeing him as a "white savage" with a "murderous spirit" in need of civilization and uplift that only industrial progress could bring.[41] And the "toughs" directed their hostility toward both local and outside developers in their Saturday afternoon melees. The guard enhanced the dominance of the developers, whether locals or outsiders, over those who preferred life as it had been; its attempts to preserve a peaceful business climate by curbing unruly displays furthered the goals of both newcomers and natives who did not see things the same way as their fractious mountain brethren.

But even the internal stability brought by the home guard could not ensure the continued prosperity of Big Stone Gap as forces originating outside the town threatened its collapse. The nationwide depression of the early 1890s quickly reduced boom to bust, imperiling the dreams and efforts of the Wise County developers. The *Post* blamed speculators for exacerbating the economic crisis by buying and selling town lots on "the same principle the crazed gambler puts his last dollar on the wheel of fortune." Concerned only about making big profits and not about the growth and development of the town, and frequently overinvesting in town lots without improving them, these speculators "helped to retard [the town] and work directly against its interest as well as their own." As a result of the bust, the Big Stone Gap Colliery shut down its operations, and its workers found their wages "just, true, due, and wholly unpaid," for which they had to bring suit. Both the Big Stone Gap Improvement Company and the Appalachia Steel and Iron Works, the gap's major employers, went under, paralyzing businesses that depended on them and freezing credit throughout the town. R. C. Ballard Thruston, holder of the liens on all lots sold by the improvement company, recalled and repossessed title to seventy-two lots bought by speculators who could not make their payments.[42] An observer from Cincinnati declared: "The recent failures there have practically bankrupted the town and the immediate neighborhood. It is worse than bankruptcy. It is practically starvation."[43]

But the roots of industry reached too deeply into the Wise County soil to be swept away so quickly. Only a few months into 1893, the improvement company reemerged, a new furniture factory began operations, and the Virginia Coal and Iron Company began work on Stonega, a major mining operation not far from Big Stone Gap. In a few years the Virginia Company had thirty-five coking ovens in full operation. The Big Stone Gap *Post* assured its readers that "after two years or more of great financial depression the country over, and in this new community particularly, the downgrade has finally been reached, and the ascent up the hill of prosperity begun." Recovery, according to the *Post*, came despite the recklessness of speculators and because of businessmen who "did not come expecting to see a magic city, made up of crystal palaces, spring up in a night, but came to wait for that which commonsense told them time was sure to bring—the upbuilding of a prosperous and thriving manufacturing and industrial city." The *Post* and the economic development it represented were "here to stay."[44]

If Wise County never became the center of a new, dynamic, and powerful industrial South, it did undergo fundamental social, economic, and demographic changes. As the recovery continued and the coal mines regained their strength, industry displaced agriculture as the core of the Wise County economy: in 1903 the county produced over 2.5 million short tons of coal and over 1.5 million short tons of coke, three times the production of any other Virginia county. The new demand for labor in the factories caused the population to rise from 5,939 in 1880 to 9,345 in 1890 and 19,653 in 1900. The ethnic homogeneity of Wise County broke down as well, as the foreign-born population went from a total of 3 in 1880 to 393 in 1900, and the black population rose from 101 (2 percent) in 1880 to 1,965 (10 percent) twenty years later.[45] Coal miners by 1900 accounted for almost a third of all occupations, farmers about 28 percent (although the number of farmers actually increased slightly from 1,145 in 1880 to 1,276 in 1900), and various other occupations ranging from iron furnace laborers, railroad workers, and timber workers to lawyers, company executives, and county officials accounted for the remaining 40 percent. The mining industry absorbed more and more of the land area, and by 1900 the land left in the county for farms had dropped to 118,270 acres and the tenancy rate had doubled to 30 percent.[46]

Despite the change in economic emphasis, however, farming had not lost its economic viability. While the average size of farms dropped from 213 acres to 93 acres between 1880 and 1900, the average amount of improved acreage declined only slightly from 35 acres to 33 acres. The loss of acreage to coal interests came more from the hillsides and ridges than

the bottomlands: those who lost their bottomlands to the coal companies either moved elsewhere or gave up farming. In fact, farmers who
still owned their land (still a fairly high 70 percent) probably did as well
or better than they had in 1880, at least monetarily, by responding to the
high demand for farm produce in the towns and mining camps. The *Post*
encouraged farmers to work to meet this new demand and extolled the
rise in the living standard of those who complied. As the *Post* remarked
in 1890,

> Formerly the small farmers of Southwest Virginia were of all men most
> miserable. . . . They raised but little and there was but little demand for
> that little. . . . It is different now. The multitude of thriving towns in this
> section furnish an excellent home market for everything the farmer can
> raise—from a cow to a chicken. . . . And, of course, the demand for all
> the farmer can make will increase with the growth of the towns and the
> enlarged development of the mining and manufacturing interests of this
> section.

The interdependence of local farming and the coal industry became
evident in the changing nature of tenancy: in 1880, 89 percent of all tenants were sharecroppers, but by 1900 that figure had dropped to 53 percent.[47] The remaining 47 percent paid cash rent for their land, which
allowed them greater flexibility than the cropper in land use decisions
and greater independence from the landowner. The rise in rent-tenancy
also reflected the extent to which monetary standards had permeated
mountain society. Landlords in a cash economy would much prefer hard
money to farm produce as their fee; crop payments had to be resold
in order to bring a profit, and rents guaranteed a fixed return. Monetary measurements of value gradually replaced more subjective standards even for farmers who did not own the land they cultivated, and
an agricultural system which had based its exchange relations primarily
on "communal self-sufficiency" in 1880 now derived its prosperity from
linkages to the market.[48]

The insider-outsider dichotomy stressed by colonialist historians is
only one of many lines of cleavage opened up by coal industrialization
in the Appalachians. Wise County natives often resented the intrusion of
arrogant "furriners" who established themselves in powerful positions
without giving much consideration to the social norms and structures
already in place. The stiff-arming tactics used by the Virginia Coal and
Iron Company generated much hostility, and the railroads incurred the
wrath of many a farmer who saw little benefit in freight trains running
through their best fields and over their best cattle. But the appearance of

a substantial portion of the native population in the ranks of the developers blurs the easy distinction between locals and outsiders and raises fundamental questions of definition. Do we consider longtime Wise County resident R. P. Dickenson, who first fought with the N&W over the right-of-way through his property and then joined it in the construction of Coeburn, an outsider or an insider? Or J. J. Kelly and Thomas Rutherford, who felt the heavy hand of the Virginia Coal and Iron Company in 1880 and then speculated in Big Stone Gap town lots in 1890? Why are the striking brickworkers, who came not from the communities surrounding Big Stone Gap but across the state line in Tennessee, natives, while speculators from mountain counties of Kentucky are not? And what of Rufus Ayers, developer par excellence, who came to Big Stone Gap from neighboring Scott County? While outsiders supplied much of the investment capital that fueled Wise County's development, the colonialism model cannot explain these contradictions.

Economic development created social distinctions based on economic or class differences that had not existed in the same ways earlier. Individuals had to assess their responses toward their changing world and redefine what was respectable or made economic sense for their families. These redefinitions led to a melting of boundaries between insider and outsider cultures, and many locals acted with equal comfort in both worlds. At least one agent for the Virginia Coal and Iron Company apparently quite enjoyed traditional community-based pastimes such as "corn shucking, log rolling, or a quilting frolic at Flanary's, Joe Kilbourn's, or John Kelly's"—three of the more capitalistic mountain natives.[49] Outside capitalists may have turned up their noses at the "backwards" mountain farmer, but they embraced as their own the "many prominent people who were natives of this section of Virginia who were alive to the great opportunities awaiting them."[50] Conflict, then, arose between developers and antidevelopers, between those who had the capability and desire to benefit from the exploitation of resources and those who had neither.

Conflict also arose among different industrialist groups jostling for advantage, causing dissension and discord that ultimately doomed the dream of Big Stone Gap leading the New South to national prominence. While the interests of speculators, industry, and railroads usually coincided and built on each other, they sometimes ran at cross-purposes. That is why Rufus Ayers and the *Post* struggled constantly to channel the often competing projects of the industrial elements toward the benefit of Big Stone Gap. Gap boosters experienced much anguish and frustration when they realized that most of their potential allies cared more about personal gain than for grand schemes of Southern rejuvenation.

NOTES

1 Quoted in Bill Hendrick, *Big Stone Gap: The Early Years* (Big Stone Gap, n.d.), 9, 11. Hendrick cited the Big Stone Gap *Herald* as the source and 15 May 1880 as the date, but plans for furnaces, railroads, and the town itself did not exist until almost ten years later.

2 Big Stone Gap *Post*, 9 Oct. 1891, p. 2, 15 Aug. 1890. The *Post*, edited by Louisville, Kentucky, native Colonel C. E. Sears, took over for the defunct *Herald* in August 1890.

3 John Gaventa, *Power and Powerlessness: Quiescence and Rebellion in an Appalachian Valley* (Oxford: Clarendon Press, 1980), 258–60; Helen Lewis and Edward Knipe, "The Colonialism Model: the Appalachian Case," in Helen Lewis, ed., *Colonialism in Modern America: The Appalachian Case* (Boone, N.C.: Appalachian Consortium Press, 1978), 22–23.

4 See especially Altina Waller, *Feud: Hatfields, McCoys, and Social Change in Appalachia, 1860–1890* (Chapel Hill: Univ. of North Carolina Press, 1988). She contended that even Pikeville, the seat of Pike County, Kentucky, was a different world culturally from the Tug Valley, home of the Hatfields and McCoys. It is important to note that while earlier accounts of mountain society denigrated its otherness, the colonialist historians have celebrated it as an alternative to an American culture dominated by an impersonal and materialistic capitalism. I do not mean at all to disregard Appalachian cultural distinctiveness, which did and does exist; I do mean, however, to locate mountain culture and history in broader contexts that the mountaineers themselves understood. See also Robert Weise, "The Sale of Mineral Rights on Right Beaver Creek, Kentucky" (M.A. thesis, Univ. of Virginia, 1990), on mountaineers' outside contacts.

5 Gaventa, *Power and Powerlessness*, and Lewis and Knipe, "The Colonialism Model: The Appalachian Case," have presented the most extreme version of the colonialism thesis. Lewis and Knipe contended that Appalachian society resembled "an Asian or African country in its economic foundations" (17), and Gaventa referred to the mountaineers as "rebels of industrialization" (62). Ronald Eller's *Miners, Millhands, and Mountaineers* (Knoxville: Univ. of Tennessee Press, 1982), and Altina Waller's *Feud* are much more sophisticated works, but the authors still chose to emphasize insider-outsider confrontation. Durwood Dunn's *Cades Cove* (Knoxville: Univ. of Tennessee Press, 1988) and Charles Martin's *Hollybush: Folk Building and Social Change in an Appalachian Community* (Knoxville: Univ. of Tennessee Press, 1984) have explored better than the others the complex interaction between mountaineers and economic change, but they have not received much attention.

6 U.S. Bureau of the Census, Wise County manuscript census, 1880, National Archives (NA). In 1882 the Virginia legislature approved the incorporation of Mineral City, which, unplatted and undeveloped, existed only in the minds of certain industrialists. Big Stone Gap arose on the same spot six years later.

7 The only businessmen known by name before 1880 are Charles Franklin
Bond, William Davis, Henderson Dotson, Morgan Lipps (also a Meth-
odist preacher and the county clerk), and Creed Flanary. James T. Adams
Papers, box 105, Appalachian Archives, Clinch Valley College, Wise, Va.;
U.S. Bureau of the Census, Wise County manuscript census, 1880.

8 U.S. Bureau of the Census, *The Tenth Census of the United States, 1880*,
vol. 3., *Agricultural Statistics* (Washington, D.C.: GPO, 1883); Wise County
Personal Tax Book, 1880, Wise County Courthouse, Wise, Va. The tax
books list all taxpayers, including nonfarmers—it can be assumed that the
percentages of farmers who owned sheep, cattle, and swine were higher than
these books indicate.

9 Other corporations included the Virginia and Tennessee Coal and Iron
Company, the Chamberlain and Miller Company, the Cumberland Land
and Timber Company, the Tinsalia Coal and Iron Company, the Southwest
Virginia Mineral Land Company, and the Virginia, Tennessee and Carolina
Steel and Iron Company. For the formation of the Virginia Coal and Iron
Company, see E. J. Prescott, *The Story of the Virginia Coal and Iron Company* (Big Stone Gap: Virginia Coal and Iron Company, 1946), 19–37. Con-
veyances of property in fee and mineral and timber rights to these corporations are recorded in the Wise County Land Deeds, book 10:354, 8:297–
309, 11:15, 12:191–206, 268–370, 13:219, 20:88. Wise County Courthouse, Wise. Rufus Ayers is no relation to Edward Ayers, one of the editors of this book.

10 Most of the original purchases made by the Virginia Company came from
the region in the southwest corner of the county on the Kentucky border and
surrounding Looney Creek and Callahan Creek, with its tributaries Mud
Lick Creek, Kelly Branch, and Preacher Creek. This region contained parts
of various Revolutionary War patents, totaling about 100,000 acres, owned
by the H. C. Kane family, the John Olinger family, and Patrick Hagan, an
Irish lawyer living in Scott County. E. K. Hyndman, the Virginia Company
agent, bought the Kane-Olinger tract in 1881 at a sheriff's auction, when
the tract was put up for sale due to unpaid debts or property taxes. Hagan
conveyed 25,000 acres of his property to Hyndman for one dollar per acre
that same year (Prescott, *The Story of the Virginia Coal and Iron Company*,
24–29; Wise County Land Deeds, 5:382, 384).

11 Prescott, *The Story of the Virginia Coal and Iron Company*, 12. The most
serious challenge to the Virginia Company's holdings came from Christian
Van Gunden (probably not a native of Wise County), who in 1888 bought
part of the Olinger tract for $6,000. His claim, defeated in 1892, held up
mine production in the best coal lands on Callahan Creek (ibid., 61–64).

12 Wise County Land Deeds, 5:503. On Callahan Creek and its tributaries, six
farmers received 50¢ per acre of minerals, and eight received no additional
compensation.

13 Prescott, *The Story of the Virginia Coal and Iron Company*, 46.

14 G. V. Litchfield made 104 coal buys near Cranes Nest and Toms Creek between 1886 and 1891. He sold these holdings eventually to Cranes Nest
Coal and Coke Company and the Virginia and Tennessee Coal and Iron
Company. F. A. Stratton, of Johnson City, Tennessee, purchased minerals
on 108 tracts between 1887 and 1900 (Wise County Land Deeds, Grantee
Index and book 7:143–488, 10:25–172 [Litchfield], 7:371–506, 8:30–231,
10:1–384, 11:305–457 [Stratton], 8:254–389 [Flanary and Hagan].

15 Chancery File 1175, and Common Law Files 813.5, 928, 930, 987, 998, 1190, Wise County Circuit Court, Wise. On the case of heirs of M. T. Orrender v. the South Atlantic and Ohio Railroad (1892), see Common Law File 931, ibid. The Big Stone Gap *Post* noted that Orrender was "horribly mangled, nearly every bone in his body being broken and his brains scattered along the track for some distance" (23 Oct. 1891, p. 1).

16 Wise County Land Deeds; see, for example, book 7:187, 189, 8:18, 10:542–52, 14:62, 200, 356, 396, 16:78, 18:138, 20:193, 23:54.

17 Commissioners whose names could be found in the 1885 Wise County Personal Tax Book averaged $404.32 in taxable wealth, compared to a county average of $125.70. Fourteen commissioners were not listed in the 1885 tax book, although seven of these had family names common in Wise County.

18 Wise County Land Deeds, 20:274, 278, 291, 25:68.

19 Kincaid Herr, *The Louisville and Nashville Railroad* (Louisville: L&N, 1943), 119.

20 Wise County Land Deeds, 8:86, 319, 10:535, 539. Hiram Kilgore, F. A. Ashworth, and R. P. Dickenson all were involved in condemnation hearings with the railroad, and all later speculated in Wise County's industrial boom. See also Gregg Michel's chapter 5 above, on Hickory Hill, which depended on rail transportation to avoid the ups and downs of the local economy and to connect the plantation with the larger market.

21 See Wise County Land Deeds, 25:77; see also ibid., 12:5, 14:358, 20:321, 24:35, 61, 25:72, 77.

22 Prescott, *The Story of the Virginia Coal and Iron Company*, 71–75.

23 Wise County Land Deeds, 23:398, 26:277, 29:241; Luther Addington, *The Story of Wise County* (Wise County: School Board of Wise County, Va., 1956), 181.

24 John Fox, Jr., *Blue-Grass and Rhododendron* (New York: Scribner's, 1909), 215, quoted in Hendrick, *Big Stone Gap*, 13; "Old-timer" quoted in ibid., 17; Wise County Land Deeds, books 12–27. See also Elizabeth Atwood's chapter 7 above on the boom times around Luray Caverns.

25 Wise County Land Deeds, 12:285, 15:36.

26 Big Stone Gap *Post*, 5 Dec. 1890, p. 1, 17 Oct. 1890, p. 4, 22 Sept. 1890, p. 2, 5 Sept. 1890, p. 2, 22 Aug. 1890, p. 2.

27 Ibid., 15 Aug. 1890, p. 1.

28 Ibid., 12 Dec. 1890, p. 2.

29 Ibid., 12 Sept. 1890.

30 Wise County Land Deeds, 5:484, 486, 521, 12:217, 16:1, 18, 18:237, 239, 27:373.

31 Ibid., 16:138, 157, 353, 17:271, 18:344, 19:50, 158, 21:119, 27:170; J. M. Hillman, "Saint Paul," in Addington, *The Story of Wise County*, 199–200. Throughout this chapter, the identification of a specific investor as a "local" comes from linking names on the Grantee Index of the Wise County Land Deeds with names on the 1885 tax list. Anybody who appears on both lists, representing boom and preboom periods, I dub a "local." Sometimes, investors had last names common in Wise County, but the first names cannot be corroborated in the tax lists; I consider these investors probable Wise County natives, but they are not included as such in the text.

32 Wise County Land Deeds, 10:535, 28:35, 63, 29:409, 431, 30:215, 347, 365, 440, 31:134, 33:9, 68, 34:11, 101, 117, 183, 191, 35:362, 189, 38:73, 169, 40:245, 41:214, 216, 42:117, 430, 44:241, 46:435, 49:287, 51:215, 52:158, 53:189, 54:144; Addington, *The Story of Wise County*, 187–88. Only a year earlier, in 1887, the N&W had to resort to a condemnation hearing to secure its right of way through Dickenson's land, but that disagreement did not prevent the two parties from cooperating on the Coeburn project. Coeburn was named for the N&W's chief engineer, W. W. Coe, and a judge from Lebanon, Virginia, W. E. Burns.

33 For Tacoma, see advertisement in the Big Stone Gap *Post*, 15 Aug. 1890 and following issues, and Wise County Land Deeds, 18:394, 20:366-82, 21:66–368, 22:97–397, 23:125–374, 24:19, 389, 25:38–393, 26:177–293, 27:192–270, 28:1–230, 29:36–404, 30:344, 31:104–295, 34:50, 35:451, 40:285, 41:307, 331, 333. One of the local investors, Judge W. T. Miller, acted as secretary for the Tacoma Improvement Company. For Norton, see ibid., 26:229–349, 27:163–374, 28:38, 231, 29:19-418, 30:296, 356, 435, 31:88, 348, 34:76–310, 36:84, 38:75–333, 39:362, 40:402–5, 41:234, 370, 42:158, 377, 43:225, 44:232, 45:211.

34 Fourteen other family names common in Wise County appear on the Grantee Indexes, but the first names cannot be linked precisely with names in the tax books.

35 Wise County Personal Tax Book, 1885; Hendrick, *Big Stone Gap*, 42. Designation of certain investors as farmers rests on the assumption that those in the tax lists who owned horses, livestock, and farm implements probably derived their sustenance from farming. This is, of course, only a means of informed guessing at occupation, but not much else is available. The 1890 manuscript census is no longer extant, and the 1880 census was compiled too early to be of much use.

36 Fox, *Blue-Grass and Rhododendron*, 217.

37 Ibid., 218.

38 Ibid., 210–11; Addington, *The Story of Wise County*, 177; Hendrick, *Big Stone Gap*, 32; Big Stone Gap *Post*, 31 July 1891, p. 2.

39 Lewis, "Family, Religion, and Colonialism in Central Appalachia," in *Colonialism in Modern America*, 121; Eller, *Miners, Millhands, and Mountaineers*, 210.

40 Big Stone Gap *Post*, 12 Sept. 1890. A total of six men served as lieutenants. See also Charles A. Johnson, *Wise County, Virginia* (Norton, Va.: Norton Press, 1938).

41 See Fox, *Blue-Grass and Rhododendron*, 207–37.

42 Big Stone Gap *Post*, 5 Jan. 1893, p. 2, paraphrased in Hendrick, *Big Stone Gap*, 37–38; Wise County Land Deeds, 33:242–62, and Grantee Index.

43 Cincinnati *Tribune*, 1893, quoted in Hendrick, 25–26, and in the Big Stone Gap *Post*, 15 June 1893, p. 2. The *Post* vehemently objected to the comments, saying "a low-down, mean, mallicious statement has been made; one that was as black as the blackest midnight darkness of perdition; one that was so infernally contemptible and offensive that it almost tainted the air in which it was repeated."

44 Prescott, *The Story of the Virginia Coal and Iron Company*, 66; Big Stone Gap *Post*, 8 Dec. 1892, p. 1, 25 May 1893, p. 2; Hendrick, *Big Stone Gap*, 26–28.

45 John Leggett Pultz, "The Big Stone Gap Coal Field of Virginia and Kentucky," *Engineering Magazine* 27 (Oct. 1904): 85; Eller, *Miners, Millhands, and Mountaineers*, 75; U.S. Bureau of the Census, *The Tenth Census of the United States, 1880*, vol. 1, *Population*, and vol. 3, *Agriculture* (Washington, D.C.: GPO, 1883); U.S. Bureau of the Census, *The Eleventh Census of the United States, 1890*, vol. 1, *Population* (Washington, D.C.: GPO, 1895); U.S. Bureau of the Census, *The Twelfth Census of the United States, 1900*, vol. 1, *Population*, and vol. 5, *Agriculture* (Washington, D.C.: GPO, 1902). The official population of Wise County in 1880 was 7,772, but that included 1,833 in the Walker District, which became part of Dickenson County later that year.

46 U.S. Bureau of the Census, Wise County, manuscript census, 1880, NA; ibid., 1900, NA; Dean Andrew Herrin, "From Cabin to Camp" (M.A. thesis, Univ. of Delaware, 1984), 24.

47 Big Stone Gap *Post*, 12 Sept. 1890, p. 2; U.S. Bureau of the Census, *Tenth Census*, vol. 1, *Population*, and vol. 3, *Agriculture*, and *Twelfth Census*, vol. 1, *Population*, and vol. 5, *Agriculture*; Herrin, "From Cabin to Camp," 24. In 1900, 62.2 percent of Wise County farms were operated by owners, 6.8 percent by part owners, 0.3 percent by owners and tenants, and 0.8 percent by managers, equaling 70.1 percent.

48 See Eller, *Miners, Millhands, and Mountaineers*, for an exposition of "communal self-sufficiency" in preindustrial Appalachia. The concept is overdrawn and the conclusions are suspect, but the term will suffice for these purposes.

49 Hendrick, *Big Stone Gap*, 7–8. Creed Flanary and John Kelly both speculated in Big Stone Gap town lots, as did several Kilbourns, though the name "Joseph" cannot be linked with certainty to any of them.

50 Statement of William M. McElwee, who arrived in Big Stone Gap in 1889 to open a bank, quoted in Hendrick, *Big Stone Gap*, 42.

9

BETH BARTON SCHWEIGER

Putting Politics Aside:
Virginia Democrats and
Voter Apathy in the
Era of Disfranchisement

VIRGINIA DEMOCRATS GATHERED IN RICHMOND'S ACADEMY
of Music just before the November elections of 1905 confident that the
state's new constitution had restored integrity to Virginia politics. Party
leaders and their wives listened as speaker after speaker anticipated the
party's triumph over political corruption in this first test of disfranchisement laws under the 1902 constitution. "We now have a chance for honest elections in this state and that chance came through a Democratic
constitution made by Democratic hands," Governor A. J. Montague told
his well-heeled audience in typically grandiose fashion. "I support the
Democratic party because it stands for the things that make for the
betterment of the condition of mankind." [1]

Just five years earlier, such self-congratulatory rhetoric was rare among
Democrats. "Honest elections" seemed out of reach for a party in the
grip of political corruption, and speeches and newspaper columns lamented the decline of state politics. Politicians moved uneasily among
constituents quick to pronounce them guilty by association with the corrupt political system. "Fraudulent elections inevitably produce political
bosses and political bosses produce rotten and corrupt government. This
is what we shall have in Virginia unless we put an end to fraudulent elections," the Richmond *Daily Times* warned. Party leaders worried that
well-publicized charges of corruption in state elections might draw federal intervention. And with increasing numbers of well-to-do whites refusing to vote, they also worried that an effective opposition could be
mustered to evict Democrats from state office. Virginia Democrats, unlike those in other Southern states, had seen strong challenges from third
parties twice in the past three decades. First the Readjusters of the 1870s
and 1880s and then the Populists of the 1890s built a viable political
opposition in part on charges of Democratic corruption. Political cor-

ruption, the Populists had charged, would weaken the moral fabric of their society and "demoralize our whole people."[2]

By the 1890s Democrats were faced with unprecedented rates of voter apathy across the state. The party might have been pleased if the majority of the nonvoters were undesirable poor whites and blacks. But the white businessmen, farmers, and professionals who had traditionally formed the backbone of the Democratic party exhibited a disturbing lack of interest in elections, forcing the party to seek the source of this apathy.

All signs pointed to political corruption as the root cause of voter apathy, and universal manhood suffrage as the root cause of corruption. Democrats quickly made black voters the scapegoats of their campaign against corruption. As the preferred targets of corrupt white politicians, blacks were blamed almost exclusively for the deplorable condition of the state political system. By the time Democrats called for a referendum on a constitutional convention in 1900, they had publicly declared their intention to end the black vote. Attorney General William A. Anderson, after his nomination to the 1901 constitutional convention, stressed that Democrats wished above all to purify state elections by disfranchising blacks and poor whites. "If fraud and corruption are not checked, sooner or later they will pervade the whole body politic," Anderson cautioned.[3]

Historians have long acknowledged a tradition of voter apathy in the Solid South of the late nineteenth and early twentieth centuries, but apathy has rarely played an active role in explanations of the timing and causes of disfranchisement. Instead, interpretations have focused on Democratic racism and whether disfranchisement was a reality even before conservatives adopted the new constitution. All have concluded that disfranchisement was an unqualified triumph for Southern conservatives. This chapter stresses the limits of Democratic power, arguing that the party sought black disfranchisement not as an end in itself but to restore high rates of voter participation among whites. Neither racism, a persistent factor in Virginia politics, nor party competition, a nonissue in Virginia after 1893, can stand alone as explanations for why disfranchisement occurred when it did. By the turn of the century, escalating voter apathy persuaded Democrats to end the black vote in the hopes of luring prosperous whites back to the polls. But voter apathy continued unabated well into the twentieth century, and disfranchisement fell short of being an uncontested triumph for Virginia Democrats. Even in the Solid South, voter behavior limited the power of party.[4]

In the world of Virginia politics at the end of the nineteenth century, ending black suffrage in order to lure well-heeled white voters back to the polls made perfect sense. Few white Virginians doubted that universal manhood suffrage was unnatural or that it was the primary source of the corruption that choked the state's election campaigns. Neither did they doubt that unchecked political corruption eventually would infect their entire society. In their view, politics both shaped and reflected public morality, and a new constitution could improve the moral tone of life in Virginia for the new century.

Politics was an integral part of life in Virginia following the Civil War, a period when partisan activities reached unprecedented heights throughout the country. Party allegiance revealed more than voting preference; it reflected an individual's values, character, and even race. As one Norfolk editor insisted, "the Democratic party means the reputable white people." Betrayal of party loyalty could mean loss of business, employment, credit, or even one's welcome at church. Writing in 1899, a journalist noted that to call a man a "crank, a rascal, a liar, an arrant rogue, an unnatural father or an ungrateful son" in print was not libelous. But "to charge a man with being a Democrat when he is publicly known as a Populist is a libel because it affects his social and business standing."[5]

Most Democratic party leaders were men of business, professional, or farming background. Of the eighty-eight Democratic delegates at the 1901 constitutional convention, sixty-two were lawyers and twenty-one were farmers; the other five included merchants, bankers, and a minister.[6] The party rank and file faithfully contributed to party coffers, attended party meetings and rallies, and engaged in partisan gossip.

Women's place in the world of late nineteenth-century politics indicates how deeply politics permeated life in Virginia. Although they would not gain the franchise for another two decades, women's activities, ideas, and presence shaped the state's political culture. Women's temperance societies were intimately tied to political power structures in the state, and groups such as the United Daughters of the Confederacy flourished on political symbolism.[7] Married women found that their husbands' political activities helped to define their own position in the community, and partisan newspapers lured female readers with society and fashion sections. Although barred from conventions, women frequently attended political rallies, where they were welcomed with such amenities as "comfortable seating."[8] Their presence helped to legitimate the party agenda, and leading Democrats understood that women carried tremendous political weight in the state. Women's support could only strengthen the Democratic cause.

Virginia Democrats participated in a tightly organized party struc-

Fig 9.1. Accomack County Democrats entertain black voters at an oyster bake in 1889. (Courtesy of the Virginia State Library and Archives, Richmond)

ture. Rallies, conventions, and elections arrived as predictably as the seasons and were part of the rhythm of life in the Old Dominion. October brought a full schedule of rallies in anticipation of November elections. Richmond newspapers, the semiofficial mouthpieces of the state Democratic party, kept track of such gatherings across the state. "The political world will be stirred from the centre out Friday in old Powhatan," the Richmond *Dispatch* declared in an advance for a speech by Senator John W. Daniel in October 1897. "Major Daniel nearly always attracts attention among the Southside people, and they lay other things aside to wait on his patriotic and eloquent words."[9] Virginians often traveled considerable distances to glimpse the face of a well-known political figure such as Daniel. Special cut-rate railroad fares often eased the burden of travel costs.

Once the crowd arrived, rallies stretched into leisurely day-long socials (see fig 9.1). Such festive gatherings were rare for most Virginians, and they often lingered until well past sunset discussing the day's events. Usually held outdoors, rallies typically included a speech of several hours' length followed by "an old-fashioned Virginia dinner arranged on long tables in an orchard near the speaker's stand."[10] The next day, newspapers detailed the crowd's size, who was present, and whether the speeches were well received. Often, the speech of a particularly important figure was published in its entirety. Holidays such as the Fourth of July and Confederate Memorial Day were also self-consciously political celebrations, resounding with rhetoric and adorned with colorful banners and Sunday attire. These displays of party spirit underscored the inclusiveness of the state's political system and affirmed the common, if loose, ties binding political insiders with their constituents.

Party conventions, held in the summer months, offered a more exclusive atmosphere. Convention delegates assembled in a designated host city to pound out their platform in debates that inevitably spewed more smoke than fire. Here the Democratic party shed its populist image and retreated behind closed doors with the characteristics of a private male club. This atmosphere of consensus reinforced delegates' belief that the party stood only for what was decent, hardworking, and prosperous in the state. In 1900 a Norfolk editor made a telling connection between the convention and the health of Virginia society, noting that "there is always something more or less inspiring about a convention . . . it puts to rout any belief that our citizenship is degenerating." [11]

Spring primaries and fall elections brought the high tide of political activity each year, testing the statewide Democratic party organization. Defeat at the polls "will not be the fault of the managers of the state headquarters, for not in years has there been greater activity in sending out literature and assigning of speakers to arouse the voters out in the rural districts," one paper reported in 1897. Another election year found the Democratic headquarters busy with "ten lady typewriters working at breakneck speed, addressing envelopes, writing letters and sending out literature." [12] The day after the vote, newspaper headlines declared the winners. Tallies of the vote by precinct were usually published within the week, and editorials lauding the victors, usually Democrats, lingered for several weeks after the election.

The whirl of activity surrounding conventions, rallies, and elections persisted through the 1870s and 1880s in spite of growing political corruption and declining voter turnout. Virginians had lived with corrupt politics since the first days of conservative rule in 1869, and with the appearance of the Readjuster movement in the late 1870s, all parties apparently resolved anew to use any means possible to win votes. Throughout this period, indulging in election fraud brought neither social nor political disadvantage. Bribery, stuffing ballot boxes, appointment of drunken and unethical election judges, and even murder occurred frequently. Such methods were accepted as a necessary part of politics in the period. Between 1874 and 1900 Virginia elections were challenged sixteen times in the U.S. House of Representatives on charges of election fraud.[13]

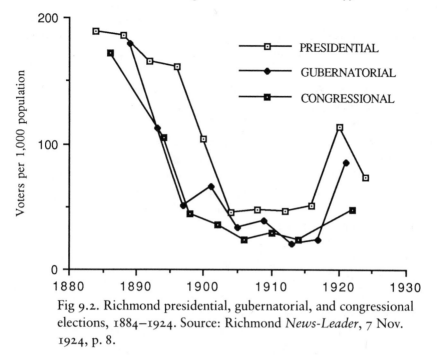

Fig 9.2. Richmond presidential, gubernatorial, and congressional elections, 1884–1924. Source: Richmond *News-Leader*, 7 Nov. 1924, p. 8.

By the early 1890s Virginia Democrats could no longer ignore dramatic declines in voter participation, particularly in state and local elections. In Richmond, for example, the total vote in congressional races plummeted 70 percent from almost 13,000 to just under 4,000 votes between 1886 and 1898. Similarly, in gubernatorial contests, the vote fell 69 percent from just over 14,000 to 5,700 between 1889 and 1901 (see fig 9.2). Tallies in presidential contests did not show such a dramatic decline, but they also dropped, especially after the mid-1890s. The difference between voter interest in national and state contests is illustrated by the turnout on Election Day in November 1888. More than 300,000 men voted in the presidential race, while a referendum for a state constitutional convention held the same day drew just 66,000 voters.[14]

Democrats' shrill denunciations of voter apathy filled newspaper columns and speeches as puzzled politicians tried to lure constituents back to the polls. Virginians continued to attend party rallies and picnics but curiously chose to ignore the polls on election day. Politics became increasingly divorced from suffrage. A halfhearted attempt by the Virginia legislature to clean up electoral practices through the Anderson-McCormick Act of 1884 was clearly ineffective. Virginians saw this supposed reform act for what it was and became even more vocal in their criticism of the system, claiming that political fraud endangered "the moral sense of the people."[15]

Falling voter participation coincided with Democrats' growing unease about the state's decline from the past. By the 1890s rapid population growth and economic change were transforming life in the state. Many Virginians, regardless of partisan affiliation, viewed these changes with marked ambivalence. They embraced progress even as they clung tenaciously to more familiar patterns of life. Although they expressed fears that urbanization would erode their traditional rural life-style, they were among the most vocal boosters of the small successes of their own hometowns. In this New South, rural and urban images mingled in strange ways, as in the apparently urbane Richmond in 1897, when a newspaper editorial called for a halt to the driving of livestock through the city's streets on Sunday. Cracking whips and shouting herdsmen were disturbing worshipers at church services. Politically, the growth of a town class throughout Virginia during the 1880s permanently altered paths to political power and pushed a new rhetoric of small-town boosterism and progress into state political contests.[16]

The strains caused by demographic and physical changes in postwar Virginia coincided with heightening racial tensions. White Democrats' disdain for universal manhood suffrage, particularly among blacks, is well documented. White supremacy was a persistent theme of Democratic rhetoric throughout this period, and the party publicly expressed their views of black voters with few reservations. "Scientific" studies purporting to prove black inferiority fueled white certainties of the decline of blacks, freed for three decades from the "disciplining" of slavery.[17]

The 1890s saw the emergence of a new generation of politicians. Born during war and Reconstruction, these men were representative of the new era. But they turned continually to the past to legitimize their political agenda, rewriting history as they did so. This era witnessed what C. Vann Woodward has called the "invention of the Old South." Champions of the Lost Cause in Virginia, usually members of the more established families in the state, often found they were preaching to the converted with their finely orchestrated rhetorical campaigns. Confederate veterans' reunions and funerals had striking visibility in late nineteenth-century Virginia. At the death in 1897 of Major Lewis Ginter, a prominent Richmonder, for example, the local paper published his will in four columns on the front page and offered detailed coverage of the funeral. Such rituals developed out of mixed motives. Clearly, many Virginians jealously guarded memories of the past, but Democratic leaders also sought political gain by clothing their party with the nostalgia of the Lost Cause.[18]

Democrats soon found, however, that even appeals to Confederate sentimentality failed to pique voter interest. As celebration of the Lost Cause reached a fever pitch, particularly in Richmond, voter participation continued to decline. The silent electorate made Democrats look uneasily to the recent past, when agrarian unrest had taught them that the costs of an unhappy electorate could be high. Democrats believed the Populist problem had been solved, but they knew the issues that had fueled the agrarian cause could easily resurface.

Scholars have long puzzled over Populism's short life in Virginia. The Farmers' Alliance and its heir, the Populist party, made little immediate impact on the state's political order. Although Virginia's tradition of agrarian organization dated from the antebellum period, the Alliance's decision to form a separate party in 1892 quickly brought its demise. Traditional views have pronounced the Populists' failure as inevitable in light of the Democrats' imposing strength.[19] Closer inspection, however, reveals that the Democrats' unease over the agrarian cause was justified. In the end, Populism deeply changed the political landscape of the state, forcing Democrats to redefine their strategy by the end of the 1890s.

The agrarian cause in Virginia, as in other Southern states, grew out of the unfulfilled promises of New South prosperity made to a perpetually depressed rural economy. By 1890 farm laborers in the state averaged just 28 percent of the wages earned by common laborers in other industries. The mainstream Democratic leadership appeared to align themselves solidly with the interests of the new town class, the railroads, and the growing, if still small, group of Southern industrialists. The political and social importance of the farm was eroding, and by the late 1880s farmers were ready to shake up a political system which no longer seemed accountable to their interests. The political parties, one rural Virginia paper declared, "only favor measures for the moneyed few, while the Alliance is protesting, and fighting for that which will benefit all mankind alike." By August 1890 the Alliance had organized in eighty-seven Virginia counties and counted about 30,000 members.[20]

Clearly, founders of Virginia Populism were far from ready to abandon politics as a forum for reform. But the gap between the Democratic and the Populist vision of political ideals was wide. Alliancemen assumed that even the most honest man, once elected, could not escape entanglement in corrupt state politics. "A representative is pledged to reform certain abuses," the *Virginia Sun* explained in 1892. "Under the blandishments of the lobby he weakens, and fails to redeem his pledges. He goes back home, and with affected nonchalance waves the matter aside." By contrast, Democrats spoke of their candidates only as "respectable gentlemen."[21]

The Kent Bill controversy of 1892 provides an example of how agrarian defeat eroded voter participation in Virginia. The bill proposed stricter regulation of railroads, and farmers readily supported any move to squelch the power of railroad magnates, with whom they continually sparred over freight rates. Railroad regulation became the unifying issue for Alliancemen statewide. Even the conservative Shenandoah Valley region affirmed the spirit of railroad reform as "productive and of great good to the Commonwealth," and by some estimates five out of six Virginians supported the bill.[22]

After two years of highly controversial public debate, a weakened version of the bill passed with Democratic support in 1892. Farmers were furious at the Democratic compromise. The Kent Bill will "become the battle cry of the next state campaign and the party of reform will sweep on to victory," the *Virginia Sun*, paper of the Alliance, angrily predicted. "A more popular issue could not have been provided."[23]

But the calls for action went unanswered. Within one year, support for the newly founded Populist party had fizzled out. Instead of boosting many Virginia farmers' resolve to push for reform, the Kent Bill controversy fueled many Virginians' cynical assessment of party politics. The episode proved to many agrarians that mainstream politicians would not tolerate attempts at serious reform.

Thus, even before the Alliance officially became the Populist party, agrarians had a formidable opponent in voter apathy. Low voter turnout clearly hurt the fledgling party, and in the end Populists had no more success in wooing growing numbers of nonvoters back to the polls than their Democratic rivals. In 1893, in the first gubernatorial race to list a Populist candidate, white Virginians stayed away from the polls in unprecedented numbers. White participation shrank by one-half from 1892 to 1893, while an estimated two-thirds of the eligible blacks had failed to vote. The Populists still managed to seat ten members of the General Assembly and to gain 41 percent of the popular vote for the governorship. But three-quarters of the nonvoters in this election were white, a dramatic change from previous years. Coupled with the Populists' dismal showing in the 1892 presidential election, these results crippled the party. Alliancemen's hopes for reform were laid to rest, and after 1893 many disdained all party activities.[24]

For the Democrats, Populism proved to be both a boon and a curse.

The Democratic machine flourished by the mid-1890s. The demise of Populism, for which the Democrats took much credit, had made their party less accountable to the electorate than ever before, and Democratic candidates knew they faced only token opposition at the polls.

But the party's renewed strength proved to be its primary weakness. The 1893 victory was a hollow one for Democrats. Virginians had seen the failure of one opposition party too many since the early 1870s, and by staying away from the polls, they now cast a vote against the entire political system. The seeming impenetrability of the Democratic fortress had seriously compromised voters' sense of political efficacy, their belief that their vote could influence the outcome of elections. Critical to voters' participation, efficacy is a fragile attitude; without the rigor of party competition, it cannot survive. Thomas Jefferson had voiced similar concerns a century earlier. "In every free and deliberating society," he wrote, "there must, from the nature of man, be opposite parties, and violent dissensions and discords." Without political parties, Jefferson believed, there could be no true self-government. After 1893 no viable alternatives to the Democratic party existed in Virginia for the first time since the Readjuster movement. Many voters, convinced they could not break the Democrats' grip or even shift the party's course, simply stayed home on election day.[25]

Curiously, the Populist episode left the Democrats uneasy. Instead of perceiving diminishing numbers of voters as a sign of their strength, Democrats worried over their inability to attract voters' attention. The Democrats' insecurity, which many scholars have discounted, was genuine. Virginia Democrats had seen more serious challenges to their rule than any other Southern Democratic organization since Redemption. The demise of the Readjusters strengthened the Virginia Republican party in the 1880s. As late as 1886 Republicans won six of ten state congressional seats. The agrarian movement, too, appeared more threatening to Virginia Democrats than its small numbers suggest. Populism had attracted an unusually high number of well-to-do rural residents, including doctors and wealthy farmers whom the conservatives had traditionally counted loyal members. After 1893 many of these men professed loyalty to no political party, and their loss diminished Democrats' respectability among their traditionally rural constituency.[26]

In their speculations about the causes of voter apathy after 1893, Democrats concluded that voters were fed up with political corruption. Criticism of the tradition of corrupt politics in the state had gained important support for opposition parties during the past three decades. But the Populist threat finally prompted Democrats, who long had openly justified use of corruption to stay the black and Republican threat, to reevaluate their strategy. They passed the Walton Act of 1894, a much-touted reform bill which established the secret ballot and ensured that state officials, not parties, were in charge of printing the ballots.[27]

The failure of Populism, then, accelerated rates of declining voter participation in the state and drew the Democrats' attention afresh to corruption and voter apathy as political issues. Smarting from the apathy of even their most upstanding white constituents in 1893, Democrats began to revise their strategy. For the rest of the decade, the party would try to polish its image by self-consciously distancing itself from corruption. Populism's impact on Virginia politics thus long outlived the movement itself.

But the new strategies did not bring voters back to the polls. The Walton Act, instead of ending the decline in voter participation, continued and even accelerated it. Turnout continued to decline, reaching epidemic proportions by the late 1890s. "The campaign in Virginia is very, very dull," one editor wrote in 1897. "It is difficult to arouse the average voter to a pitch of enthusiasm over any measure," another observed. That same year the Richmond *Planet*, the newspaper of the black community, detected "an apathy among all classes the like of which has not been seen in many years before. The colored vote was similarly affected." By 1901 just half of all eligible voters cast ballots in the gubernatorial race.[28]

The pervasive mistrust of the political process by the 1890s drew many to distinguish between politicians and statesmen. In her popular novel completed in 1900, *Voice of the People*, Virginia novelist Ellen Glasgow noted this contrast in her portrayal of a poor white who climbed to the governorship of Virginia. "He had gone to Richmond to meet an assembly of statesmen; he had found a body of well-intentioned but unprofitable servants. The day when a legislator meant a statesman was done with; it meant merely a man like other men, to be juggled with by shrewder politicians or to be tricked by the more dishonest ones." Politicians also found increasingly vocal critics in the clergy. "We have all grown hardened to the cry of the political demagogue," a Methodist pastor wrote in 1900. "We have heard the story before, and we gave him a smile—but no vote!"[29]

Democratic leaders were puzzled and disappointed by their constituents' aversion for politics. Apathy among blacks was expected as a sign of their unfitness for political participation, and Democrats frequently cited low black voter turnout as reason for taking the franchise away from them. But the party could hardly advocate the same measures in the face of an uninterested prosperous white electorate. Instead, they chided white voters' laziness and argued that "bad government is almost invariably due to carelessness and neglect on the part of voters." The fruits of indifference would inevitably allow "professional politicians to take advantage and manage to run in their candidate while the better men are defeated."[30]

Party leaders warned of certain Democratic defeat and the threat of "Republican rule" and "negro rule" if Virginians did not vote. Dismissing the possibility that rhetoric was a true reflection of Democratic fears, historians have generally viewed this alarmist rhetoric as a smokescreen used by party leaders to obscure their frankly racist desire to end the black franchise.[31]

As scholars have concluded, disfranchisement was spurred by racism. But party rhetoric clearly points to a deeper motive for eliminating poor voters in the state, both black and white: Democrats initiated disfranchisement in a genuine reform spirit to lure "qualified" prosperous whites back to the polls. This can explain what has so far eluded historians: why it took thirty-five years for Virginia Democrats to decide to end the black vote. Conservatives believed the survival of their political system hinged on wooing whites back to the polls.

White voter apathy was particularly problematic for Democrats. The party counted on high turnouts to determine the number of Democratic delegates to congressional and state conventions.[32] And after 1893 the party was especially uneasy that voter silence could mean another reform movement was stirring. A high turnout was required if elections were to be a reliable measure of public opinion. Fundamentally, however, Democratic politicians sought to rally voters around the cause of disfranchisement because they perceived that politics and politicians were losing influence in the everyday life of Virginians. Much like the agrarian reformers of the decade before, Democrats moved toward voter reform to bolster a tradition they feared was disappearing.

By the turn of the century, Democrats found themselves in the curious position of trying to entice voters to abandon "careless indifference" from one side of their mouth while condemning unrestricted suffrage as "a serious menace to the peace and prosperity of the state" from the other. Voters were able to decipher these contradictory messages. They knew the party was encouraging only the prosperous men of the state to vote, while hoping that poor white and black men would stay home. This was apparent in the party's charge in 1897 that voting contributed to the difficulties of the poor. "Industrious and frugal Virginians have something else to do besides wasting their time at country stores discussing politics and cheap money . . . they can easily make themselves better off if they will drop politics and go to earnest work."[33]

Some Democrats were perceptive enough to realize that the party's domination of state politics somehow contributed to voter apathy. "The certainty of Democratic victory benumbs our opponents and their inactivity produces apathy in our own ranks," one editor observed. Another account from 1897 notes that "the Republicans are aware that their fight is a hopeless one and the Democrats are suffering from a severe attack of over-confidence." But party leaders easily dismissed these views, convinced that political competition would neither benefit the party nor increase voter participation. Democrats aimed to dominate the competition, not foster it.[34]

With their diagnosis in hand, Democrats quickly seized upon universal manhood suffrage as the root cause of corruption and, in turn, voter apathy. Black suffrage "polluted the sources of governmental power" and created a "mass of reeking corruption of the social and political order" of Virginia, Democrats argued. Although the question of whether poor whites should have the vote was more controversial, many Virginians agreed with William A. Anderson, who believed that since there was "no excuse" for white illiteracy, illiterate whites did not deserve the vote.[35]

Because Democratic politicians believed legislation had a fundamental effect on social ethics and relations, they expected that franchise restriction would restore old standards to the state's social order. Rewriting the state's constitution would not only eliminate universal manhood suffrage and restore voting as a privileged activity among well-to-do white men in the state. Democrats also believed it would also teach poor blacks and whites their place. Disfranchisement, then, was the perfect reform. It would both solve the "negro question" and restore well-to-do white men's confidence and participation in the political process.

Although disfranchisement had already survived the test of Southern courts, Virginia conservatives approached the prospect of a constitutional convention carefully, and for good reason. Public divisions over calling the convention recalled earlier cleavages of the Readjuster era. A constitutional referendum in 1897 had failed badly, with just 31 percent of the 122,000 total votes cast in favor of the measure.[36] The 1897 referendum had not been supported wholeheartedly by the party, but after this defeat Democrats began building support for another referendum. By 1900 support for the referendum was strong among white voters in counties with large black populations, so the party focused much of its efforts on the counties of the Piedmont region. Party rhetoric concentrated on persuasion, praising voters' ability to make the correct choices at the polls. "The people of Virginia can always be depended upon to do the right thing in the long run. They are honest, sensible, and patriotic, and they are not easily led by demagogues and rainbow chasers." Democrats even tried to temper their normally racist rhetoric. "It requires no courage for a newspaper conducted by a white man to attack the negro, for the white man knows he will not be called to account," the Norfok *Virginian-Pilot* reassured voters in May 1900. "This suffrage question is one that needs to be looked at in a dry light." [37]

The constitutional referendum of 1900 stood as a final critical test of interest in the franchise, because the intentions behind the Democratic movement for a new constitution were widely known. Passing the referendum assured sharp limitations of voter eligibility. Nevertheless, just 138,000 of an estimated 425,000 eligible voters participated. Significantly, that number would roughly equal the voter turnout of 131,000 in the 1904 presidential election after disfranchisement. Those most threatened by the referendum apparently stayed away from the polls.[38]

The victory momentarily overwhelmed Democrats' worries about the small turnout, and they turned to nomination of convention delegates. Returns revealed 56 percent favored a new constitution, boosting party confidence that theirs was a popular reform movement, in spite of the small turnout. "In the name of the great patriots of Virginia, whose memory we cherish," the Richmond *Times* declared in anticipation of the convention, "let us for this time put politics aside." In this appeal for nonpartisanship, misguided Democrats overlooked the lessons those "great patriots," including their beloved Jefferson, had learned. The founders knew that putting politics aside would compromise democracy in their young nation, and Virginia politics after the turn of the twentieth century confirmed their judgment.[39]

If Democrats were pleased when the constitutional convention met in June 1901, Richmond society was delighted by the diversion it created. The convention transformed city life for many while the delegates were in town. Hotels filled to overflowing and the city's social life flourished. In the sultry summer months, committees met only a few hours each day, leaving plenty of cooler evening hours for socializing. After a year of these deliberations, delegates resolved their differences over the suffrage amendment to create a constitution which U.S. Senator John Daniel praised "as colorless as a pane of glass." [40]

Article II of the document completely revised state suffrage laws. In 1902 and 1903 voter registrars would admit any male over the age of twenty-one who could read "any Section of this Constitution," "give reasonable explanation of the same," and pay a property tax of at least one dollar annually or who could show proof that he was a Confederate veteran. After 1904 any man who had not registered in 1902–3 would be asked to pay an annual poll tax of $1.50, apply for registration in his own handwriting without aid, and "answer on oath any and all questions affecting his qualifications submitted to him by the officers of registration, which shall be reduced to writing."[41]

By November 1904 those who had attended the convention were confident that their new constitution had successfully ended universal manhood suffrage. Voter turnout plummeted almost 50 percent between the presidential contests of 1900 and 1904, from 264,000 to 131,000. In state elections, vote totals dropped off by an even greater margin, falling by 78 percent between the gubernatorial elections in 1901 and 1905.[42]

Democratic editors showered the party with praise. "The new Constitution has done its work well," the Lynchburg *News* declared triumphantly. "It seems almost wonderful that a plan of suffrage so satisfactory in its operation should have been devised." Republicans immediately charged registrars with refusing to register their party members, while all Democrats, literate or not, were enrolled. Their protests fell on the deaf ears of an emboldened Democratic leadership. At last, it seemed, they could afford to ignore the Republicans. The carefully crafted constitution virtually eliminated Democrats' need for corrupt practices to gain or maintain office.[43]

Democrats extended their vision of political reform to public schools almost immediately after the convention. Convinced that the new political order required a new kind of citizenship, the State Board of Education in 1904 ordered that "civil government" courses be taught at the high school level. Newly revised textbooks published for this purpose explained the new constitutional law of the state and stressed the importance of individual responsibility in upholding good government. Party leaders and publishers did not dwell on the fact that many of the young men in these classes would not be able to vote under the new constitution.[44]

Like Virginia Democrats, scholars have concluded from the sharp drop in voter turnout that disfranchisement was a triumph for conservatives. They argue disfranchisement easily achieved, and even surpassed, Democrats' intentions by restricting suffrage more severely than any time before in the state's history. But these interpretations do not take into account the voluntary nature of voting. A sharp drop in voter turnout does not mean that all of those who did not vote were barred from the polls.

Interpretations of disfranchisement have generally centered on the debate, first raised by political scientist V. O. Key in 1949, over whether disfranchisement was a legal or extralegal phenomenon in the South. Key argued that disfranchisement actually began in the 1870s, after white conservatives regained political control in the region through fraud and intimidation. The extralegal process was capped between 1890 and 1910 with formal legal restrictions passed in every Southern state. For Key, legal disfranchisement was the "roof rather than the foundation of the system" of suffrage restriction, which depended on "more fundamental political processes" than the law.[45]

But J. Morgan Kousser, in the most comprehensive study of Southern disfranchisement, took a very different position. He argued that disfranchisement was primarily a political phenomenon, prompted by the Democrats' desire to squelch potential opposition at the polls, and that the disfranchising laws themselves dramatically curtailed voter participation. Using sophisticated estimation techniques, Kousser computed voter turnout before and after disfranchisement, concluding that blacks and poor whites stopped voting only after forced to by strict new voter registration provisions. The new constitution, not extralegal white intimidation and violence, he argued, disfranchised black Virginians. Disfranchisement was not, therefore, a "fait accompli."[46]

More recently, Joel Williamson has argued that disfranchisement was motivated primarily by Southern whites' obsessive fears of black domination. He believed, like Key, that blacks had long abandoned the polls because of extralegal pressure from whites. White conservatives, therefore, did not need disfranchisement to keep blacks from voting but simply to "show explicitly and blatantly the power of whites."[47]

These legal and extralegal arguments may be reconciled. Some Virginians, many of them black, were prevented from voting by white intimidation before constitutional disfranchisement, while new laws kept many more away from the polls after 1902. Turnout did fall among white and black voters after disfranchisement, and logic points to the laws as a likely cause for some of the drop in turnout.

But this debate does not address the twenty-year trend of plummeting voter turnout among whites in the years leading up to 1901. Nor does it explain the timing of disfranchisement. Long before legal restrictions were enacted, many Virginian voters, not all poor or black, simply stopped voting, especially in state and local contests.[48] But perhaps most importantly, the legal-extralegal debate ignores the persistence of voter apathy after disfranchisement laws were passed.

When voter apathy is considered as an important variable in the disfranchisement equation, it becomes clear that disfranchisement was not a total victory for the Democratic party. The Democratic party would not have groped for new strategies to get out the vote in 1905, the very time when the triumphs of disfranchisement were supposed to be evident, if all was well. Yet just before the November election that year, party leaders sent a letter to all wards in Richmond noting that "the energy of the voter is spent and apathy seems to be quite general. We are all exceedingly anxious to have a full vote cast and request you to amuse the voters of your precinct, giving particular attention to the apathetic." [49]

In fact, the gubernatorial election of 1905 shattered Democratic hopes that eliminating the black vote would create a "new beginning" in state politics, allowing a "royal fight of white man against white man in which the Democrats and Republicans may test their steel freely." That year, by conservative estimates, 21 percent of registered voters turned out. In Richmond, fewer than half of the estimated 7,000 eligible voters cast ballots in the November general election. The Norfolk *Virginian-Pilot* reported a "very light vote" in Newport News and a "much smaller vote than expected in Suffolk." [50] Democrats obviously did not expect the percentage of all Virginians who voted to match predisfranchisement turnouts. Instead, the references to a light vote show that Democrats expected a higher percentage of qualified voters to turn out than before disfranchisement. That the party's public denunciations of voter apathy continued after disfranchisement indicates voter reform had not diminished white voter apathy. In 1905, and thereafter, even voters who met the strict requirements of the new constitution simply continued a trend begun twenty years earlier: they disfranchised themselves.

Democrats attributed poor turnouts across the state to "the absence of soul-stirring issues," but they could not hide their disappointment and dismay. Newspapers reveal a puzzling range of Democratic responses. The *Times-Dispatch*'s leading editorial on 8 November protested that "it is inconceivable that the people of Virginia should have such little interest in their own affairs." Refuting the idea that disfranchisement was a consciously partisan ploy on the part of Democrats, the Norfolk *Virginian-Pilot* argued that "on the contrary, the Democratic party lost more white votes by the new Constitution than did the Republicans." Norfolk and Richmond papers both blamed nonvoters for their own predicament. "Most of those who were disfranchised were responsible for it themselves . . . by failure to pay the poll tax or negligence to register." [51] The *Times-Dispatch* summed up Democratic dismay at persistent voter apathy. "It is remarkable to us that any qualified voter, least of all a poor man, should decline to vote because he chances to be dissatisfied with any statutory act or any political situation. The sensible thing is for voters to take their grievances to the ballot box for that is the only way they can accomplish a change. They can certainly accomplish nothing good for themselves by the let-alone policy."[52]

All of these responses indicate that Democrats were caught off guard by continuing voter apathy after disfranchisement. Although in theory disfranchisement was designed to exclude only those voters whom Democrats believed were unfit for the franchise, in practice the restrictions accelerated the trend of nonparticipation among state voters. The new laws discouraged many who might have just met qualifications because they feared public humiliation before election officials. Disfranchisement also institutionalized, for all practical purposes, the one-party system in Virginia. Democratic control was not only a tradition in the state after 1902, it came very close to being constitutional law. The Fredericksburg *Journal* frankly admitted that "beneath this seeming apathy there might be a feeling of disgust at Democratic means and measures."[53]

Virginia's new constitution not only ensured the state Republican party's impotence, it also deeply altered the tone and style of politics within the Democratic party. After disfranchisement, the frequency of political coverage in local newspapers dropped significantly, for example.[54] Disfranchisement freed politicians from the hard work of reaching the voting masses in Virginia.[55] In effect, it clothed the entire political process with the guise of exclusivity formerly found only at party conventions. After disfranchisement, Democratic leaders found their audiences more often at private fund-raising dinners than on the courthouse steps. Party rhetoric also reflected this new privatization of politics. Candidates and elected officials no longer focused their efforts on persuasion. Party leadership was less concerned with public opinion than with the opinion of party insiders.

This shift was anticipated by the very means Democrats used to adopt the new constitution in 1902. In order to win the 1900 referendum, Democrats had agreed to two conditions: that the constitution would be submitted to the voters for approval and that no person or descendent of any person registered to vote before 1861 would be disfranchised. Yet Democrats turned their backs on the first of these promises. Rather than submitting the constitution for voter approval, they adopted it by proclamation. The move reflected party insiders' growing conviction that the political process should be controlled largely by the party machine.

The proclamation of the state constitution, a breathtaking breach of public trust by the Democrats, stirred practically no controversy. A smattering of lawsuits brought by blacks who were disfranchised failed to pass the court system controlled by the Democrats.[56] But white voters deprived of their say in enacting the new constitution expressed no public reservations about the proclamation. The silence implies approval by some Virginians; it also shows that many voters' sense of efficacy had been completely destroyed by the time the convention ended. The same voter apathy that motivated Democrats to end universal manhood suffrage allowed them to achieve their goal easily.

The proclamation of the new constitution foreshadowed future attitudes of both political leaders and voters in Virginia. Throughout the nineteenth century, Virginia Democrats publicly revered theories of popular political participation, even if they sometimes failed to practice them. Disfranchisement allowed the party to discard public reverence of those ideals. After 1905 Virginia politics became, both in theory and in practice, the pursuit of the privileged.

In 1905, when a Virginia election official asked a white registered voter why he refused to "exercise his high right of citizenship," the man quickly replied, "Dog law. I'm not going to vote for people who make laws to tax my dog." The editor relaying this story was disgusted that "any qualified voter should decline to vote. Such men have the idea that they are spiting the state or some political party. The fact is they are spiting themselves."[57]

After 1905, from behind the closed doors of party conventions and gatherings of the party faithful, Virginia Democratic leaders began to blame the electorate for their apathy, distancing themselves from the people they claimed to serve. "The ballot is the only weapon a poor man has. It is like a gun in the hands of a soldier," the *Times-Dispatch* observed.[58] Conventional wisdom said that if an armed soldier refused to use his weapon in the face of an enemy attack, he was a coward. In their increasingly shrill denunciations of Virginia voters, Democrats ironically echoed their criticisms of black voters a decade earlier. Those who did not vote refused their civic duty, they argued. The voters, not party leaders, were to blame for political apathy, they insisted.

But their audience was simply not listening. And in the face of their failure to lure white men back to the polls, Democrats turned away from voters and toward the inner circle of their political machine. Party rhetoric became increasingly focused on internal party matters, and politics took on an increasingly exclusive cast as public accountability fell to an all-time low. Politics faded from the pages of even the most partisan newspaper.

If Democrats realized their expectations for disfranchisement had not been fulfilled, no hint of it emerged publicly for more than two decades. But in 1924, just before the April primary, editors of the Richmond *News-Leader* suggested that the 1902 constitution was to blame for Richmond's

> worst scandal—the failure of her citizens in the fundamental of representative government. . . . It is useless to attribute the smallness of the vote to apathy or to indifference. They are effects, not causes. The basic trouble is that qualification under the Virginia constitution involves more than the average voter—or the average voter in any state—is willing to do in the absence of bi-partisan conflict. Plainly put, in seeking to preserve the rule of whites by excluding the negroes, Virginia has fastened upon herself the rule of a minority of whites. In disfranchising the negroes, she has led tens of thousands of whites to disfranchise themselves.[59]

The editors went on to ask: "Is the complete disfranchisement of the negro worth what it has cost?" The question was hardly the beginning of a voting reform movement. For most white Virginians, the answer was apparently yes, indicating that the party had succeeded in drawing the boundaries of political activity so closely to the party machine that even eligible voters did not see the point of participating.

In 1901 Virginia Democrats set out to free the state's democratic system from both an uneducated, uninterested electorate and the growing apathy of qualified, upstanding white men. Their success in sharply restricting the electorate has obscured their unsuccessful attempt to end voter apathy and partisan corruption. Instead of freeing the political process, their new constitution placed the heart of the democracy, the franchise, in a bondage which would not be broken for the next sixty years.

NOTES

D. Alan Williams proved a valuable advocate for this chapter at its conception. Edward L. Ayers, with his patient encouragement and criticism, has endured its countless drafts with professionalism and good cheer.

1   Richmond *Times-Dispatch*, 30 Oct., 2 Nov. 1905.

2   Richmond *Daily Times*, 28 Oct. 1897; Virginia *Sun*, 14 June 1893, quoted in C. Vann Woodward, *Origins of the New South* (Baton Rouge: Louisiana State Univ. Press, 1951), 327.

3   William A. Anderson Papers, box 38, Acc. 5462, Manuscripts Division, Special Collections Department, University of Virginia Library.

4   The most influential study of disfranchisement in the South is J. Morgan Kousser, *The Shaping of Southern Politics: Suffrage Restriction and the Establishment of the One Party South, 1880–1910* (New Haven: Yale Univ. Press, 1974). Kousser sought to revise the classic work of political scientist V. O. Key, *Southern Politics in State and Nation* (New York: Knopf, 1949).

Other studies of disfranchisement and Virginia politics of the period in-clude: Allen W. Moger, *Virginia: From Bourbonism to Byrd* (Charlottes-ville: Univ. Press of Virginia, 1968); Raymond Pulley, *Old Virginia Re-stored: An Interpretation of the Progressive Impulse* (Charlottesville: Univ. Press of Virginia, 1968); Ronald Edward Shibley, "Election Laws and Elec-toral Practices in Virginia, 1867–1902: An Administrative and Political His-tory" (Ph.D. diss., Univ. of Virginia, 1972); Ralph Clipman McDanel, *The Virginia Constitutional Convention of 1901–1902* (Baltimore: Johns Hop-kins Univ. Press, 1928); William C. Pendleton, *Political History of Appala-chian Virginia* (Dayton, Va.: Shenandoah Press, 1927); Andrew Buni, *The Negro in Virginia Politics, 1902–1965* (Charlottesville: Univ. Press of Vir-ginia, 1967); Wythe Holt, "Virginia's Constitutional Convention of 1901–02," (Ph.D. diss., Univ. of Virginia, 1979).

5   Norfolk *Virginian-Pilot*, 17 May 1900; Woodward, *Origins of the New South*, 348; Augustus J. Munson, *Making of a Country Newspaper: Being a Detailed Statement of the Essentials to Success in Newspaper Making* (Chi-cago: Dominion Co., 1899), 87.

6   A total of 100 delegates attended the convention (Moger, *Virginia: From Bourbonism to Byrd*, 187).

7   See Angie Parrott's chapter 10 below.

8   Richmond *Dispatch*, 19 Oct. 1897.

9   Ibid., 24 Oct. 1897.

10   Ibid., 29, 31 Oct. 1897.

11   Norfolk *Virginian-Pilot*, 1 May 1900.

12   Richmond *Times-Dispatch*, 26 Oct. 1897, 26 Oct. 1905.

13   The Readjuster movement was peculiar to Virginia politics. This group, ini-tially a faction in the Conservative party, formed a coalition of farmers, poorer whites, and blacks who supported readjustment of the huge state debt after the war. The "Funders," who became the Democratic party in 1883, pushed for full repayment of the state debt (Shibley, "Election Laws and Electoral Practices," 84, x–xi; Key, *Southern Politics in State and Nation*, 540). For an example of how white political corruption affected some black Virginians, see Lawrence L. Hartzell's chapter 6 above.

14   The turnout for the 1888 constitutional referendum compared favorably with the 40,000 votes in congressional elections in Oct. 1865, the poor-est showing ever in the state's history (Shibley, "Election Laws and Elec-toral Practices," 16).

15   Speech of A. P. Thom, "The Inevitable Readjustment of the Law," before the Virginia State Bar Association, Aug. 1893, quoted in ibid., 157. The Anderson-McCormick Act of 1884 was a series of amendments to the exist-ing law that placed control of nearly all of the electoral system in the hands of the majority party, or the Democrats, including the appointment of elec-tion judges.

16   Between 1870 and 1900 the state's population grew by 51 percent, while the urban population more than doubled. Virginia had 1.22 million residents in 1870 and 1.85 million in 1900. The urban population grew from 146,000 in 1870 to 340,000 in 1900 (U.S. Bureau of the Census, *Historical Statistics of the United States*, 1 [Washington, D.C.: GPO, 1976]: 36; Richmond *Dis-patch*, 2 Nov. 1897). David L. Carlton, *Mill and Town in South Carolina*,

1880–1920 (Baton Rouge: Louisiana State Univ. Press, 1982), describes one example of how town growth affected local politics in the New South.

17 Dewey Grantham, *Southern Progressivism: The Reconciliation of Progress and Tradition* (Knoxville: Univ. of Tennessee Press, 1983), 122–27.

18 Richmond *Dispatch*, 7 Oct. 1897. For more on "the invention of the Old South," see C. Vann Woodward, *The Burden of Southern History* (Baton Rouge: Louisiana State Univ. Press, 1960), chap. 1; "The Search for Southern Identity"; Grantham, *Southern Progressivism*; Joel Williamson, *Rage for Order: Black/White Relations in the American South since Emancipation* (New York: Oxford Univ. Press, 1986). For a discussion of the new generation of Southern leaders, see David Herbert Donald, "A Generation of Defeat," in Walter Fraser and Winfred Moore, eds., *From the Old South to the New: Essays on the Transitional South* (Westport, Conn.: Greenwood, 1981).

19 The two works that have explored Virginia Populism in detail are William DuBose Sheldon, *Populism in the Old Dominion: Virginia Farm Politics, 1885–1900* (Princeton: Princeton Univ. Press, 1935), and William Allen Link, "Cavaliers and Mudsills: The Farmers' Alliance and the Emergence of Virginia Populism" (M.A. thesis, Univ. of Virginia, 1979). Link argued that the fragile coalition of agrarian interests in Virginia was shattered by the Alliance's entrance into politics.

20 Link, "Cavaliers and Mudsills," 2–3; Pulley, *Old Virginia Restored*, 36; Quicksburg, Va., *Union*, 28 June 1890, quoted in Link, "Cavaliers and Mudsills," 25. Virginia membership in the Alliance was well behind that of other Southern states. In Georgia, for example, the Alliance gained more than 100,000 members between 1887 and 1891 (C. Vann Woodward, *Tom Watson, Agrarian Rebel* [1938; rept. New York: Oxford Univ. Press, 1978], 136; Link, "Cavaliers and Mudsills," 44).

21 *Virginia Sun*, 13 Feb. 1892; Richmond *Times-Dispatch*, 3 Nov. 1905.

22 Link, "Cavaliers and Mudsills," 48, 55; New Market *Shenandoah Valley*, 10 March 1892. Robert C. Kent of Southwest Virginia introduced his bill in 1888 calling for the strengthening and expansion of the state's railroad commission, first established in 1877 (Link, "Cavaliers and Mudsills," 49).

23 *Virginia Sun*, 13 Feb. 1892.

24 Link, "Cavaliers and Mudsills," 63, 66; Shibley, "Election Laws and Electoral Practices," 152; Kousser, *The Shaping of Southern Politics*, 173. In 1892, 57 percent of nonvoters were black and 43 percent white; in 1893, 25 percent of nonvoters were black and 75 percent white (Link, "Cavaliers and Mudsills," 64).

25 Kenneth Prewitt, "Political Efficacy," in David L. Sills, ed., *International Encyclopedia of Social Science* (New York: Macmillan, 1968), 225–27; Saul K. Padover, *Jefferson: A Great American's Life and Ideas* (New York: Harcourt Brace Jovanovich, 1970), 107.

26 Link argued that the Virginia Alliance was successfully able to woo wealthy members of the influential Farmers' Assembly in the early 1890s (Link, "Cavaliers and Mudsills," 17–21, 38–39, 42). Kousser also stressed the tenuousness of Democratic strength in Virginia through the 1890s (Kousser, *The Shaping of Southern Politics*, 172).

27 Link, "Cavaliers and Mudsills," vii–viii. Because Kousser stressed the

agency of laws in restricting voter participation, he interpreted the Walton law as a significant example of the success of legal restrictions. His regression estimates show that the act significantly cut Republican party voting and that black turnout fell from 46 percent to 2 percent of the black male population from 1893 to 1897. Such results were anticipated and celebrated by Democrats. But the decrease in black and Republican voting rates was not matched by an increase in participation among the prosperous whites whose support the Democrats coveted, and therefore, the Walton Act should be interpreted as a limited success for the Democrats.

28 Richmond *Dispatch*, 20 Oct. 1897; Richmond *Times*, 20 May 1900; Richmond *Planet*, 6 Nov. 1897; McDanel, *Virginia Constitutional Convention of 1901–1902*, 16. V. O. Key found a similar dramatic drop in voter participation in Texas following the 1896 presidential contest. By 1902 Texas voter participation had been cut in half from 1896 levels (Key, *Southern Politics in State and Nation*, 534–35).

29 Ellen Glasgow, *Voice of the People* (New York: Doubleday, Page, 1902), 312; Rev. W. W. Royall of Chase City, Va., in the Richmond *Christian Advocate*, 19 April 1900.

30 Richmond *Times*, 7 April 1900.

31 Here historians have generally ascribed to the view that the obvious is not the "real reality." See Alan Megill, "Recounting the Past: 'Description,' Explanation, and Narrative in Historiography," *American Historical Review* 94 (June 1989): 631.

32 Richmond *Dispatch*, 29 Oct. 1897.

33 Richmond *Times*, 7, 6 April 1900; Richmond *Times*, 26 Oct. 1897.

34 Richmond *Dispatch*, 20, 21 Oct. 1897. For a subtle examination of issues surrounding voter apathy in the North, see Michael E. McGerr, *The Decline of Popular Politics in the American North, 1865–1928* (New York: Oxford Univ. Press, 1986).

35 Woodward, *Origins of the New South*, 327; *Report of the Proceedings and Debates of the Constitutional Convention* (Richmond: Hermitage Press, 1906), 2:3032; Shibley, "Election Laws and Electoral Practices," 219.

36 Key, *Southern Politics*, 546, 543. By the time Virginia Democrats called for a constitutional convention to reform voter registration, disfranchisement was far from a new idea in the South. In 1890 Mississippi legislators had been the first to rewrite the state constitution to restrict voting, and other Southern states followed. With the exception of Texas, every Southern state had statutes designed to limit the franchise through a variety of means by 1900. For a concise summary of voter reform in the period, see Kousser, *The Shaping of Southern Politics*, 239.

37 Richmond *Times*, 6 Feb. 1900; Norfolk *Virginian-Pilot*, 13 May 1900. For a discussion of regional support of disfranchisement, see Key, *Southern Politics*, 546.

38 The final tally was 77,362 for and 60,375 against the referendum (McDanel, *Virginia Constitutional Convention of 1901–1902*, 16). Scholars, including Kousser, have questioned the accuracy of these returns, citing widespread fraud. Only correctly marked ballots—with the Democrats' narrow definition of "correctly"—were counted. But there is no reason to believe that fraud distorted these results any more than other elections of the period.

Lawrence N. Powell has suggested that fraud was so prevalent in the New South that the tallies of all elections should be reexamined (Powell, "Correcting for Fraud: A Quantitative Reassessment of the Mississippi Ratification Election of 1868," *Journal of Southern History* 55 [Nov. 1989]: 631–58). Two decades after the referendum, an observer in Appalachia recalled that most whites in the state had opposed the constitutional convention, but "their will was defeated by the machine with large majorities procured with the peculiar machine methods." In fact, all but seven of the counties west of the Blue Ridge voted against the convention (Pendleton, *Political History of Appalachian Virginia*, 443).

39 Key, *Southern Politics*, 543; Richmond *Times*, 4 Feb. 1900.

40 "The Work of the Constitutional Convention," speech of U.S. Senator John Daniel to the Virginia State Bar Association, 5 Aug. 1902, quoted in Shibley, "Election Laws and Electoral Practices," 243. The Virginia Constitution of 1902 was also notable for its creation of a State Corporation Commission and closer regulation of corporate activity in the state. Scholars have puzzled over this seemingly progressive reform by the same delegates who embraced disfranchisement.

41 Virginia, *Constitution of 1902*, Article II.

42 U.S. Bureau of the Census, *Historical Statistics of the United States*, 1079. In 1901 the Virginia gubernatorial vote totaled 198,000; in 1905 it was 43,100 (Moger, *Virginia: Bourbonism to Byrd*, 179; Richmond *Times-Dispatch*, 9 Nov. 1905).

43 Lynchburg *News*, 1 April 1905; Pendleton, *Political History of Appalachian Virginia*, 457.

44 For more about the philosophies that these texts expressed, see William A. Link, *A Hard Country and a Lonely Place: Schooling, Society, and Reform in Rural Virginia, 1870–1920* (Chapel Hill: Univ. of North Carolina Press, 1986), 157–58, and Angie Parrott's chapter 10 below. Examples of these texts include William F. Fox, *Civil Government of Virginia: A Textbook for Schools Based upon the Constitution of 1902 and Conforming to the Laws Enacted in Accordance Therein* (New York and Chicago: Richardson, Smith, 1904); Royall B. Smithey, *Civil Government of Virginia* (New York and Cincinnati: American Book Company, 1904); and Howard L. McBain, *How We Are Governed in Virginia and the Nation* (Richmond: Bell Book and Stationery Co., 1908).

45 Key, *Southern Politics*, 553, 533.

46 In Virginia overall voter turnout fell by 54 percent from 1900 to 1904, according to Kousser. White voter turnout fell by 48 percent, while his calculations show that black turnout actually fell to nothing. The latter figure illustrates the unpredictability of Kousser's methods (Kousser, "Ecological Regression and the Analysis of Past Politics," *Journal of Interdisciplinary History* 4 [1973]:237–62; Kousser, *Shaping of Southern Politics*, 241).

47 Williamson's emphasis on white racism does address an omission in Kousser's interpretation, which does not explain the Democratic party's persistent interest in disfranchisement throughout the 1890s, a time when the party's growing strength precluded a viable opposition party (Williamson, *Rage for Order*, 152).

48 Kousser mistakenly assumed that all those who did not vote after disfran-

chisement could not. He himself conceded that figures alone could "never logically prove causation" (Kousser, *Shaping of Southern Politics*, 242). For a critique of Kousser's use of ecological regression estimation techniques, see Lee Benson, "The Mistransferance Fallacy in Explanations of Human Behavior," *Historical Methods* 17 (Summer 1984): 118–31, and Kousser's reply, "Must Historians Regress? An Answer to Benson," ibid., 19 (Spring 1986): 62–81.

49 Richmond *Times-Dispatch*, 6 Nov. 1905.

50 Ibid., 9 Nov. 1905; Norfolk *Virginian-Pilot*, 8 Nov. 1905. Determining an exact number of registered voters eligible for the elections immediately after disfranchisement is difficult, given the lack of accurate figures and the complexity of the registration procedure. McDanel, in *The Virginia Constitutional Convention of 1901–1902*, estimated, based on newspaper accounts, that 276,000 whites and 21,000 blacks were registered to vote. State records show that 254,000 paid their poll tax that year. To vote, Virginians had to both register and pay the tax. Because 297,000 registered and 254,000 paid the poll tax, total registration must have well exceeded 200,000. Using the conservative figure of 200,000, however, the 1905 gubernatorial vote of 43,000 represented a 21 percent turnout. Kousser's estimate of a 40 percent turnout for the 1904 presidential election in Virginia represents the percentage of the entire white male population who voted, not the percentage of registered voters who turned out. He did not examine the 1905 gubernatorial election (McDanel, *Virginia Constitutional Convention of 1901–1902*, 50–51; Kousser, *The Shaping of Southern Politics*, 226).

51 Richmond *Times-Dispatch*, 9, 8 Nov. 1905; Norfolk *Virginian-Pilot*, 21 Feb. 1905.

52 Richmond *Times-Dispatch*, 11 Nov. 1905.

53 Fredericksburg *Journal*, 11 Nov. 1905.

54 The analysis was conducted using content analysis, a systematic counting of units within a block of text. See Bernard Berelson, *Content Analysis in Communications Research* (New York: Hafner, 1971). Of a sample of fifteen Richmond papers picked randomly in a four-week period near the general elections of 1897 and 1905, the average number of political stories printed in 1897 was 14.6; that dropped to 8.1 for 1905. Only articles devoted to state and local politics were counted.

55 Kousser, *Shaping of Southern Politics*, 227.

56 See Lawrence L. Hartzell's chapter 6 above for more on black political participation, and Buni, *The Negro in Virginia Politics*, for a discussion of black politics after disfranchisement.

57 Richmond *Times-Dispatch*, 9 Nov. 1905.

58 Ibid.

59 Richmond *News-Leader*, 1 April 1924.

10

ANGIE PARROTT

"Love Makes Memory Eternal": The United Daughters of the Confederacy in Richmond, Virginia, 1897–1920

BETWEEN 2:00 AND 2:05 P.M. ON THE AFTERNOON OF Monday, 3 June 1907, trains throughout the South slowed to a halt, and the region's business and commerce stopped momentarily as people all across Dixie focused their attention on events in Richmond, Virginia. On that day, thousands of people flooded the city to witness the long-awaited unveiling of the monument to Jefferson Davis, the Confederacy's only president. An estimated 200,000 people were on hand for the festivities, which began with a magnificent parade of over 1,000 Confederate veterans dressed in gray. As one spectator later recalled, "it was the greatest parade I ever saw & which took an hour & a half to pass one point. From our standpoint it looked as if there were acres of people standing close together." After the parade Davis's only surviving daughter, Margaret Howell Hays, and her two young sons unveiled the statue "as the Richmond Howitzers boomed a presidential salute, fireworks and balloons bearing Confederate flags sailed skyward, a chorus and band rendered a rousing chorus of 'Dixie,' and thousands of spectators roared their approval."[1]

Perhaps the most enthusiastic spectators were Richmond's United Daughters of the Confederacy (UDC), whose hard work and undying enthusiasm had made the monument a reality. In 1896, after a much-celebrated design competition, a joint memorial association of Richmond civic leaders and the United Confederate Veterans announced plans for an elaborate marble structure costing an estimated $210,000. But three years later the association had collected only $20,000. Realizing their failure, the members of the all-male association reluctantly appealed to the Daughters of the Confederacy to take over the project, asking that they "assume the responsibility of erecting the monument, and relieve the obligation of the Veterans, as they found they had promised more than they could accomplish."[2]

Although some Daughters feared that such an undertaking was "too great for ladies to handle by themselves," the UDC answered the veterans' appeal with enthusiasm and soon doubled the amount collected by the memorial association. The women also adopted a more practical plan for the monument, costing an estimated $70,000, one-third the amount needed for the original design. Daughters all over the South raised money for the project by holding bazaars and fairs, selling buttons, calendars, and baked goods, and sponsoring picnics and dances. The Richmond chapter alone raised $5,960, more than any other chapter in the UDC, and by the spring of 1906 construction on the monument was underway. Succeeding where their male predecessors had failed, the Daughters of the Confederacy stood proud on the afternoon of 3 June 1907. As Governor Claude A. Swanson of Virginia reminded the crowd assembled at the unveiling, "this magnificent memorial is a gift from the United Daughters of the Confederacy, whose loyalty to the Confederate cause is ardent and lasting, and whose splendid qualities and patriotism are sufficient to stimulate and make great and glorious any people."[3]

By 1907 the people of the South had long been known for their unwavering loyalty to the Confederacy. Indeed, the fall of the Confederacy evoked greater unity among the former rebels than had the war itself. Black Southerners, of course, had very different opinions regarding the Civil War and its aftermath. But for most whites, defeat somehow rendered the Confederate cause even more noble, and in the decades following Appomattox the Confederacy began to assume legendary proportions. The myth of a just war heroically waged dominated the Southern mind, as the Confederate war effort became synonymous with self-sacrifice, unity, and valor. At the same time a related tradition, that of the idyllic Old South, also gained credence. Frustrated by the realities of life in the postwar era, white Southerners increasingly came to visualize the antebellum South as a land of grace and plenty, peopled by chivalric gentlemen, beautiful ladies, and happy, carefree slaves. A combination of these two myths, along with the attitudes and emotions they brought forth, gradually shaped the white South's interpretation of the Civil War; rather than forsaking the fallen Confederacy, white Southerners romanticized the Old South, glorifying its gallant heroes and idealizing the principles for which they fought. By the end of the nineteenth century, the Lost Cause had been resurrected, and the "Confederate celebration" was under way.[4]

The primary champions of the Lost Cause were the thousands of women who joined the United Daughters of the Confederacy. Formally organized 10 September 1894 in Nashville, Tennessee, the UDC united into one body the various Ladies Memorial Associations and Confederate women's groups that had sprung up throughout the South in the years since the war. Unlike male organizations such as the United Confederate Veterans (UCV) and the Sons of Confederate Veterans (SCV)—both of which suffered from shrinking membership totals and declining interest—the UDC had a wide popular appeal among Southern women and grew rapidly during its early years. In 1900, only six years after its formation, the UDC boasted roughly 17,000 members in 412 chapters, and by 1920 membership had climbed to well over 68,000. Women of Confederate descent organized chapters in almost every state of the Union and even in such remote points as Mexico City and Paris. Thus, by the turn of the century the task of keeping the Lost Cause alive came to rest in the delicate yet strong hands of the United Daughters of the Confederacy.[5]

Mourning and grieving for the dead had long been the responsibility of Southern women, and as the struggle for the Davis monument suggests, memorial work most often occupied the UDC during the organization's early years. Building upon the efforts of the various postwar memorial associations, UDC chapters across the region continued to express their sorrow by erecting monuments, both large and small, to commemorate the heroes of the Lost Cause. But unlike the earlier Confederate women's groups, which remained devoted almost exclusively to memorial work, the Daughters of the Confederacy boldly assumed a much broader purpose:

> The objects of this association are historical, educational, memorial, benevolent, and social: To fulfill the duties of sacred charity to the survivors of the war and those dependent upon them; to collect and preserve material for a truthful history of the war; to protect historic places of the Confederacy; to record the part taken by the Southern women in untiring efforts after the war in the reconstruction of the South, as well as in patient endurance of hardship and patriotic devotion during the struggle; to perpetuate the memory of our Confederate heroes and the glorious cause for which they fought; to cherish the ties of friendship among members of this Association; to endeavor to have used in all Southern schools only such histories as are just and true.[6]

While the many monuments built by the UDC became the group's most celebrated and visible achievements, it was the Daughters' many other endeavors that kept the Lost Cause truly alive. Comprised almost exclusively of women from the middle and upper classes—women commanding ready access to schools, newspapers, and legislative chambers—the

UDC exercised a powerful influence in the South, shaping public opinion for decades. In their enthusiastic and persistent efforts to glorify the antebellum South and immortalize the heroes of the Civil War, the Daughters not only preserved the memory of the Confederacy but also perpetuated the ideals of the past. Dedicated to the motto "Love Makes Memory Eternal," the United Daughters of the Confederacy functioned to ensure that the conservative traditions of the Old South would endure the progressive changes of the New South.[7]

Nowhere was the conflict between progress and tradition more keenly felt than in Richmond. The capital of the former Confederacy, Richmond was at the very center of the Confederate celebration. By 1920 the "Queen City of the Confederacy" supported several memorial and social organizations and boasted numerous Confederate monuments and memorials—including the famous Monument Avenue lined with statues of Lee, Davis, Jackson, and Stuart. Alongside these constant reminders of the past, though, appeared undeniable signs of change and prosperity, such as the nation's first electric streetcar system, installed in 1886. As one visitor to the city perceptively observed, these conflicting visions created a unique feeling of tension in Richmond: "standing there in the shadows of the classic old Capitol one has a stronger feeling of the blending of generations. This is the very heart of the Old South, and yet it is also the heart of a modern city. On every side rise tall buildings; the clang of traffic and the roar of business ring in the ears."[8]

The Old South flavor of Richmond was due in large part to the efforts of the city's United Daughters of the Confederacy. In the three and a half decades when the organization was at its height, the women of Richmond organized no less than six UDC chapters. Thousands of women from Richmond's leading families joined these chapters, making the UDC one of the city's most respected and visible women's groups. But unlike many of Richmond's other women's groups, which often used their influence to effect social change and implement progressive reforms, the Daughters of the Confederacy sought only to preserve the past: " 'The New South' is a term distasteful to us. We are not desirous of putting off the old and putting on the new, for we would prefer to believe that the old South shall never die, but shall endure for aye in our hearts and lives and institutions, and that its gentle spirit shall ever pervade and embrace our whole reunited country." Wholly dedicated to the traditions and ideals of the Lost Cause, Richmond's Daughters of the Confederacy worked to protect their city's past in an era of rapid change.[9]

In their efforts to keep the Lost Cause alive, the Daughters of the Confederacy early recognized the necessity and value of education. As one member explained, this aspect of their work was significant indeed: "In this day of public school education[,] a fair and just account of the war between the sovereign states must and shall be given to the rising generation and every women in our ranks has an influence to wield in the matter." Working through the local schools, both public and private, Richmond's Daughters of the Confederacy established a "proper" under-standing of the Old South and its struggle for independence. The chapters often began by adorning classrooms with visible reminders of the Con-federacy, such as battle flags, photographs, and busts of military heroes, with a particular emphasis on Virginia's veterans. In order to pique the students' interest in Southern history, the Daughters frequently spon-sored essay contests, with cash prizes, on topics such as the "Confed-erate Navy," "Jefferson Davis," and "The Priorities of Virginia." They also contributed liberally to school libraries, presenting subscriptions to the *Confederate Veteran* and other popular periodicals and copies of ap-proved histories such as the popular *Women of the South in War Times*. Finally, the Richmond chapters of the UDC sponsored various lectures and presentations at local schools, heard by thousands of students annu-ally.[10]

In all of these activities the UDC endeavored to present the "true" story of the Civil War. Like most white Southerners during this period, Richmond's Daughters of the Confederacy held that the war of 1861–65 was not a "Civil War" at all but a "War Between the States," wholly ini-tiated by the North and fought over purely constitutional issues. In pam-phlets, textbooks, and lectures, the UDC sought to convince students that secession was just and that to "say or teach, that slavery was the cause of the Civil War, with its assumption of superior moral status on the one side and obstinate turpitude on the other, indicates a failure to grasp fun-damental facts of American history. It is a singular misrepresentation to make it appear that emancipation, an incidental outcome of the armed conflict, was the principal point in contention either during the war or in the decades before it." The true cause of the war, according to the UDC, was not slavery but the "disregard, on the part of the States of the North, for the rights of the Southern or slave-holding states."[11]

The Daughters were also quick to defend the valor of the Confederacy, claiming that the South lost the war not because it lacked sufficient will or military ability but because it possessed fewer troops and inadequate supplies. "There is no record in all the world's history," read one widely distributed pamphlet, "of any army that endured more privations with greater fortitude, or fought more bravely than the soldiers of the Confed-eracy. . . . Not only did the Confederates have greatly inferior numbers, but they were poorly armed, often scarce of ammunition, and scantily fed and clothed." In white classrooms all over the city, Richmond's Daughters of the Confederacy sought to inculcate the traditions and ideals of the Old South by persuading schoolchildren that their fathers and grandfathers had been neither traitors nor cowards but had fought valiantly for a just cause.[12]

The subject of slavery was also a major educational concern for the Daughters of the Confederacy. Like a substantial majority of white Southerners during this period, they still felt the need to defend the region's "peculiar institution." As one Daughter explained, the UDC had a unique and urgent responsibility in this regard:

> We have amongst us some who can tell us from their own experiences what the institution of slavery was, and what it meant to them and to the negroes under their control. In those days we never thought of calling them slaves. That is a word that crept in with the abolition crusade. They were our people, our negroes, part of our very homes. There are men and women still living who know these facts and who can give them to us, but they are fast passing away, just as are the men and women who lived during the War Between the States.

In Virginia, the mother of slavery, the urge to justify the system was particularly intense. In their work Richmond's Daughters assured children that their ancestors had actually been opposed to slavery, that "the colonies of Virginia and Georgia had strongly opposed its first introduction, but after the Constitution of the United States had recognized the slaves as property and the wealth of the South was largely invested in negroes, they did not feel it was just to submit to wholesale robbery." Even more important, especially in the minds of former slaveholders and their descendants, they sought to discredit abolitionists' accounts of cruelty to slaves and to convince students that masters had treated slaves "with great kindness and care in nearly all cases, a cruel master being rare, and one who lost the respect of his neighbors if he treated his slaves badly. Self-interest would have prompted good treatment if a higher feeling of humanity had not." In return, the Daughters claimed, slaves were "faithful and devoted and were always ready and willing to serve" their masters.[13]

While the classroom was their primary educational focus, the Daughters of the Confederacy also reached many white school-age children by forming auxiliary chapters. Recognizing that "the perpetuity of their own organization depended upon enlisting the active interest of the boys and girls of Confederate descent," each of Richmond's UDC chapters organized a Children of the Confederacy group. The youngsters who joined these auxiliaries, most of whom were girls, were sure to receive a "proper" education, participating in UDC educational activities both in and out of the classroom. Led by their own junior historians, the Children of the Confederacy studied a variety of topics, including "Negro Folk Tales," "Secession and the Result," and "Heroes of the Confederate Navy." Upon adulthood, the boys and girls who belonged to these auxiliary groups usually joined either the SCV or the UDC, making devotion to the Lost Cause a lifelong affair. Through these junior chapters, the UDC was able to educate white children "properly," while at the same time providing for its own institutional perpetuation.[14]

Finally, the UDC's interest in education extended well beyond instruction for youngsters. Beginning in 1910, the national and state organizations established a number of scholarships at various colleges and universities for the descendants—both male and female—of Confederate veterans. Richmond's UDC chapters donated liberally to these scholarship funds, helping to fulfill the educational goals of numerous young women and men at normal schools, small colleges, and professional schools. In addition to these contributions, many individual chapters also instituted their own scholarships. For example, Lee Chapter endowed a scholarship fund at Stonewall Jackson's alma mater, Virginia Military Institute, and upon the death of its founding president, Mrs. Norman V. (Janet) Randolph, Richmond Chapter established a generous scholarship in her name at the College of William and Mary. Stonewall Jackson Chapter provided aspiring students with yet another source of financial assistance with the establishment of the Jennie Gunn Ball Student Loan Fund.[15]

In "this day of public school education," Richmond's United Daughters of the Confederacy exerted a powerful influence in the city's educational system, effectively controlling the educational experiences of thousands of children. In the minds of even the most inattentive of schoolboys, the constant stream of UDC-sponsored essay contests, library books, pictures, and lectures re-created the grand civilization of the Old South and the courageous principles of the Confederacy. For those few lucky enough to receive UDC scholarships and for the hundreds who joined the Children of the Confederacy, the impact of the UDC's proSouth propaganda was even greater. On every level, though, the effect was the same; the educational work of the UDC allowed the Daughters to shape interpretations of the Southern past, carefully deleting any unpleasantness and forever embellishing any virtues.[16]

While educational work occupied much of their time and energy, the

Daughters of the Confederacy also functioned far beyond the walls of the schools. Waging the battle for "true" history, the Daughters extended their influence well into the public arena, seeking to establish a "proper" understanding of the Confederacy on a grand scale. As one member explained, the need for the UDC's historical work grew more pressing each day:

> Friends, we are making and preserving history, saving the records of forty years ago, and the night cometh when no man can work. Each year that passes makes our task more difficult. One by one our noted statesmen and warriors, eye witnesses and participants in our gallant fight pass from us into the silence beyond. Let every daughter help her Chapter Historian, let her collect authentic anecdotes from fathers and mothers, who lived and worked and suffered and died for the Confederacy. Let each daughter keep her eyes on the newspapers of the country to collect information and data. To the future historians such records would be a mine of untold treasure.

Encouraged by their chapter historians, Richmond's Daughters confirmed and preserved Confederate records, collected memoirs and reminiscences, donated relics to the Confederate Museum, compiled scrapbooks full of various memorabilia, and wrote and distributed historical essays and pamphlets. The chapters also devoted a portion of each meeting to historical study, as outlined by the UDC Year Book. Written and distributed by the national and state historians, these booklets provided chapters with suggested topics for study. Typical suggestions included: "Religion in the Army," "Songs of the Sixties," and the ever-popular "Stories of Faithful Slaves." In addition to these monthly programs, the chapters also held "historical evenings," dedicated to the discussion of Southern history and often attended by members of the community.[17]

Most importantly, the UDC monitored popular interpretations of the Civil War. Inspired by the motto "Loyalty to the Truth of Confederate History," the Daughters had four main goals in this regard: "do not let anyone, individual or newspaper say 'Civil War' without correcting it to 'War Between the States,' refer to Confederates as 'rebels,' endorse any book or legislative measure without full knowledge, [or] neglect the work in our schools." Richmond's chapters of the UDC enthusiastically set out to accomplish these goals. In books, newspapers, pamphlets, and lectures, the Daughters kept the Lost Cause alive by effectively subduing its critics. As a former commander of the Grand Army of the Republic warned his comrades, these efforts proved remarkably successful: "you must stand ever ready to combat the baleful influence of that other group of women, the Daughters of the Southern Confederacy. . . . I have had ample opportunity to see the workings of this influence and it is one that we must guard against. There are still those that believe that the Stars and Bars stood for something pure and noble."[18]

The heated controversy over the infamous "Boyson essay" best demonstrates the goals, methods, and impact of the Daughters' historical agenda. As a part of its work, the UDC frequently sponsored essay contests on a variety of topics. In 1908 a group of eminent Southern historians judged a UDC competition at Columbia Teacher's College for the best essay on the "South's Part in the War Between the States." In this contest, the judges awarded the $100 cash prize to Christine Boyson, a native of Minnesota. The Daughters of the Confederacy, however, were outraged by the judges' choice. Openly contradicting the UDC's idyllic vision of the past, Boyson portrayed the Old South as "backward," maintaining that "intellectually, the [antebellum] South was practically dead. Most of her people were densely ignorant." Even more outrageous, Boyson charged that Virginia's beloved General Lee was a "traitor," in that he aided "the enemies of his own country." The Richmond chapters of the UDC led the loud and angry public protest raised against the committee's choice, praising the intellectual vitality of the Old South and defending the honor of General Lee. The white Southern public agreed, and the Daughters finally gained a formal, albeit reluctant, apology from the judges.[19]

In their battle for "true" history, the UDC wielded a powerful influence. And as their reaction to the Boyson essay shows, they were not above bending history and even historians to their animating purpose— keeping the memory of the Confederacy alive. While most white Southerners of the period viewed the Lost Cause as just, the women who joined the UDC proved particularly virulent in their devotion to the Confederacy. The Spanish-American War successfully reconciled most Southern men to the Union, but the white women of Dixie long remained noted for their enduring sectionalism. As one male commentator observed proudly, "our noble women, who are not going to be 'reconstructed,' maintain undying devotion to Dixie, and its sad yet glorious memories." Richmond's Daughters of the Confederacy were certainly no exception. For years the city's UDC chapters persistently petitioned the General Assembly to abolish the legal observation of Lincoln's birthday, and Richmond's Daughters were among the most vocal opponents of the proposed reunion (endorsed by the UCV) of Union and Confederate forces at Appomattox. Even death, it seems, could not weaken the Daughters' devotion to the Lost Cause: Richmond Chapter unanimously resolved that "a small silk Confederate flag be placed in the hand of each daughter carried from us into death." With such steadfast loyalty and unwavering commitment, the UDC not only protected but also redefined the Southern past.[20]

Despite the Daughters' social prominence and institutional success, the UDC was only one of many women's organizations active during this period. Indeed, the dawn of the New South saw a dramatic increase in female activism, as women all across Dixie banded together in a variety of organizations, seeking to effect social change. In Richmond groups such as the Young Women's Christian Association (YWCA), the Women's Christian Temperance Union (WCTU), the Instructive Nurses Visiting Association (INVA), and several women's clubs and church circles embraced a wide variety of progressive social reforms, virtually transforming society. While the city's Daughters of the Confederacy were certainly among this new class of female civic leaders, they usually employed their exalted position for far more conservative purposes. Eschewing social activism and opposing many progressive reforms, the UDC struggled to preserve the traditions of the Old South in a rapidly changing new century.[21]

Chief among these activities was the benevolent work of the UDC. Following the Civil War, thousands of Confederate veterans were left homeless, penniless, and physically disabled. Time and time again, the UDC stepped in to provide both financial and emotional support for these aging heroes and their dependents. Working through the city's Soldiers' Home and Home for Needy Confederate Women, Richmond's UDC chapters were especially active in this regard, donating much of their time and energy, along with a large part of their annual expenditures, to relief efforts. The chapters also shared their generosity with worthy recipients throughout the South and occasionally provided relief for deserving non-Confederates. Somewhat ironically, even a few of Richmond's black citizens benefited from the benevolence of the UDC. Inspired by their own stories of faithful slaves, Lee Chapter members, for example, "upon discovering that a number of 'war-time mammies' were in the City Home . . . decided to look after them and help them."[22]

For countless veterans and their dependents the benevolent work of the UDC met very real and pressing needs. But in comparison with the relief work undertaken by other women's groups, the UDC's efforts seem meager at best. Carefully gauging their generosity according to the "worthiness" of the recipient and doing little to address the actual causes of poverty, Richmond's Daughters of the Confederacy virtually ignored most of the city's ever-expanding needy population. Fortunately, organizations such as the WCTU, the YWCA, and the various women's clubs and church circles provided desperately needed aid to thousands of Richmonders. Even more important, with the emergence of the social welfare movement, many of Richmond's female civic leaders began working to ameliorate the circumstances that bred poverty in the first place. The INVA, for example, advocated health reform as a means to end poverty, offering free classes in home nursing and family hygiene, while the YWCA promoted job training and gainful employment. Dedicated to abolishing poverty, rather than merely abating its effects, these and numerous other women's groups made a vast difference in the lives of countless Richmonders. But fixated on the antebellum era, the Daughters of the Confederacy continued a tradition of benevolence clearly at odds with realities of life in the New South.[23]

While the Daughters of the Confederacy shunned most progressive measures, they did occasionally aid in reform efforts. Many of Richmond's Daughters, it seems, were particularly interested in education, and not merely as another arena for UDC propaganda. In 1913, for example, the city's UDC chapters came out in full and active support of a statewide movement for coeducation at the University of Virginia, joining the Virginia Division in heartily endorsing a "co-ordinate college for women, in the environs of the University of Virginia . . . so connected with the University academically, as to be able to use its teaching staff, library, and laboratories." Although this campaign ultimately failed, the Daughters also engaged in other, less futile efforts. Even Richmond Chapter, widely known for its avoidance of non-Confederate activity, had a soft spot for education. On several occasions, the chapter was remarkably receptive to financial appeals from groups such as the Industrial League of the South and the Southern Woman's Alliance Association, making generous donations without the usual debate on the appropriateness of the endeavor or any regard to the genealogy of the recipient.[24]

Despite their active interest in education, Richmond's Daughters of the Confederacy hardly distinguished themselves as leaders in the city's growing educational reform movement. The Richmond Education Association formally inaugurated this crusade by implementing a variety of reforms, such as much-needed renovations to the city's dilapidated public high school and a vastly improved curriculum. Other women's groups soon joined in, virtually transforming the Richmond educational system. The WCTU, in its battle to abolish the consumption of alcoholic beverages, naturally placed heavy emphasis on education. As early as 1887, that organization campaigned for mandatory "Scientific Temperance Education" in public schools, and by 1892 compulsory education for all children under fourteen years of age had been added to their re-form agenda. Richmond's branches of the YWCA were actively involved in yet another aspect of reform—adult education. The YWCA offered a variety of extended education classes to the city's young working women, including instruction in cooking, sewing, recreation, and Bible study. In later years, the YWCA even offered courses in sex education and began discreetly distributing birth control devices to its members. The UDC, of course, either avoided or openly opposed all these progressive reforms.[25]

While the benevolent and "reform" activities of the UDC certainly provide ample evidence of the Daughters' conservatism, nowhere is their perspective more readily apparent than in the group's stance on the most pressing woman's issue of the late nineteenth and early twentieth centuries—woman suffrage. Some Northern women worked for the vote well before the Civil War, but because the reform was so closely associated with abolitionism, the idea of woman suffrage was anathema in the antebellum South. It was not until the turn of the century, with the rise of female activism and an increase in female employment, that the Southern suffrage movement gained real strength. As the capital of Virginia, Richmond soon became a battleground for the state movement, and suffrage leaders found ready and enthusiastic support among the city's many women's groups. The WCTU, the YWCA, the various woman's clubs, and even a few church circles joined in the fight for the vote. But the suffrage movement also met with determined resistance. Despite many changes in the status of Southern women, traditional ideals of womanhood remained firmly in place, and many Southerners, male and female alike, felt women neither needed nor wanted the vote. Troubled Southern race relations made the issue even more volatile, as antisuffragists charged that giving the vote to all women would increase the political power of Southern blacks.[26]

Predictably, the UDC rejected the idea of woman suffrage during the early years of the movement. While the Daughters certainly enjoyed the social freedoms that accompanied the rise of the New South, they were staunchly opposed to giving women the vote. Instead, UDC leaders advocated the use of more conservative methods, reminding members that the domestic sphere was still woman's most powerful area of influence: "If there is a power that is placed in any hands, it is the power that is placed in the hands of the Southern woman in her home. That power is great enough to direct legislative bodies—and that, too, without demanding the ballot." Of even greater concern to the UDC was the effect woman suffrage might have on the Southern way of life. As one Daughter heatedly explained at the 1911 national convention, giving women the vote could only result in a breakdown of society: "No daughter of the Confederacy will be a suffragette. No veteran will permit female Negro suffrage—if it brings on another war. For when the cook comes to the meeting and puts on her bonnet quick, and goes to the polls and votes for Dr. Booker T. Washington as President of the United States, or says 'you gets you another cook,' the women will be in the saddle with sabre and pistol galore." [27]

Despite the UDC's strong opposition, the suffrage movement continued to gain strength and respectability throughout the South. Many women who had once been opposed to woman suffrage gradually came to support the idea, and a growing number of women's organizations placed increased pressure on the various state legislatures. Many Daughters of the Confederacy may have been among those who eventually joined the movement. In towns and states throughout the South, UDC members could later be found actively campaigning for woman suffrage. Even so, neither the national nor any of the state organizations ever came out in open support of the measure. Moreover, a substantial number of UDC members, many of them high-ranking officers, continued to oppose suffrage. Thus, while it is impossible to evaluate fully the Daughters' position on woman suffrage, it is clear that the UDC felt it best to maintain the stance it took on most progressive issues—avoidance. Even in an era which saw sweeping changes in the lives of American women, the United Daughters of the Confederacy clung to the traditions of the past. [28]

On the morning of 3 June 1988 a small crowd, dressed in faded Confederate gray and worn antebellum hoopskirts, gathered dutifully around the Jefferson Davis statue on Richmond's Monument Avenue, waiting for the annual Massing of the Flags ceremony to begin. After a brief prayer and a rendition of the "Star Spangled Banner," the ceremony commenced, and these Sons and Daughters of the Confederacy solemnly set about assembling and raising the flags of the former Confederate states. With the flags in place, the winsome Children of the Confederacy then led a heartfelt salute to the Stars and Bars: "I salute the Confederate flag with affection, reverence, and undying remembrance," followed by a duet of the always popular "Bonnie Blue Flag." After an inspiring speech on the life of Jefferson Davis delivered by a former commander of the SCV and a rousing chorus of "Dixie," the flags were retired and the crowd slowly began to disperse. [29]

While the crowds are much smaller and the ceremony less spectacular than those of 3 June 1907, the Massing of the Flags Ceremony, held annually since 1965, has become a tradition in Richmond, a gentle reminder that in some hearts and minds the Lost Cause still lingers on. And even though many Richmonders of today may care little about Davis, or the Civil War for that matter, few can escape the constant reminders of their city's history. The monuments built by the UDC and UCV still stand proud, and Virginia's tourism industry thrives on attractions such as the Museum of the Confederacy and the various battlefields surrounding the city. Finally, though decidedly smaller than at the turn of the century, the major Confederate organizations, including the UDC, the SCV, and the Children of the Confederacy, are still active in Richmond today, carrying on their work in parades, memorial ceremonies, and chapter meetings.[30]

The credit for much of this interest in the Old South belongs to the city's United Daughters of the Confederacy. During the early years of this century, when the organization was at its height, Richmond's six UDC chapters were among the most active and influential women's groups in the city. Through its memorial, educational, historical, benevolent, and social activities, the UDC sought to preserve what it saw as the city's most valuable asset—its Confederate past. In parks and cemeteries, classrooms and lecture halls, books and newspapers, even veterans' homes and poor houses, the Daughters of the Confederacy worked to sustain the Confederate celebration.

While this celebration inevitably waned, the legacy of the Daughters' work endured. Constantly bombarded with the UDC's pro-South propaganda and idealized interpretations of the past, the vast majority of white Southerners refused to question the prevailing social or racial order well into the twentieth century. Rather, the region's many inequalities—white supremacy, racial segregation, and extreme poverty—seemed just, even necessary. Moreover, as one Union veteran cautioned his comrades, the Daughters' influence may have reached well beyond the Mason-Dixon line, affecting the nation as a whole: "I warn you that they are busy everywhere spreading their propaganda. Even in Washington they are active." The UDC, so efficient in promulgating a pro-South perspective, insulated generations of white Southerners, of white Americans even, from both the realities of the past and the obligations of the present. Not only in Richmond, Virginia, but throughout the South and across the country, the United Daughters of the Confederacy functioned to ensure that despite the fall of the Confederacy, the Old South would never truly die.[31]

NOTES

Several people helped to bring this chapter to fruition. I would like to thank Professor Cindy Aron of the University of Virginia for her guidance, patience, and wisdom while directing my master's thesis. Professor Edward Ayers, also of the University of Virginia, proved to be not only an inspiring teacher but also a skillful and careful editor. As coeditor, John Willis provided ready support and valuable insight. I also received assistance from the many librarians and archivists I encountered while doing my research. Guy Swanson, Archivist and Curator of Manuscripts at the Museum of the Confederacy, was especially helpful in my search through the museum's uncatalogued UDC materials. Mrs. Richard Wetzel, Librarian at the UDC's Caroline Meriwether Goodlett Library, provided valuable information about Richmond's UDC chapters. Finally, I would like to thank my fellow graduate students, parents, and friends for their support and encouragement.

1   "An Account Written by Mrs. Moffett in the Back of a Book of Confederate War Songs," p. 1, in Jefferson Davis Monument Vertical File, Valentine Museum, Richmond (VM). For the history of the Davis monument, see John H. Moore, "The Jefferson Davis Monument," *Virginia Cavalcade* 10 (Spring 1961): 29–34, and Jefferson Davis Memorial Association, *Souvenir Book of the Jefferson Davis Memorial Association and the Unveiling of the Monument, Richmond, Virginia, June 3, 1907*, arranged by Alice M. Tyler (Richmond: Whittet and Shepperson, 1907), Virginia State Library and Archives, Richmond (VSL).

2   *Minutes of the 6th Annual Convention UDC* (1899), 65.

3   Unidentified newspaper clipping in Jefferson Davis Monument Vertical File, VM; speech by Governor Swanson quoted in Moore, "Jefferson Davis Monument," 34.

4   Southern images of the Civil War underwent several changes in the postwar era, beginning with bitterness and finger-pointing in the 1860s and 1870s and gradually moving by the 1890s toward a view of the Confederacy at once stoic and sentimental. Many historians have studied the development and nature of these attitudes. Gaines M. Foster, *Ghosts of the Confederacy: Defeat, the Lost Cause, and the Emergence of the New South* (New York: Oxford Univ. Press, 1987), has suggested that the Lost Cause was primarily a cultural movement, easing social tensions in the late nineteenth-century South. Barbara L. Bellows and Thomas L. Connelly, *God and General Longstreet: The Lost Cause and the Southern Mind* (Baton Rouge: Louisiana State Univ. Press, 1982), and Charles R. Wilson, *Baptized in Blood: The Religion of the Lost Cause 1865–1920* (Athens: Univ. of Georgia Press, 1980), have emphasized the religious nature of the Lost Cause and argued that it served as a "civil religion" for Southerners. Roland G. Osterweis, *The Myth of the Lost Cause, 1865–1900* (Hamden, Conn.: Archon, 1973), also emphasized the religious nature of the Lost Cause but placed it in the larger context of postwar Southern Romanticism. Susan S. Durant, "The Gently Furled Banner: The Development of the Myth of the Lost Cause" (Ph.D. diss., Univ. of North Carolina, 1972), suggested that the Lost Cause served as a psychological salve for the defeated white South.

The terms "Lost Cause" and "Confederate celebration," the latter of which was coined by Foster, are used here interchangeably to refer to the postwar interest of white Southerners in the Confederacy and the antebellum South.

5   According to the UDC Constitution, women eligible for membership included the "widows, wives, mothers, sisters, nieces, and lineal descendants

of such men as served honorably in the Confederate Army, Navy, Civil Service, or of those men unfit for active duty who loyally gave aid to the cause; also women and their direct descendants, wherever living, who can give proof of personal service and loyal aid to the South during the war." Information regarding the origin and history of the UDC is in Mary B. Poppenheim et al., *The History of the United Daughters of the Confederacy* (Raleigh, N.C.: Edwards & Broughton, 1925), 1–18. For trends in UDC membership, see Margaret N. Price, "The Development of Leadership by Southern Women through Clubs and Organizations" (M.A. thesis, Univ. of North Carolina, 1945), 83. On the importance of the UDC in the Lost Cause, see Osterweis, *Myth of the Lost Cause*, 92–93; John C. Ruoff, "Southern Womanhood, 1865–1920: An Intellectual and Cultural Study" (Ph.D. diss., Univ. of Illinois, 1976), 95, 98–99; Wilson, *Baptized in Blood*, 25–26, 32–33.

6 Constitution of the United Daughters of the Confederacy, 1903, VSL. On the traditional role of Southern women as mourners, see Patricia R. Loughridge and Edward D. C. Campbell, "Life after Death: Mourning in the Old South and the Confederacy," *Women in Mourning* (Richmond: Museum of the Confederacy, 1984). On the role of women in postwar memorial work, see Foster, *Ghosts of the Confederacy*, 37–39; Mrs. Anne Bachman Hyde, "United Daughters of the Confederacy," *Confederate Veteran* 13 (Jan. 1915): 15. For information on individual memorial associations, see Confederated Southern Memorial Association, *History of the Confederated Memorial Associations of the South* (New Orleans: Graham, 1904).

7 On the influence of the UDC, see Price, "Development of Leadership," 86–89. While many historians of the South briefly mention the UDC in their work, no thorough study of the organization exists. Foster, *Ghosts of the Confederacy*; Price, "Development of Leadership"; and Ruoff, "Southern Womanhood," offer the best information on the UDC. Patricia Fay Climer, "Protectors of the Past: The United Daughters of the Confederacy, Tennessee Division, and the Lost Cause" (M.A. thesis, Vanderbilt Univ., 1973), focuses on the work of the Tennessee UDC but does little to evaluate the larger function of the UDC. On the exclusive nature of the UDC, see Foster, *Ghosts of the Confederacy*, 171; Ruoff, "Southern Womanhood," 100; Price, "Development of Leadership," 60; Durant, "Gently Furled Banner," 161.

8 Garnett Askew, quoted in Christopher Silver, *Twentieth-Century Richmond: Planning, Politics, and Race* (Knoxville: Univ. of Tennessee Press, 1984), pp. 17–18. On Confederate monuments and organizations in Richmond, see Wilson, *Baptized in Blood*, 18–19. Michael B. Chesson, *Richmond after the War, 1865–1890* (Richmond: Virginia State Library, 1981), 171–72, and passim, argued that rather than moving into the New South, the people of Richmond lingered instead in the past, making Richmond the "old city of the New South." Christopher Silver showed that Richmond did experience notable growth in the late nineteenth and early twentieth centuries and argued that many Richmonders were firmly committed to the New South vision of progress, but a lack of "public commitment to underwrite the costs of expansion" hampered any progress in this regard (Silver, *Twentieth-Century Richmond*, pp. 17–52).

Several historians have dealt with the complex relationship between the New South and the rise of the Lost Cause. Paul M. Gaston, *The New South Creed: A Study in Southern Mythmaking* (New York: Knopf, 1970), and

C. Vann Woodward, *Origins of the New South, 1877–1913* (Baton Rouge: Louisiana State Univ. Press, 1951), showed that the Lost Cause was very much a product of the New South and was often used by New South leaders to support their programs. Jonathan Wiener, *Social Origins of the New South: Alabama, 1860–1885* (Baton Rouge: Louisiana State Univ. Press, 1978), argued that the popularity of the Lost Cause is evidence of the postwar persistence of the antebellum planter class and indicates a weakness in the New South rhetoric. Durant, "Gently Furled Banner," 178–79, pointed out that the popularity of the Lost Cause was possible only with the prosperity of the New South.

9   Historical Records of the UDC, vol. 6, Eleanor S. Brockenbrough Memorial Library, The Museum of the Confederacy, Richmond (EBML). Drawing on the success of organizations such as the Hollywood Memorial Association and the Confederate Memorial Literary Society, Richmond women formed six UDC chapters between 1897 and 1930: Richmond Chapter (11 Nov. 1897), Chesterfield Chapter (22 Oct. 1904), Lee Chapter (28 Oct. 1911), Stonewall Jackson Chapter (20 Jan. 1920), Elliott Grays Chapter (21 July 1925), and Janet Randolph Chapter (16 May 1927). Like the national organization, the Richmond UDC enjoyed its greatest popularity between 1913 and 1921, with an average membership of 1,843 per year. Participation peaked in 1918, with 2,053 Daughters citywide, and then slowly began to decline, dropping to 1,365 by 1930. Histories of each of these chapters were recorded in 1937 and are in Virginia Historical Society, Richmond (VHS); see Mrs. B. A. Blenner, "Origin of Richmond Chapter, UDC"; Mrs. J. M. Hillsman and Mrs. Thomas J. Starke, "History of the Stonewall Jackson Chapter UDC"; Alice Whitley Jones and Catherine Temple Lynch, "A Brief History of the Janet Randolph Chapter UDC"; "History of the Elliott Grays Chapter No. 177 Virginia Division UDC"; "The History and Some of the Highlights in the Administrations of the Presidents of Lee Chapter UDC." While complete membership lists for all of these chapters are unavailable, evidence from Richmond Chapter suggests that the UDC drew a significant portion of its membership from Richmond's elite; see Richmond Chapter UDC Treasurer's Roll and Minute Book, 1919–21, EBML.

10 *Minutes of the 6th Annual Convention Virginia Division UDC*, 1900, 12–13. On UDC educational work, see Poppenheim, *History of the UDC*, 95–127, and Osterweis, *Myth of the Lost Cause*, 111–17. Information on educational activities of the various chapters is in individual chapter reports in *Minutes of the Annual Convention Virginia Division UDC*, 1897–1930.

11 Matthew Page Andrews, *The Women of the South in War Times* (Baltimore: Norman Remington, 1920), 15; Jefferson Davis Chapter UDC, Galveston, Tex., *UDC Catechism for Children* (1904), VSL, p. 1, a pamphlet which was reprinted by a Staunton, Virginia, chapter of the UDC and widely distributed to schoolchildren all over Virginia.

12 *UDC Catechism for Children*, p. 10.

13 Historical Records of the UDC, vol. 2, EBML; *UDC Catechism for Children*, p. 4. Foster, *Ghosts of the Confederacy*, 140, 156–57, 190, has suggested that the UDC's interpretation of slavery supported Southern racial orthodoxy of the period and that overt references to white supremacy were rare in the group's activities, as a more paternalistic attitude was adopted. For other perspectives on Virginia slavery, see chapter 2 by John Willis and chapter 5 by Gregg Michel above.

14 On the Children of the Confederacy, see Poppenheim, *History of the UDC*, 181–89. Each of the Richmond UDC chapters formed junior auxiliaries: Lee Junior Chapter (1912), Richmond Chapter Grandchildren of the Confederacy (1912), Chesterfield Junior Chapter (1912), Stonewall Jackson Chapter Children of the Confederacy (1926), Manchester Chapter Children of the Confederacy (1932), auxiliary to Elliott Grays Chapter UDC. In 1927 Richmond Chapter formed another auxiliary, the Richmond Junior Chapter, which later became Janet Randolph Chapter. Information on the activities of the various Children of the Confederacy chapters is in individual chapter reports in *Minutes of the Annual Convention Virginia Division UDC*, 1912–30.

15 For information on the UDC's efforts to promote higher education, including a breakdown of financial assistance offered, see Price, "Development of Leadership," 74–77.

16 The UCV and the SCV were also active in educational work. In 1892 the UCV established a committee to review textbooks, and the SCV organized a similar committee in 1898. Herman Hattaway, "Clio's Southern Soldiers: The United Confederate Veterans and History," *Louisiana History* 12 (Summer 1971): 227, 235, has shown that Virginia's veterans were especially active in this regard. Even so, educational work was primarily the responsibility of women.

17 Speech by Mrs. Anna M. D. Yeatman, *Minutes of the 6th Annual Convention Virginia Division UDC*, 1900, p. 12. On UDC historical work, see Foster, *Ghosts of the Confederacy*, 116–26; Poppenheim, *History of the UDC*, 135–41; Price, "Development of Leadership," 77–79. Information on historical activities of the various chapters is in individual chapter reports, *Minutes of the Annual Convention Virginia Division UDC*, 1897–1930; "Historical Year Book, 1917–1918," UDC Vertical File, Caroline Meriwether Goodlet Library, Memorial Building to the Women of the Confederacy, Richmond (CMGL). For the program of a typical historical evening, see Mrs. J. Enders Robinson, "Three Papers Written for and Read on the Third Historical Evening" (1911), VSL.

18 "Virginia Division UDC Historical Year Book, 1927–1928," p. 2, EBML; "GAR Speaker Hits Confederacy Group," unidentified newspaper clipping in UDC Vertical File, CMGL. Davies, *Patriotism on Parade*, 262–66, has shown that the GAR and other Union groups actively protested against the Lost Cause and its pro-South propaganda. Hattaway, "Clio's Southern Soldiers," 236, argued that in comparison to other Confederate groups, the UDC was much more devoted and much less subjective in its historical work.

19 Morgan P. Robinson, "Concerning the Boyson Essay and Its Defence," in *Historical Records of the UDC*, vol. 4, EBML. On the controversy surrounding the Boyson essay, see Foster, *Ghosts of the Confederacy*, 186–88; *Minutes of the 17th Annual Convention Virginia Division UDC*, 1909, 29–31.

20 Editorial, "The Spanish War and Dixie," *Confederate Veteran* 6 (Nov. 1898): 512; Minutes of Richmond Chapter UDC, 14 April 1915, 12 Sept. 1923, EBML. On the intense sectionalism of Southern women, see Davies, *Patriotism on Parade*, 41, 265–66; Foster, *Ghosts of the Confederacy*, 172; Ruoff, "Southern Womanhood," 85–88.

21 On the rise of female activism in the South, see Price, "Development of Leadership"; Anne F. Scott, *The Southern Lady: From Pedestal to Politics*,

1830–1930 (Chicago: Univ. of Chicago Press, 1970), 186–201. On Virginia women in particular, see Suzanne Lebsock, *"A Share of Honour": Virginia Women, 1600–1945* (Richmond: Virginia State Library, 1987), 105–25.

22 *Minutes of the 27th Annual Convention Virginia Division UDC*, 1923, p. 182. On UDC relief work, see Poppenheim, *History of the UDC*, 189–210; information on benevolent work of the various chapters is in individual chapter reports in *Minutes of the Annual Convention Virginia Division UDC*, 1897–1930.

23 On Southern women in the social welfare movement, see Dewey Grantham, *Southern Progressivism: The Reconciliation of Progress and Tradition* (Knoxville: Univ. of Tennessee Press, 1983), 200–17; on Virginia women in the movement, see Lebsock, *A Share of Honor*, 105–18.

24 *Minutes of the 18th Annual Convention Virginia Division UDC*, 1913, p. 25; Minutes of Richmond Chapter UDC, EBML. On the Coordinate College League, see Anne Hobson Freeman, "Mary Munford's Fight for a College for Women Co-ordinate with the University of Virginia," *Virginia Magazine of History and Biography* 78 (Oct. 1970): 481–91. The interest of the UDC in educational reform was not as far removed from traditional practice as one might think; Catherine Clinton, *The Plantation Mistress: Woman's World in the Old South* (New York: Pantheon, 1982), 123–38, has shown that antebellum women of the planter class had a keen interest in education.

25 Progressive women's groups such as the WCTU often campaigned for a wide variety of reform measures; see, for example, Anastasia Sims, " 'The Sword of the Spirit': The WCTU and Moral Reform in North Carolina, 1883–1933," *North Carolina Historical Review* 64 (Oct. 1987): 394–415. On the Richmond Education Association, see T. J. Jackson Lears, "Patricians Close Ranks: Richmond on the Eve of the Twentieth Century" (M.A. thesis, Univ. of North Carolina, 1972), 37–40; Lebsock, *A Share of Honour*, 115. On the Richmond WCTU, see Mrs. Howard M. Hoge, "History of the Virginia Women's Christian Temperance Union" (1937), VHS. On the Richmond YWCA, see Naomi C. Chappel and Ellen V. Gilchrist, "History of Richmond YWCA" (1937), VHS; Lebsock, *A Share of Honour*, 113, 130.

26 On the origins of the Southern woman suffrage movement and the tensions unique to it, see Grantham, *Southern Progressivism*, 209–17; Scott, *Southern Lady*, 165–84; Aileen S. Kraditor, *The Ideas of the Woman Suffrage Movement* (New York: Norton, 1981), 163–65. On the Virginia campaign in particular, see Lebsock, *A Share of Honour*, 120–25; Amy L. Marschean, " 'Glory in the Flower': The Impact of Woman Suffrage in Virginia" (M.A. thesis, Univ. of Virginia, 1988).

27 Mildred Lewis Rutherford, in Historical Records of the UDC, vol. 4, EBML; Lloyd C. Taylor, "Lila Meade Valentine: The FFV as Reformer," *Virginia Magazine of History and Biography* 70 (Oct. 1962): 482.

28 Scott, *Southern Lady*, 180, said that by 1916 the UDC was actively campaigning for suffrage but provided no evidence to support this. The Minutes of Richmond Chapter UDC, EBML, contain no references to woman suffrage. On attitudes of individual UDC members toward woman suffrage, see Mary E. Massey, "The Making of a Feminist," *Journal of Southern History* 39, no. 1 (Feb. 1973): 3–22; Price, "Development of Leadership," 83–85.

29 On the Massing of the Flags Ceremony, see John Edmonds, "Pomp and Circumstance: For Those Who Won't Forget," *Commonwealth Times*, 23 June–13 July 1981, and programs of the ceremony, both in the Jefferson Davis Monument Vertical File, VM.

30 Richmond has had as many as ten UDC chapters since 1897, five of which are active at present—Richmond-Stonewall Jackson Chapter (combined in 1964); Lee Chapter; Janet Randolph Chapter; President Davis Chapter (formed 8 Oct. 1953); and Matthew Fontaine Maury (formed 12 Dec. 1958)–Centennial Chapter (formed 16 April 1961) (combined in 1984)—with a total membership of approximately 400–500 members. The Chesterfield, Elliott Grays, and General Stuart (formed 21 Aug. 1953) chapters have disbanded in recent years. At present, the UDC has approximately 27,000 members nationwide.

31 "GAR Speaker Hits Confederacy Group," unidentified newspaper clipping in UDC Vertical File, CMGL.

EDWARD L. AYERS

Conclusion: If All the
South Were Virginia

THOSE WHO HAVE READ MORE THAN ONE OF THE CHAPTERS
in this book will see that the authors adhere to no single school, interpretation, or set of priorities. While Melinda Buza, in the first chapter,
stresses the reassuring bonds of sentiment that connected elite white Virginians across differences of gender and age, Angie Parrott, in the final
chapter, stresses how daughters' sentimental memories of their fathers
stifled historical memory a century later. While John Willis argues for
a strong tradition of secular honor and barely subdued anger among
enslaved Virginia blacks, Gregg Michel finds that Hickory Hill slaves
often acted more from careful economic calculation than from opportunities for revenge during the war. While Lloyd Benson stresses the way
enlistment in the Confederacy followed the contours of age and family
structure in Orange County, Kevin Ruffner argues that diverse soldiers
remained bound together throughout four years of hardship. While Lawrence Hartzell argues that Petersburg blacks maintained an abiding faith
in politics after Reconstruction despite attempts to deny them the vote,
Beth Schweiger stresses black and white Virginians' widespread disillusionment with politics. And in perhaps the most overt difference, Rob
Weise portrays many of the mountain people of Wise County as willing
participants in the industrial transformation of their community while
Elizabeth Atwood emphasizes the negative effects of Northern capital in
Page County.

The diversity, even apparent contradictions, among these chapters is
part of the view of history this book intends to encourage. The authors
of these chapters have repeatedly turned toward explanations that stress
tension and ambiguity. They offer readings of history that differ in subtle
and significant ways from some of the more influential interpretations of
Southern history during the last couple of decades.

Focusing this book on Virginia suggests one strategy for a new view
of the South, for these chapters self-consciously explore what are widely

recognized as the margins of the region, places where boundaries of economy and culture remained especially ambiguous. "The South," after all, is an abstraction, an idea which comes in and out of focus depending on its context. Seen together, these chapters show that the study of obviously problematic places in the South can help us see how political, economic, and cultural boundaries overlapped and diverged. If we ignore such places—if we define the South only in terms of its difference from the North, or if we see white Americans as essentially the same because all were receptive to capitalism and racism—we miss the complexity of the South's position within the nation. Every place in the South felt the tension between the power and identity of the locality and the power and identity of the nation. Every place in the South was problematic.

Many commentators have suggested that explanations of major Southern institutions such as slavery and segregation must become more sensitive to geographic variation and change over time. The study of places along the many borders of the South may help considerably in this endeavor. Instead of purging case studies of any taint of non-Southernness and focusing only on plantation districts, historians might profitably turn to the kind of anomalous places explored in this book—mining towns, tourist attractions, declining cities, wheat plantations. General accounts might devote more attention to the early frontier, to cities, and to states such as Kentucky, West Virginia, and Florida. Studies might examine Southerners of both races who moved to the North and the West or investigate manifestations of Southern culture that became part of the national culture. It is clear, in other words, that the lines between the South and the rest of the country remained in constant flux throughout the nineteenth century, and we might do more to explore those shifting boundaries, those edges of the South.

While there is nothing particularly disturbing about enlarging our field of study geographically, other aspects of this book may trouble readers. Some of the contributions may imply unwelcome political connotations, an uncritical acceptance of the nineteenth-century South on the terms of its most privileged residents. Why study the personal lives of the Virginia gentry, slaves who rejected the Christian church, widespread loyalty to the Confederacy, the eagerness of mountaineers to profit from the exploitation of their own counties, or apathy among poor and aggrieved voters? None of these questions, after all, fits the agenda of much of the best Southern history written in the last half century, which has sought to redress the injustices of the past by sympathetically chronicling the struggles of the oppressed.

Indeed, in a sort of poetic justice, the wrongs of the Southern past have inspired some of the best and most invigorating historical scholarship in America. A parade of seminal books—stretching from W. E. B. DuBois's *Black Reconstruction* (1935) to C. Vann Woodward's *Origins of the New South* (1951), Kenneth Stampp's *Peculiar Institution* (1956), Eugene Genovese's *Political Economy of Slavery* (1965), Lawrence Goodwyn's *Democratic Promise* (1976), and Joel Williamson's *The Crucible of Race* (1984)—has placed the theme of overt or covert conflict between genders, races, and classes at center stage. These books draw much of their power from their moral energy, their outrage at the way so many people in the South were denied the dignity due them as human beings and as Americans. These authors, whatever their politics, took as their major task the unmasking of injustice and the celebration of resistance; they punctured the self-serving pretensions of various Southern elites and debunked the racist and arrogant myths of earlier twentieth-century scholars who shared and perpetuated those pretensions.

The deep engagement and democratic ideals of these critical historians have inspired the authors of this volume. But the edges of some revisionist arguments have become dull from too much handling; what began as risky attacks have, through no fault of their authors, been domesticated into rhetorical conventions. Within academe, at any rate, there is scarcely a scholar who challenges the centrality of overt and relatively straightforward conflict among well-defined groups as the foundation of the Southern past. Struggles of class, race, and gender have become accepted at face value.

Even as we maintain our insistence that the lash on the slave's back, the war fought to perpetuate human bondage, and a profoundly undemocratic politics were central to the South's history, maybe we can also add new perspectives to these and other parts of the Southern past. One task of the next generation of Southern historians is to continue the job begun by our predecessors of conveying a sense of the full humanity of the people who lived in the nineteenth-century South. Achieving that goal demands that we see relationships of power in more complex terms and develop a more supple vocabulary to describe the many different kinds of networks within which people lived. The people of the nineteenth-century South moved among any number of simultaneous processes, transformations, and retrogressions; historians should attempt to embrace multiplicity and contradiction, not shove them aside.

The first two chapters in this book suggest two—among many—ways that we might approach fundamental, though incommensurable, divisions of the antebellum South: gender and race. Melinda Buza's study argues that the tensions earlier scholars have found between men and women in the Old South were all too real and that the pace and risks of childbearing conspired with cultural expectations to divide males and females in fundamental ways. But Buza also shows that the gentry of the early antebellum South longed to be emotionally united with their mates, not merely to live in businesslike marriages that conveniently consolidated landholdings or produced heirs. Whether written by male or female members of the elite, their letters betray little sense of their authors as slaveholders, domineering patriarchs, or submissive helpmates. Buza suggests that we see these people as situated in complex webs of relationships, consciously using lessons learned from same-sex friendships to help them with relations across gender lines.

Buza's chapter raises many questions about this class of white Southerners. What are we to make of the apparent disjunction between their powerful class role as slaveholders and their tenuous personal conceptions of themselves? Do we accept their apparent lack of animosity toward the other gender without reservation, or do we see their rhetoric of romantic love as embedded in relationships that were already, unquestionably, asymmetrical and unequal? Any satisfactory explanation for these questions will have to account for evidence of amity as well as conflict between the genders, will need to take into consideration the stages of life of men and women, will need to look at the ways this class changed its view of itself as the years passed and as its progeny peopled much of the South and North.

John Willis's study raises similar questions and possibilities about the slaves so often ignored in the personal correspondence of the gentry. Many influential historians speak of the slaves as a Christian "community," united in a struggle against their oppression, drawing emotional strength from their deep faith. But Willis discovers that on a plantation where Christianity was encouraged by the owner, where a profession of Christianity might even bring freedom, a majority of slaves refused to profess the religion. Instead, it seems, slaves' own version of "honor," a harsh secular standard, claimed more followers than did Christianity. In Willis's chapter, slaves were divided among, as well as within, themselves. Does such a portrayal diminish the black struggle for their humanity, or does it strengthen it? Must we speak of slaves as more noble and religious than their masters if we are to restore moral balance to history? If one discovers and reveals divisions in the slave community and fault lines in slave culture, does that revelation betray them? We need more portrayals of slave life that make room for the differences and disjunctions on the thousands of farms and plantations where slaves lived. Instead of talking about variations in slave life as so many epicycles within a coherent system of paternalism or capitalism, we need to examine the ruptures in slaves' experiences, the sharp breaks between generations, believers and nonbelievers, men and women, the old colonial South and the new cotton South. Slavery was always based on brute force, but it always remained as complex as human beings themselves.

The relationships among white men in the Old South might seem easier to categorize, since they were uncomplicated by overt divisions of gender or race. Yet ever since the days of the abolitionists, observers have wondered why nonslaveholding white men did not chafe more at the arrogance and power of slaveholders. Some historians have pointed out that the planters in fact shared considerable political power with their poorer neighbors; others have talked of the unifying effects of economic patronage and kin ties; others have argued for an ideological hegemony in which the limits of political discourse precluded any discussion of the justice and wisdom of slavery. Lloyd Benson has attempted to get at these questions through another common strategy of the chapters in this book: painstakingly building an interpretation from the mundane evidence of daily experience. Through an intensive use of local maps and records, Benson is able to show that divisions among white men of various levels of wealth were mediated not only by kin, business, and political ties but also by occupational diversity and shared, though obviously unequal, access to some of the most fertile land in their neighborhoods. In other words, the white society of this part of the South saw class divisions qualified by economic as well as political and cultural complexities. We need to construct our ideas of class from a close, local attention to landholding and occupation as well as slaveholding; we need to understand just how class divisions "felt" before we can judge the extent to which they had to be mediated by other bonds among white men.

Historians often have looked at the Civil War for evidence of class divisions in the South. While earlier generations of white Southerners found in the Confederacy evidence of the fundamental unity and solidarity of the white South in its most vulnerable time, historians have increasingly found evidence of profound disaffection. The records of the Confederate governors are filled with lamentations from desperate farm wives and their soldier husbands about the deprivations visited on them by the new Southern state, and the military records are filled with evidence of desertion and resentment. Kevin Ruffner suggests a way to reconcile the older and newer views, to reconcile unity and division. His study of the 44th Virginia Regiment offers ample evidence of desertion, of disloyalty, of disgruntlement—even as the study argues that no simple divisions of class account for those patterns. Ruffner finds age and marital status better predictors of desertion than whether or not a man was a slaveholder. As in Benson's Orange County, class took on its full meaning only in the context of these other attributes. Being a nonslaveholder at the age of nineteen was no particular mark of inferiority, especially if a young man was unmarried, educated, or living at home with his parents. But being a nonslaveholder at forty-five, when a man had a wife and several children to support and could look forward to little prospect of acquiring slaves, meant something else altogether. That is one reason so much of our evidence of class division in the Confederacy comes from women's letters, one reason so much desertion grew out of desperate attempts to get home to help wives and children. Class can best help us understand the South when we locate class as fully as we can within all the other kinds of relationships among which white Southerners lived.

Black Southerners may be even more resistant to easy generalizations than their white neighbors. The full dimensions of that complexity have been masked, though, by our usual sources on nineteenth-century blacks: contemporary white portrayals, autobiographies of exceptional blacks, twentieth-century oral histories. While these sources have proved extremely rich in the hands of gifted historians, they have obvious and insurmountable limitations. Gregg Michel offers another perspective on black life in the South with his exhaustive use of plantation records. By exploring the structure of both the slave and free black work force that evolved at Hickory Hill over nearly half a century, Michel is able to show the many decisions blacks faced when opportunities for freedom arrived. While slave families had appeared strong in the late antebellum period, as the most thorough historians of the black family in slavery have argued, the disruptions of war at Hickory Hill dramatized the conflicts within those families: several husbands fled for freedom, leaving their wives and children behind. Other divisions also testify to profound differences among the blacks who had lived in an unusually stable slave community, as some stayed on the plantation for years after the war while others abandoned Hickory Hill at the first opportunity. Blacks, like whites, acted on a complex set of desires and needs, some of which involved loyalty to other blacks, some of which turned on narrow self-interest, and some of which accommodated white people's money, power, and persuasiveness. A full account of Southern history must take all these things into consideration.

The diversity of black life in the South becomes even more apparent in the city, as the chapter here by Lawrence Hartzell makes clear. Petersburg's experience emphasizes, among other things, the distinction between economic and political power in the nineteenth century. Even though historians often conflate the two kinds of power into "white supremacy" or "elite domination," Hartzell's study makes it clear that political and economic structures intersected at unpredictable angles. Petersburg blacks gained political power at times when state and national structures created opportunities for local ambition and skill to work. Those times, though, seldom fell into synchronization with economic change. As a result, black leaders in Petersburg found themselves constantly negotiating between different kinds of aspirations, different kinds of possibilities. Sometimes it seemed to make sense to push hard for political power and rights, while at other times it made more sense to keep a low profile, to put energies into business, family, or voluntary associations and forgo politics. The black "community" was constantly pulled apart as opportunity varied so much from one year to the next and from one person to another.

The experiences of the people in the mountains of Wise County reveal another variation on the problems and opportunities posed by the increasingly integrated national economy of Gilded Age America. The white people of southern Appalachia entered the era after the Civil War in far more advantageous circumstances than did former slaves. With about eight of ten heads of households owning the land they farmed, men in the mountains spoke with considerable unanimity on political matters. Yet over the course of just a few decades their counties were transformed into places where large industrial corporations controlled much of the land and exerted decisive political power. Historians of the mountains thus face a different problem from historians of the black belt: explaining the loss of land and control in a place where locals were once so empowered. Appalachian historians have tended to portray the transformation as one of raw force and chicanery, of interlopers and natives. Robert Weise, though, suggests that by looking more closely we find a far more complex pattern of accommodation and initiative on the part of local people. The class lines that divided Appalachia cut across the native population as well as between outsiders and insiders. New classes of mountaineers developed with astonishing speed, it seems, as differences in religiosity, ambition, contact with the outside world, age, and location in the county led some mountain people to embrace the new order even as others spurned it. The process of incorporation was a persistent one, as every new generation confronted, and confronts, the same decisions of how best to live in an industrial Appalachia.

The chapter on the Luray Caverns by Elizabeth Atwood would seem to pose fewer problems for the received wisdom than most of the preceding chapters. Her account of the coming of outside capital to the Shenandoah

Valley, after all, fits widely held ideas about the colonial economy in the New South. The struggles in Page County were fought between large railroad companies and local landholders, profits flowed out of the community and into the accounts of large Northern-based corporations, little long-term development came as a result of the opening of the caverns. Atwood's contribution to our collective effort of revision comes more in her choice of topic than in her argument. Tourism, and leisure in general, have not been deemed worthy subjects for historians wrestling with the important questions of Southern history. Despite tourism's status as a major industry of the twentieth-century South, the subject does not fit our ideas of what the South was "really" like in the nineteenth century and is thus shunted aside. Historians who keep making the South seem simpler than it was ignore all the noise of change that fails to fit the classic list of important things to study, a list in large part borrowed from the progressive historians of the early twentieth century. Studies such as Atwood's prompt us to enlarge our conception of the South and stop ignoring the many kinds of experiences people confronted there.

While tourism in the New South has been slighted, politics in the region has been studied exhaustively. We have studies of the political histories of virtually every Southern state (including Virginia) after Reconstruction, studies of Populism, studies of disfranchisement. Some of the battles over Southern politics have been fought close and hard by historians, so Beth Schweiger's chapter enters a crowded and dangerous battlefield to raise questions most historians have not asked. Is it possible that the Democrats, for all their power, did not exercise as much control over the political environment in which they worked as we have thought? Were they concerned about the atrophy of the electorate even as they gloated over the demise of their opposition? Most of the literature on the New South portrays the Democrats in bold tones, almost superhuman in their ability to control voters, anticipate change, and get what they wanted. Schweiger suggests that we need to take what Democrats said more seriously, that we need to examine their anxieties and failures as well as their victories. Like Michel and Hartzell, Schweiger also portrays postwar blacks as a complex and divided group, adapting quickly to political change in ways that many Americans did in the late nineteenth century but that are now deemed inappropriate. Schweiger's picture of New South politics is painted in subtle colors, with intricate brushwork.

The chapter on the United Daughters of the Confederacy, by Angie Parrott, ends our book on a fittingly ironic note. Parrott shows how the UDC struggled for control of the Southern past by trying to wrest history from arrogant Yankees unwilling to acknowledge the justice and valor of the Southern cause. In this process, the UDC not only suppressed the unpleasant parts of Virginia's past but also ignored what were for them disquieting parts of the present. While other women's groups in Richmond worked to redress many of the problems facing the urban South at the turn of the century, the UDC used its considerable resources to consecrate a highly selective view of the past. Parrott's chapter vividly demonstrates that visions of the past guide our actions in the present, legitimating some and invalidating others.

The ten chapters in this book attempt to do just the opposite of what the women in Angie Parrott's chapter attempted to do. We hope to work toward a more expansive view of the Southern past. It has long been clear that a history which leaves out women, blacks, and the poor of every description is not merely incomplete but badly distorted. We have taken that conviction and extended it in other dimensions as well. It is not enough merely to include those disinherited from the past, merely to celebrate their resistance and endurance. Historians should take them seriously enough to document their lives in full, to notice as many of their dilemmas and decisions as we can, even when the decisions were not always what we would have them be. Scholars might be more interested, too, in looking at places that seem peripheral on the usual maps of significant historical activity, places not held to be typical or emblematic of some larger coherence we would impose on the past. We should be willing to allow for loose ends, openings, and paradoxes in our portrayals. We might begin disassembling our totalizing metaphors, our assumption that relatively smooth systems of one sort or another contained the past.

One consequence of adopting a view of the South which makes room for some of the disjunctions, anomalies, and disquieting patterns we suggest in this book might be a vision of the past more engaging to people of today, people who find the South a place where old and new are thrown together in incongruous patterns. It is easy for young people in the region, whether white or black, to think that the Southern past broke in two in the 1960s, when a simple and repressive society left over after slavery became a society which revolves around television and fast food. Perhaps we can show them not only that the present is still shaped by the domination that marked the nineteenth-century South—the usual, and important, moral of the region's history—but also that the past was in many ways as complex and interesting as our own South. By opening our story of the past to new possibilities, we may also encourage faith in new possibilities for the future.

Index